CATHOLIC RECORD SOCIETY

PUBLICATIONS

(RECORDS SERIES) VOLUME 73

ST GREGORY'S COLLEGE, SEVILLE, 1592–1767

By

Martin Murphy

CATHOLIC RECORD SOCIETY
1992

Printed in Great Britain by
Hobbs the Printers of Southampton

CONTENTS

		Page
Preface		vii

1.	Historical Introduction:
	  I The English Years, 1592–1693
	  II The Irish Years, 1710–1767
		1

	Notes	31
2.	Sources and Abbreviations	38
3.	The Archives of St Gregory's	43
4.	Alumni of St Gregory's, 1592–1767: An Alphabetical List	48
5.	Martyred Alumni	105
6.	English Jesuits in Andalusia, 1592–1660	106
7.	Andalusian *impresos* relating to English Catholic affairs, 1590–1670	115
8.	Extracts from the Annual Letters	123

Documents

1.	The Mission oath (ed. Mgr Henson)	128
2.	A Scotsman before the Inquisition, 1594	131
3.	Henry Piers: an Anglo-Irishman at Seville, 1597–8	135
4.	Francisco de Peralta's Defence of the English College, 1604	142
	Spanish text	142
	Translation	152
5.	Joseph Creswell and his Spanish Jesuit opponents: The Evidence of Andrew White, S. J., October 1612	163
6.	A petition for an English Rector, 1613	168
7.	William Whichcott's Letters from England, 1616	170
8.	Henry Gerard's Stir, 1693	182
9.	Richard Richardson's will, 1730	187
10.	A petition for the restitution of the College buildings, 1792	193

Appendix: The Espinosa legacy	199
Index of persons	203
Index of places	215

PREFACE

'The Cinderella of the Colleges', which 'remains the enigma it has always been'. Thus Godfrey Anstruther described St Gregory's, Seville, in the second and third volumes of his *Seminary Priests*. It is to be hoped that this volume will go some way to solving this enigma, throwing light upon a hitherto obscure corner of recusant history. It may be of interest also to historians of Seville and students of Anglo-Spanish relations during an eventful period. Perhaps it will provide the materials for a more informed assessment of the legacy of Robert Persons. A glance at the notes will show that the historical skeleton contained here has had to be assembled painfully from *disjecta membra*. Other material may still lie buried in Spanish archives for a future historian to disinter.

This work rests on foundations laid by others, particularly by Canon Edwin Henson, Rector of St Alban's College, Valladolid, who turned his lonely vigil at the college during the Second World War to advantage by setting the archives to order. The handsome bound blue volumes of Seville documents in the Valladolid archives are a testament to his patient labours. In the absence of any formal registers, such as existed for St Alban's, he combed through account books, legal documents, receipts and records of mass stipends to assemble what became known as 'Henson's list', a tentative MS index of Seville students pieced together from stray scraps. This list was used by Anstruther when compiling the volumes of his *Seminary Priests*, and was the basis for the register of Seville students in the period 1591–1605 published by Henson in collaboration with A. J. Loomie in Volume 9 of *Recusant History*. Anstruther cast his net wider by consulting the ordination registers of the Seville archdiocese, though he overlooked some entries and was frequently frustrated by the vagaries of Spanish transcribers of English surnames—a problem which requires for its solution the combined skills of the code-breaker and the phonetician. My task was to widen the investigation by using further sources available in libraries and archives in Seville, Granada, Simancas, Madrid and Rome.

My thanks are due first to Mr Antony Allison, then General Editor of the Catholic Record Society, who first suggested this project and sustained it with patience and support. Monsignor Ronald Hishon, the former Rector of the English College at Valladolid, allowed me the freedom of the archives and offered warm hospitality on two occasions. Professor Albert Loomie made many valuable suggestions, based on his long study of the Spanish Elizabethans and his mastery of a complex period. Fr Eduardo Moore allowed me to consult the Jesuit archives at Granada and provided ever-courteous guidance there. Fr Thomas McCoog kindly allowed me to consult his transcriptions of Jesuit catalogues at the Roman archives of the Society of Jesus which are due to be published in another volume of this series. At a late stage of this project I was fortunate to have the assistance of Professor Francisco Borja de Medina, who shared his deep knowledge of Jesuit and Andalusian history, based on many years of research in Rome. He made available his notes on English Jesuits in Andalusia and pointed me in new directions. In Rome, Monsignor Walter Drumm and his colleagues at the Beda College provided congenial hospitality.

Many others have helped the work along the way, among them Dr Manuel Moreno Alonso; Fr Thomas Flynn, O.P., Fr Francis Edwards, S.J., Dr Felipe Fernández-Armesto; Dr R. W. Truman; Fr Michael Williams; Dr Nigel Griffin; Fr John J. Silke; Fr F. J. Turner; Fr Michael Sharratt; Mr Martin Cleary, and many librarians and archivists. I am grateful to the Anglo-Spanish Society for a travel grant which made possible a visit to Rome, and to the Council of the Catholic Record Society for further assistance. Professor T. A. Birrell checked the proofs with an expert eye.

Acknowledgements are due to the following for permission to use copyright material: the Roman archives of the Society of Jesus (Annual Letters and Catalogues of the Andalusian Province); the Rector of the English College, Valladolid (Documents 1, 4, 8 and 9); Professor Pedro Herrera Puga (Document 2); Bodley's Librarian (Document 3); the archivist of Simancas (Documents 5 and 6).

The frequency of the words 'possibly' and 'probably' in the alumni list suggests how tentative must be many of the details in it. The last word has not been written. *Exoriare aliquis!*

Martin Murphy

Frontispiece: *The Triumph of St Gregory*, by Juan de Roelas, painted in 1608 to hang above the altar of the college chapel, and now at Ushaw College, Durham. A receipt in the college archives records the payment to the artist of the large sum of 1560 *reales*.

The formally grouped and crowded canvas (4.40 × 2.57m) was evidently composed to a programme, designed to harmonise the themes of martyrdom, Marian devotion, opposition to heresy, ecclesiastical training, and St Gregory's role in linking the Churches of Seville and England. St Gregory, the Apostle of England, is in the central position. In front of him kneels the royal martyr St Hermenegild, who sacrifices his royal crown rather than accept Arianism, renouncing an earthly kingdom in exchange for the martyr's palm and crown of roses which angels hold above him at the top of the picture. The kneeling figure on the right, wearing the pallium, is St Leander, Archbishop of Seville and friend of St Gregory, who dedicated to him his *Liber Moralium*. The youths in the right foreground are perhaps English students, represented as under the Archbishop of Seville's protection. To the right and left of St Gregory are ten Spanish bishop-saints who according to tradition were trained at St Leander's ecclesiastical school at Seville in the 6th century—an appropriate model for the 16th century college. For further discussion of the painting, see p.20.

1. HISTORICAL INTRODUCTION

I. THE ENGLISH YEARS, 1592–1693

Though St Gregory's had an official life of 175 years, it functioned as an English college for only a hundred, and flourished for only forty. Nevertheless its heyday (1592–c.1630) coincided with the most eventful period of English recusant Catholicism and for a brief period it occupied centre stage. Its rise and fall to some extent reproduce in microcosm the changing fortunes of its host city, Seville, which during these years began its decline from being a cosmopolitan centre of major political and commercial importance to the position of a provincial backwater living on its past glories.[1]

English trading connections with Andalusia were already strong in the late 15th century. Much of the trade went in and out of the port of Sanlúcar de Barrameda, downriver from Seville, at the mouth of the Guadalquivir. The volume of traffic with London, Southampton and Bristol was such that an English hospice of St George was founded there in 1517 on land donated by the Duke of Medina Sidonia, under the patronage of the Bishops of London, Winchester and Exeter. The Bristol merchant Robert Thorne made his fortune in Seville and was one of the financiers of Sebastian Cabot's first voyage in 1522. The money he made in Andalusian trade made possible his foundation of Bristol Grammar School. In 1530 an 'Andalusia Company' was established on terms which empowered the English residents of the Andalusian ports to meet annually and elect a 'consul' and twelve assistants. Later, in 1577, this Sanlúcar brotherhood was incorporated into a new 'Spanish Company' set up in London under a Privy Council charter, but this did not survive for long. There was opposition to it in England from other powerful trading interests such as the Merchant Adventurers, and the English community at Sanlucar itself became divided between the older residents who were Catholic in their sympathies, and the more recent arrivals who professed the reformed religion.[2] The deterioration in Anglo-Spanish relations which had begun with Henry VIII's divorce eventually, in the reign of Elizabeth, ended in open hostilities. Yet a recent study has shown that even after 1585 English cloth, tin, grain and lead continued to be exchanged for Spanish fruit, wine, oil and coin. The profit motive and old business partnerships often proved stronger than nationalistic or religious loyalties. Many English traders, from the West country particularly, were prepared to flout the embargo imposed by their government, running their goods into smaller harbours or sometimes passing themselves off as Irishmen. The *Marchants avizo*, a guide for such traders written by the Bristol merchant John Browne, was significantly published while the embargo was still in force, in 1589. The Spanish authorities, it appears, were often ready to connive at these practices. The two most powerful deterrents to trade were on the one hand the activities of the Inquisition, which regarded foreign heretics as a danger to Spanish faith, and on the other, the depredations of English buccaneers. Drake was almost as unpopular with peaceful English traders in Spain as he was with the Spanish themselves.[3]

In 1592, the year of the foundation of St Gregory's, Seville was at the apogee of its fortunes. In the hundred years since the discovery of America its population had more than doubled to well over 100,000, and it had become the biggest city in Spain, one of the ten biggest in Europe. It was the gateway to the New World, the receptacle of the fabulous wealth which the Fleet of the Indies unloaded yearly on its quays beside the Torre del Oro. In 1595 the largest treasure ever seen in the city was deposited in the Casa de la Contratación, the hub of Spain's European and Atlantic trade. Through its port passed the administrators, soldiers and missionaries who were still opening up a vast new American empire. Industry followed commerce. The abundance of precious metals from America attracted goldsmiths and silversmiths, and the increase in shipping led to a growth in the manufacture of naval supplies. It was Seville which produced the arms and gunpowder for the conquests of Cortes and Pizarro. Meanwhile, more pacific exports flowed outwards to Northern Europe, Italy, Africa, and America: wine, oil, fruit, leather, wool, cochineal, ceramics. This prosperity offered opportunities to foreign merchants, bankers and entrepreneurs, from France, Flanders, Genoa, Naples and the northern countries. One group was now diminished in numbers: the Jews. The importance of Spanish Jewry to the Spanish economy may have been exaggerated, but the massive exodus which followed the measures taken by the Catholic Kings in 1492 to enforce their conversion led to an empoverishment of society. Similar measures taken against the *mudéjares*—Spaniards of Muslim origin—also deprived the nation of valuable skills and talents. A growing obsession with purity of blood and purity of faith began to make for a more closed society.[4]

Seville's prosperity attracted also, from all over Spain, a picaresque army of beggars, rogues, adventurers and parasites hoping for a share of the pickings. Their world was brilliantly depicted in the *novelas ejemplares* of Cervantes, who in 1592 had a precarious job in Seville and was soon to be imprisoned for debt. Another contemporary novelist, Mateo Alemán, who was his fellow-inmate in prison, described the city as ruled by 'Don Dinero', 'Master Money'—a place where men respect 'not what you know, but what you possess'. In the words of the poet Góngora, Seville was 'the great Babylon of Spain'. It was this materialism which shocked St Teresa when she arrived in 1575. Bred in the austere simplicity of Avila, a provincial Castilian hill-town, she was not prepared for the worldliness, flamboyance and corruption of the big city, 'No Foundation', she wrote of the Seville Carmel, 'caused me more hardships'. She found the people initially indifferent and the clergy uncooperative, and her distaste for show was not understood by a society which judged by outward appearances. Though popular opinion turned in her favour, her views on Andalusia and the Andalusians remained unflattering.[5]

In the first half of the 16th century Seville enjoyed a remarkable degree of religious tolerance. Only one Protestant was put to death between 1500 and 1550, and theologians argued that heresy should be combated by reason. The Archbishop of Seville from 1525 to 1538, Alonso Manrique, was one of the leading Spanish Erasmists. But the tide had already begun to turn when in 1558–59 the discovery of groups of Lutheran sympathisers in Valladolid and Seville led to panic measures. Heresy was no longer a foreign phenomenon, but a local infection which had to be cauterised. 'Lutherans' were hunted down and executed at public *autos*. Spanish scholars were recalled from abroad and an Index of prohibited books was introduced to seal off the country from heresy. The leaders of the reformist movement at Seville, Juan Gil (known as Egido) and Constantino Ponce de la Puente, both graduates of the University of Alcalá and canons of Seville cathedral, advocated a doctrine of justification which could not be reconciled with the recent formulation of the Council of Trent (1547). They died in prison, but their effigies were burned at the *auto-de-fé* of 1560, when fourteen victims (including two English sailors) were burned in person. Altogether fifty-one people were executed at Seville as heretics between 1559 and 1562. One of those burned in 1562 was the Prior of the Hieronymite monastery of San Isidoro del Campo, just outside the city, which was a nest of dissidents. Twelve of its monks had already fled, making their way to Geneva or London. One of them, Cassiodoro de la Reina, the translator of the Bible, was pastor of the Spanish exiles' church of St Mary Axe from 1559 to 1564. Another, Antonio del Corro, ended his days as a prebendary of St Paul's. Persecution was responsible for a two-way traffic, from Spain to England as well as in the other direction. Though the measures of 1559–60 almost totally eliminated native Spanish Protestantism, the fear of foreign and heretical infection remained.[6]

In spite of its importance, Seville lacked a major university. It had two *colegios mayores:* Santa María de Jesús and Santo Tomás, the latter under Dominican control. Much of their time was devoted to mutual rivalry and the defence of their privileges. The Jesuits opened their first house in the city in 1554, but though called a 'college' it was, in accordance with St Ignatius' policy, intended only for students intending to join the Society. Later, external students were admitted, one of them being Cervantes, who was to pay tribute to 'the love, the solicitude and the industry' of his teachers. As the result of pressure from influential churchmen and city fathers a grammar school was opened in 1561, but the move into public education aroused misgivings among some in the Society. Writing to St Francis Borgia, the General, in 1570, the Andalusian Provincial argued that the Society's aims and interests were not being served by having to bear this increasingly demanding burden. There were other schools in the city where the young could obtain an education more suited to its worldly ethos. 'The mind of the *sevillano*', he declared, 'is acute, but volatile. Young people in this city are brought up in affluence, idleness and luxury. Every day brings new excitements on land and sea which distract from study. Seville is the stepmother, not the mother, of learning'. This was made evident, he went on, by the small number of vocations for the Society. 'Large cities are not suitable as places for study' he wrote, which was why universities were normally situated in smaller towns such as Salamanca and Alcalá. Besides, 'because our classes are so full, some leading citizens, even pious ones, are sending their sons to other schools, which means that our classes are crammed with the poor and uncultured'.[7]

One of the alternative schools referred to by this writer was that directed by the humanist Juan de Mal-Lara. At his death in 1571 persons of rank and fashion transferred their sons to the Jesuits, which led to a marked increase in the number of their pupils. They now became irrevocably committed to an educational role, and in 1572 Fr Juan Castañeda, writing to the General to appeal for more teachers, put the number of students at 700, representing 'the illustrious flower of the city's youth'.[8] In 1579, with a grant from the city fathers, the Society moved the college to a new site in the centre of the city. This large and splendid institution was dedicated to St Hermenegild. The choice of patron was significant. Hermenegild was a local hero, an Arian prince of the Visigothic era who had been converted to orthodoxy and suffered martyrdom, as a result of which his father and brother had been converted and the orthodox faith established in Spain. This ancient history took on a fresh significance in the light of the Counter-Reformation, and as a result of the Jesuit revival of his cult the feast of St Hermenegild was extended in 1586 to all the churches of Spain and Portugal. The inauguration of St Hermenegild's College in Seville was marked by a dramatic representation of the martyr's story, performed in public. This and other Jesuit plays were partly written in the vernacular and included elements of comedy and satire which appealed to a popular audience and helped to establish the college in ordinary people's esteem and affection[9].

But the Society in Seville was by no means exclusively concerned with education. Some of the fathers took the gospel out into Andalusia on rural missions. One of the most remarkable was Pedro de León, who for forty years ministered to the inmates of the prison in Seville. His frank, uncensored memoirs, written late in life at the request of his superiors, are a revelation of the city's lower depths and of the author's compassion. One of the most graphic passages is his account (reproduced elsewhere in this volume) of his attendance on a wild and defiant Scotsman who, after five years' imprisonment by the Inquisition, was given a day's notice of his trial at an *auto-de-fé*. In his zeal for souls, de León was prepared to go to far greater lengths to save his men than was normal, and here his attitude differed from that of the friars who usually attended these occasions. The Scotsman was reconciled, but after returning to prison he later went berserk and attacked the governor, with the result that he was brought to another *auto* and executed.[10]

This, then, was the city to which Robert Persons came in 1591—a place of stark contradictions between light and darkness, conspicuous wealth and desperate poverty, materialism and other-worldliness. It was a city where the aristocracy set the tone but where even the lowest retained their pride, a city immoderate in its pleasures and in its repentance, open to the outside world and yet utterly convinced that nowhere and nobody could compare with Andalusia and the Andalusians.

Persons was not the first English Jesuit to reach Andalusia. William Weston arrived in 1576, soon after joining the Society, and spent eight years in the Province, teaching Greek at the Seville college and working as a missioner in Cadiz and Sanlúcar. He went to Sanlúcar at the request of the Duke of Medina Sidonia, who wanted a chaplain for the English there.[11]

Persons' mission to Spain has been described elsewhere.[12] He went to Madrid in 1589 with a twofold purpose: to resolve the differences which had arisen between the Society and the King, and to appeal for help for the English seminaries. With characteristic skill he not only achieved both objectives but also gained the confidence of Philip II, who became a dedicated supporter of his cause. The turn of events seemed to Persons to be providential, and he seized his opportunity with both hands. The colleges at Rheims and Rome had been unable to cope with the recent rise in the number of applicants from England, and were short of funds. Persons obtained a substantial royal subsidy for Rheims, but realised that a permanent solution of the problem would be made possible by the establishment of a seminary, or seminaries, on Spanish soil. Spain could offer both physical and financial security. Taking advantage of the presence at Valladolid of a number of English students and priests, he obtained the king's permission to establish a college there. His ability to negotiate his way through the labyrinth of Spanish ecclesiastical and civil bureaucracy was remarkable, as was his gift for public relations. On the day of the college's inauguration, 1 September 1589, he published a manifesto ably designed to commend the English Catholic cause to the Spanish public. Drake's recent attacks on La Coruña and Vigo had exacerbated anglophobia. Persons was at pains to make a distinction between English Catholics and English Protestants, and to emphasise that they were more at odds with each other than Englishmen in general with Spaniards. He reminded his readers of the assistance given by English Catholics to survivors of the Armada, and encouraged them to think that a restoration of Catholicism in England was imminent.[13]

Though the opportunity at Valladolid was providential, the town was not ideal for his purposes, due to its landlocked position and its declining importance. It was natural that he should look south to Seville, with its greater wealth and better communications. In 1590 he sent two colleagues there to reconnoitre. They were well received by the Jesuit Provincial of Andalusia, Bartolomé Pérez, and reported back favourably. Ironically, the two men chosen for this mission, John Cecil and John Fixer, were soon to become double agents working against Persons for the English Government.

In the following year, 1591, Persons himself arrived in Seville with twelve newly ordained priests from Valladolid, on their way to England. He moved fast in preparing the ground for his future college. As a result of the official embargo on trade with England, the brotherhood of St George at Sanlúcar had ceased to function effectively and was reduced to a few English Catholic merchants still in residence. Persons saw the potential of St George's as a communications centre and as an entry and exit base for missioners on their way to or from England. Yielding to his powers of persuasion, the eight remaining members of the brotherhood agreed to the transference of St George's from civil to ecclesiastical use: henceforward the land, income and right to levy dues would be devoted to the upkeep of a confraternity of

English priests, the chaplains of St George, who would have a deciding say in the election of the lay consul. This was to cause much indignation among the members of the Spanish Company in London, who after the restoration of Anglo-Spanish trading relations in 1604 unsuccessfully petitioned for the return of the property and the restoration of the brotherhood to its original secular status. The consulship was to remain in Catholic hands, despite later attempts from England to promote other candidates. A key role in all this was played by the merchant Thomas James, one of the signatories to the deed transferring the property of St George's.[14]

Cardinal Allen became the patron of the reconstituted residence of St George, and Dr Thomas Stillington was installed as its first Provost. The priests there—who were seculars, not Jesuits—were entrusted by the Inquisition with the task of inspecting English ships and searching them for heretical books. Persons meanwhile conducted a personal mission to a group of ninety English prisoners who were doing hard labour at Puerto de S.María. As a result of his mission they were reconciled to the Church *en masse*, and the occasion was marked by a banquet at which the converts were waited on at table by the Adelantado, Don Martín de Padilla, and other grandees. The cabin boys among the company, some of them not yet into their teens, were removed by Persons and placed in the households of Spanish noblemen or in Jesuit colleges, as domestics. Meanwhile the support of the local establishment—the Church, the Inquisition, the civil authorities—was sedulously cultivated.

In the autumn of 1592 Persons returned to Seville with the first nucleus of students, armed with a letter from the King to the Cardinal Archbishop, urging him to give the venture his moral and financial support, but discreetly ('con secreto y disimulación').[15] With so many demands on his patronage, the King was doubtless anxious to avoid creating precedents or provoking invidious comparisons. The Cardinal, Rodrigo de Castro, prided himself on his descent from the House of Lancaster and had accompanied Philip II on his visit to England years earlier, so he had personal reasons to be well disposed to the young Englishmen. The leading figures in Sevillan society also patronised the foundation: the Dukes of Arcos, Béjar and Sessa, the Marquesses of Priego and Ayamonte, the Marchionesses of Alcalá and Tarifa.[16] On 25 November Persons, his assistant Joseph Creswell and fourteen students took possession of temporary premises in the Plaza de San Lorenzo. Only a month later, on 29 December, the young community staged an open day to mark the feast of St Thomas of Canterbury. A distinguished gathering of civil and ecclesiastical dignitaries were given a repeat perform-ance of the *fiesta* which had been held for the King when he visited the Valladolid college earlier the same year. In Persons' words, 'the Cardinal and some other great personages were intertayned with orations and speeches in Latine, at their first entrance, until the masse began. The church and court thereunto adjoyned were addressed and hanged with great store of rich cloths, and thereupon much variety of poemes and learned inventions in Latin, Greeke, Hebrue, French, Spanish, Italian and other languages wherein these students seeme to have much use and skill'. During the mass, one of the students, John Worthington, preached in Latin on the text 'Bonus pastor animam dat pro ovibus suis', pointing to the parallel between the martyr of Canterbury and those of the present day. Later four students took the mission oath while another, George Chamberlain—a future Bishop of Ypres—explained the proceedings in Spanish. The youth and learning of the students, their aristocratic bearing and their piety all made a deep impression on public opinion. The people of Seville, Persons wrote, seemed to be 'ravished as it were with a kind of admiration of them, to see so many Inglish tender youthes al bred and borne in this Queene's reigne and yet so forward and fervent in their religion as to offer themselves to al kinde of difficulties, afflictions and perils for the same'.[17] The warmth of this reception was all the more remarkable given the general feeling against the English following Drake's attack on Cadiz five years earlier and the continuing havoc wrought on Atlantic shipping by English 'pirates'.

It was equally important for Persons that he should have the support of the local Jesuits. Claudio Acquaviva, the Father General, wrote to the Superior of the Professed House in Seville, Esteban de Hojeda, requiring his cooperation, adding: 'I should very much regret the expression of any word or feeling against it (the foundation)'. The phrase betrays anxiety. As we shall see, the Professed House feared a loss of income if the new college attracted donors away from it. Besides, Persons did not endear himself to some of the local Jesuits by wishing himself upon them with the help of powerful protectors from outside. Acquaviva at any rate was fully committed to, and concerned for, the new foundation. 'Since this work is something new in Spain and entrusted to the Company', he told the Andalusian Provincial, 'it is important for our reputation that it should succeed'.[18]

The Rector of the new College of St Gregory appointed by the Provincial was Francisco de Peralta, to whom its early success was largely due. He was Rector for over twenty years in all (1592–1607 and 1612–21). It cannot have been easy for him to have Persons, and later Creswell, looking over his shoulder, as it were, but he persevered and the students responded to his commitment and affection. St Gregory's was in fact the first seminary on Tridentine lines to be seen in Seville. Though the Spanish bishops had been foremost in supporting the proposals made at Trent for a new system of priestly training, they had taken few steps to put these proposals into practice, and the education of the secular clergy was of a low standard. However, the English attended the new Jesuit faculty of theology which had been opened at St Hermenegild's College in 1584 and which offered the best and most modern teaching available. They were regarded by the local people as Jesuit, rather than secular, students.

In May 1594 the college was formally constituted by a bull of Clement VIII whereby it acquired the privileges already granted to St Alban's at Valladolid. The same year Persons successfully negotiated an annual grant of 600 ducats from the city fathers—a subsidy which was to be the mainstay of the college finances. From January 1593 it was accommodated in cramped quarters in the Plaza de la Magdalena, where the overcrowding and heat took its toll of the students' health. In 1595 a more suitable and permanent site was bought in the Calle de las Armas, a main thoroughfare leading to the centre of the city from the Puerta Reál, on its southern side, and which derived its name from Seville's thriving armaments industry. It was the very same street in which St Teresa had established her first community twenty years earlier. A large sum was spent on converting the property to institutional use. 'It will be the finest college for many leagues', Persons wrote to Acquaviva, revealing the scale of his ambitions, 'and will accommodate more than a hundred and fifty persons'.[19] The new premises, of which the college took possession in October 1595, adjoined the palace of the Duke of Medina Sidonia (who gave it access to his water supply—a precious commodity in a city so subject to drought and disease) and was only a few yards distant from St Hermenegild's. The college also acquired a country retreat outside the city at Dos Hermanas. A chapel was endowed by Ana de Espinosa, widow of Alvaro de Flores, onetime commander of the Fleet of the Indies, and opened in 1598. The benefactress and her two brothers stipulated that they and their descendants should be buried in a family vault before the high altar. This condition was to cause some legal problems much later, when a member of the family claimed rights of patronage over the chapel. He demanded the privileges which other noble patrons enjoyed, such as to be offered the first palm on Palm Sunday and the first candle on the feast of the Purification—with his coat of arms embossed on it.[20] The detail illustrates the intense competition for public dignities and marks of honour which characterised the nobility of Seville.

These years coincided with the height of the persecution in England. In April 1594 Henry Walpole, who had been one of the founders of the college and had taught there between 1592 and 1593, died a martyr's death in London. Joseph Creswell's account of his martyrdom was widely circulated in Spain and America, and in Seville the college came to be regarded as a seedbed of future martyrs. Though the spirituality of Seville had always been obsessed with death and suffering, embodied in the images of the agonized Christ and his grieving mother which were, and are, the centrepieces of the Holy Week processions, the reality of martyrdom had never been experienced at first hand. Seville was now able to suffer vicariously through these English students whose youth and ardour moved their hearts. Something of the popular veneration felt for the college can be seen in Peralta's story of the two gentlemen who travelled from Morón de la Frontera, fifty miles away, to kiss its walls.[21]

The fervour which pervaded the college itself at this time can be glimpsed in Peralta's account of the death of two students, Robert Waller and Thomas Egerton, in 1595. The former died as the result of penitential practices undertaken to obtain the grace of his parents' conversion: 'In addition to the frequent and prolonged use of the discipline (which drew blood), fasting three days a week and wearing a hairshirt, he endured next to his skin a large, spiked iron brace which would have proved fatal even to a strong constitution. This was not discovered until after his death, nor was it ever known where he obtained the instrument'. Thomas Egerton, too, died as a result of excessive self-mortification. By flaying himself with the discipline 'he had drawn so much blood that by the time it was discovered and steps were taken to remedy his condition, he was mortally consumptive. He admitted that he and other students regularly rose at midnight and took the discipline in front of the Blessed Sacrament for an hour or more'. When on the point of death, the student summoned one of the fathers to hand over his hairshirt and blood-stained discipline, saying that he was surrendering his weapons now that the battle was over. 'He looked upon the sick room as his prison cell', Peralta wrote, 'and his physical sufferings as his martyrdom'.[22]

However much this account is coloured by rhetoric and by the author's concern to satisfy a local interest in the morbid, and though a modern reader may find it strange that a religious superior should condone such practices, the account must be seen in its context. These were not normal times, and this was no ordinary seminary, preparing its subjects for a lifetime of uneventful pastoral activity. Every student knew that he might have to undergo the supreme test, which could only be prepared for by a rigorous, ascetic training of mind and body. They were made fully aware of the ordeal they might have to face when the details of Henry Walpole's torture and execution became known. Those who keyed themselves up for this mission, only to be denied the opportunity because of ill-health, may have turned to self-mortification and 'white martyrdom' as a means of expressing their solidarity with the martyrs and assuaging a sense of guilt.

The first alumnus of the college to die on the scaffold was Thomas Hunt, *alias* Benstead, executed in 1600. The details of his and other martyrdoms were publicised at Seville in news-sheets based on first-hand reports received by Creswell from England. The English spy Giles van Hardwick, *alias* William Resould, wrote to London in 1599 that 'the Jesuite Creswell hath so good intelligence that their waggeth not a strawe in the Inglishe court but he heareth of it', and that he received weekly ' a porter's burden of letters of intelligence from all places'.[23] Interest in the English martyrs existed in Seville even before the foundation of St Gregory's. The University Library at Seville preserves a manuscript translation of Dom Maurice Chauncy's account of the martyrs of the London Charterhouse, written by a monk of the Cartuja at Seville. Later, Zurbarán painted a fine portrait of Dom John Houghton for the Cartuja at Jerez between 1637 and 1639. In 1592 the Sevillan humanist and poet Fernando de Herrera wrote a life of Thomas More, dedicated to the Cardinal Archbishop, Rodrigo de Castro. But Spaniards in general saw England in the context of chivalric romance. This is evident in Cervantes' story 'The Spanish-English Lady', which represents the Elizabethan court in a highly imaginative light, more appropriate to the court of King Arthur. A popular *romance*, or ballad, published at Seville in 1606, reported the conversion of King James following visions of Santiago and of his predecessor, Queen Elizabeth, who warned him of the fires of hell in which she was being consumed. 'Send me Theatines', it reported James as writing to the King of Spain ('Theatines' being the term by which the Jesuits were popularly known). This note of fantasy is to be found even in more sober reports. A *relación* of the embassy of Don Juan de Tassis to London in

1603 describes his visit to the 'castle of Miraflores' at Greenwich, 'mentioned by Amadis of Gaul'. Though the news-sheets published by St Gregory's were more factual, they were no doubt interpreted in the light of such preconceptions.[24]

Good relations with the Inquisition were essential to the college from its beginnings. Persons had to allay initial suspicions that the presence of Englishmen at Seville might be a potential source of heretical infection. He was careful to court its favour and win its support. Its officers were invited to college functions, and it became customary for students to pay them a formal visit on arrival and departure. On one such occasion, in 1616, the students' spokesman expressed his wish 'to see the Holy Tribunal established in England and other provinces plagued by heresy, in order that by its means religion might be kept pure and undefiled, as it was in Spain'.[25] The Inquisitors for their part made frequent use of the English Jesuit fathers at St Gregory's as interpreters, attending examinations of prisoners in its prison—the Castillo de Triana—or as censors, 'expunging the poisonous books of heretics'.[26] Few Spanish clergy could speak foreign languages, whereas the English had a more international background. Persons was later to claim with some pride that after 1592 not one Englishman had been put to death by the Inquisition, since he successfully established the principle that most Englishmen could not be classed as heretics in so far as they had never actually been Catholics. It has been reckoned that between 1585 and 1604 about fifty-seven Englishmen were imprisoned by the Inquisition, but only a minority of these were detained on religious grounds. For most English traders the Inquisition was a nuisance rather than a source of terror.[27]

The presence at Seville of so many English prisoners of war provided the students of St Gregory's in its early days with many opportunities for proselytism and controversial debate—opportunities equalled by no other continental seminary. There are frequent references in the Annual Letters to students going the rounds of 'prisons, galleys, hospitals and inns', and to 'conversations' with 'heretics' held in the college hall. However the presence of so many foreigners in the city meant that the college was particularly vulnerable to spies and informers, and the English government was regularly informed of its activities. There is the case, for example, of Constantine Eckelles, who on returning to England in March 1597 reported how as a prisoner of war at Seville the previous year he and his companions had been visited in gaol by Fathers Persons, Thorne and Walpole, who had sought to convert them. As a result, Eckelles and eleven others were reconciled and released into the care of St Gregory's, for it was customary for such prisoners to be placed under supervision in religious houses. He was found work at Sanlúcar, whence he escaped.[28] It is difficult to believe that a man of Persons' intelligence could have believed that such 'conversions' were likely to be lasting, but by similar action the English Jesuits rescued many of their fellow-countrymen from the horrors of the Seville gaol. In reporting the activities of the fathers at Sanlúcar, Eckelles added the interesting information that they changed their names every month, 'so as not to be discovered'. These aliases were adopted at Seville also. Another informant about the college was Giles Arkenstall, a shipper of corn to Spain, who in 1605 offered to report to William Cecil on his conversations at St Gregory's and to supply the names of those students whose return to England was imminent.[29]

The risks of these contacts with English prisoners and traders are best illustrated by the case of Edward Squyer. He and a companion were captured on an expedition to the Indies and brought to Seville where they were set at liberty but later fell foul of the Inquisition and were sentenced to two years of confinement in a monastery, to be instructed in the Catholic faith. From this monastery, the Carmen, they visited St Gregory's nearby for 'discussions' with the fathers and students, who do not seem to have taken Squyer very seriously. According to the account written by Martin Aray, when he asserted that 'he had the Holy Ghost within him . . . the scholars laughed heartily, and so did Father Persons also'.[30] However Squyer and his companion were reconciled, and in May 1597 petitioned to be allowed to return to England, 'where we hope by God's favour to do much service to His Divine Majesty in defence of his cause'. They cited Richard Walpole as a guarantor of their *bona fides*. The Spanish hoped to exchange them for two canons of Cadiz held in England, but a few days later, to Walpole's embarrassment, they escaped from their monastery and made their way to England. There the hapless Squyer became the instrument of a carefully contrived plan to discredit the Jesuits. Walpole, it was alleged, had asked him if he could 'compound poisons', and when he admitted to a 'skill in perfumes' he was, on the strength of this modest qualification, given the recipe of a deadly unction which he was to smear on the pommel of the Queen's saddle—having gained access to the stables of the Earl of Essex, his previous employer. He bought the ingredients—opium and mercury—in London and tried them out at Greenwich on a whelp, which was not seen again and was therefore presumed to have died as a result. The deadly ointment was to be conveyed in a double bladder and handled, for safety, with a glove. The idea was that the Queen would be sure to touch the poisoned pommel with her hand, which she would then put to her mouth, with fatal results. That so fantastic a story should have gained credence is striking evidence of the state of public opinion, worked on by the government. As Walpole himself observed, if he had contemplated so important a mission, he would hardly have entrusted it to 'so weak a vessel' as Squyer. When the details of the plot reached Seville and were read out to the students, Walpole recorded that 'the first effect which it wrought was to make us all merry for two recreations, the whole matter seeming in truth rather a may game or comical representation than a thing either done or devised in earnest'. The results were more serious. The story, and the publicity given to it, by Francis Bacon among others, did much to establish the Jesuits in popular demonology as intriguing regicides. Walpole was alleged to have promised Squyer that if he succeeded in the murder of the Queen—the 'unum necessarium'—'he should exchange his present state with the state of a glorious saint in heaven'.[31]

The restoration of trade between England and Spain in 1603 led to the return to Seville and Sanlúcar of English merchants. Over one hundred of them at Seville attended the funeral of a colleague in 1605, when he was buried 'in the night in the fields' as was the custom with heretics.[32] Henceforward the fathers of St Gregory's had to contend with enemies on their doorstep. In addition there was growing opposition from within the Andalusian province of the Society. Persons' death in 1610 left the English more vulnerable, for his successor, Joseph Creswell, was less diplomatic and conciliatory. The tensions between Creswell and some of his Spanish confrères broke out into open hostilities in 1612-13, and are documented elsewhere in this volume.[33] A list of grievances against the English, circulated within the Society, reveals the animosity which had gained ground. Many of the English fathers, it was suggested, had once been heretics or schismatics, or were the sons of such, and their orthodoxy was therefore unreliable. They were 'scheming and devious', and could not be trusted to manage their own affairs without Spanish supervision. Removed from Spanish control, the colleges at Valladolid and Seville could become nests of spies. Moreover the English were always 'divided among themselves', and so needed an impartial Spanish Rector to arbitrate in their disputes. Many of the English fathers had not had a regular formation, having been trained on the mission, and—as was to be expected of men brought up among heretics—they were uncivilised and unmannerly ('tienen costumbres y modos muy bárbaros').[34] Some of these accusations were prompted by xenophobia, others by resentment of Creswell's tendency to act as though the English were independent of the Spanish Provincials. One of the charges against him was that he had told the students at St Gregory's that the Spanish Jesuits were their worst enemies. He certainly did not disguise his disdain for his enemies and what he regarded as their provincial small-mindedness. The English, he wrote pointedly to the Father General, had not entered the Society 'in order to ensure a livelihood, or to win prestige for their families, or to make a career, but rather to save souls, to help others do the same, and to serve God'.[35] He failed in his attempt to establish a separate novitiate for the English in Granada, and to have St Gregory's put under an English Rector, and the Valladolid College narrowly escaped being transferred elsewhere.[36] In spite of his vigorous campaign of self-defence he was removed from Spain at the end of 1613 and his successor as Vice-Prefect at Madrid, Anthony Hoskins, did not carry the same weight. There are signs that all was not well at St Gregory's in the years that followed. Two students left to join the Benedictines in 1613, and ten were admitted to religious orders in 1619-20. Peralta ceased to be Rector in 1621, and none of his successors won the same confidence from the students.

Nevertheless, St Gregory's continued to be supplied with small but regular intakes of students from St Omer—in spite of the dangers of the sea journey. The main hazard in early years had been the possibility of interception by English ships. Those travelling from or to England often went by way of Irish ports. But the threat of falling into the hands of pirates from the Moroccan and Barbary coasts became equally, if not more, serious. Twelve students travelling from Calais to Seville by sea in 1622 were captured by a pirate ship and taken to Alarache on the Atlantic coast of Morocco, whence they escaped only after harrowing experiences from which one of them never recovered. It is surprising that parties of students continued even after this to make the hazardous sea voyage—especially in view of the substantial ransoms which were demanded by pirate captors.[37]

The political situation was now changing in a way which affected the English Catholics in Spain generally and St Gregory's in particular. The visit of the Prince of Wales to Madrid in 1623, and the prospect of a Spanish marriage, offered the exiles one last but illusory hope of obtaining a restoration of the old religion by political means, and of returning to England in the train of a Spanish princess. The collapse of that scheme was eventually followed by a new era in Anglo-Spanish relations, which was marked by a greater pragmatism on both sides. One of the effects of the Treaty of Madrid in 1630—one of the architects of which was an alumnus of St Gregory's, John Knatchbull, S.J.—was a diminution of the dependence of English Catholics on the Spanish crown.[38] Sir Francis Cottington, the English signatory of the treaty, passed through Seville on his way home in 1631. He and his retinue of eighty were fêted by the city fathers with the customary munificence, and a contemporary account records how the ambassador, on being shown the gardens of the Alcázar, pronounced them to be 'the finest sight he had seen in Europe'. After a visit to the Cathedral, Cottington's party went on to St Gregory's, where they remained until one o'clock in the morning. The English college evidently kept Andalusian hours.[39]

As the special relationship between English Catholicism and the Spanish crown became weaker, so did St Gregory's, now increasingly isolated and irrelevant to changing needs. Seville itself was already in decline. As its river silted up, it began to yield in importance as a naval and commercial port to Cadiz, its more enterprising neighbour, which had immediate access to the Atlantic. Seville had always been subject to flood, drought and disease, and in 1649 it was devastated by a catastrophic plague which cost about 60,000 lives—almost half the population. St Gregory's did not escape, for the Annual Letters record that in 1650 eight students were sent from St Omer to make up the losses. The martyrdom of three of the college's *beati* occurred in the 1640's,[40] but their deaths went unnoticed and unrecorded in a city which had lost interest in English Catholicism and which had more immediate sufferings to attend to on its own doorstep.

One of the problems faced by the authorities was to persuade the English Provincial to send them personnel of sufficient calibre who could be spared from the mission and who would be willing to serve in what was now an isolated outpost. In 1639 the Rector of St Gregory's asked that the English Minister, who was 'unsuitable', should be replaced by a Spaniard, but the General refused the request on the grounds that an Englishman was needed to read the students' letters.[41] Clearly there was a good deal of mutual incomprehension between superiors and students. The latter frequently complained of their conditions and their complaints were relayed to Rome, where the Father General often found it necessary to write to the Rector of

St Gregory's or the Andalusian Provincial, reminding them of the need to treat the students with understanding and paternal care. As early as 1610 he wrote to the then rector, Alonso Díaz (who had temporarily replaced the gentle Peralta) of reports that had reached him that 'if the students ask for something, they frequently get the reply that since they are to be martyrs it is good for them to suffer, or that since they are poor they should be content with poor conditions. They particularly resent this last remark, since the majority of them are well-born and rich and brought up in comfort'.[42] The General's correspondence also shows that he was disturbed by rumours of extravagance and slackness within the house. In 1638, for example, he told the Andalusian Provincial of his disquiet at learning that there were currently 17 Jesuits at St Gregory's compared with only 19 students—a situation which could only lead to 'murmuring'. Too much money was being spent on fiestas and fireworks, and he had heard that the Rector had entertained sixty of his Jesuit friends to dinner on the feast of St Thomas of Canterbury—wasting the resources which should be spent on the students.[43]

No doubt some of these peccadilloes may have been exaggerated by censorious students telling tales out of school. Nevertheless it is impossible to resist the impression that St Gregory's may have been used by the Provincial as a convenient refuge for the recalcitrant or unemployable. This is confirmed by the fact that the disgraced procurator of St Hermenegild's, Andrés de Villar, was placed under house arrest there. The scandal for which he was responsible is evidence that all was not well with the Society at Seville in the mid-17th century. In 1645 it was discovered that he had been speculating on a vast scale for years with the college funds, and when some of the ships in which he had invested went down in the Atlantic the college was left with debts of 400,000 ducats. Five hundred creditors were ruined and the liquidators moved in. It was, as the Jesuit historian has described it, the worst economic débacle ever suffered by the Society.[44] The number of staff at St Hermenegild's was cut from about eighty to fourteen, and its size and status were reduced to those of an obscure provincial college. One of the attractions of Seville for English students had been the quality of teaching at St Hermenegild's, but this advantage now disappeared.

Between 1646 and 1662 the number of students at St Gregory's fell from seventeen to five. Successive Spanish Rectors found it increasingly difficult to obtain students from St Omer and to obtain their annual subsidy from the city council.[45] It was difficult to justify such a subsidy when people in Seville were dying of hunger. In 1652 there were bread riots which spread to Cordoba and other Andalusian centres. This was the Seville painted by Murillo, where an army of ragged poor depended on charity. In such a context, appeals to the memory of the English martyrs by a college which was now in fact a hostel for Spanish students, with only a few token English, rang hollow. The problems caused for the Spanish authorities by trouble-makers such as Henry Gerard (p. 182) brought the crisis to a head. The last English student to be ordained at St Gregory's, Paul Savage, left in 1693, and with his departure the college ceased to be English in all but name.

Studies

Writing about St Gregory's in its early years, the Jesuit historian Henry More wrote that 'Francisco de Peralta made a praiseworthy Rector for a good many years and was altogether acceptable to the students. Nor did the young men flock to any other place with more enthusiasm than to Seville, both for this reason and also because although the climate reached the limits of the possible where heat was concerned, they still preferred that and the studies at St Hermenegild's to those of Valladolid and Rome'.[46]

At the end of the 16th century there were four professors of theology at St Hermenegild's, three of philosophy, and one of each of scripture, moral theology, Hebrew and Greek. The teaching was characterised by a humane and modern scholasticism, and there were distinguished scholars among the professors. Melchior de Castro, who presided at a disputation in 1593 at which Richard Walpole and Henry Floyd publicly defended theses, was known for his tract *de Beatitudine*. Juan de Pineda, the Rector of St Hermenegild's in the first decade of the 17th century, had a European reputation as a scriptural scholar, whose commentaries on Job, Ecclesiastes, and the Canticle of Canticles were published at Madrid, Cologne, Venice and Antwerp. The last-mentioned work, 780 pages long, has been described by a modern historian as 'a dense jungle of erudition'.[47] He was also the principal compiler of the Spanish *Index Expurgatorius* in 1607 and 1612, and an examiner of books for the Inquisition. He had close relations with St Gregory's. A letter from Richard Walpole at Seville to Richard Verstegan in Antwerp in August 1597 has a note appended by Pineda, with instructions about the title page of his commetary on Job, for which Verstegan also did the engravings.[48] It was Pineda who preached at the solemn exequies for Doña Luisa de Carvajal held at St Gregory's in 1614. In Seville he was celebrated above all as the champion of the Immaculate Conception, in whose cause he wrote and preached. He is better known to posterity as the target of a satirical sonnet by Góngora, whose wrath he aroused by failing to award him a prize at a poetry contest in 1610. He later wrote a censorious report on Góngora for the Inquisition. Another distinguished scriptural scholar who taught at the college was Luis del Alcázar, whose commentary on the Apocalypse was published at Seville in 1603, at Antwerp in 1614 and at Lyons in 1619. Among the better-known theologians were Diego Ruiz de Montoya (d. 1632) and Diego Granado (d 1632), and the humanities were well represented by Melchior de la Cerda, Hernando de Avila and Gerónimo de Zaragoza.

In its early years, St Gregory's catered for a wide range of students, from those in their early teens to those in their late twenties, covering the curriculum from grammar and rhetoric through to theology. There seems to have been no division of labour between the various English colleges, and students were assigned to places where there was room for them. A leaflet written about 1604 to raise local funds for St Gregory's describes the course of studies there as consisting of rhetoric, poetry, Greek, 'arts' (the term used for philosophy—including logic, mathematics, physics and natural history), theology, controversy, instrumental and choral church music, and liturgy.[49]

Until about 1620 St Gregory's had an English Prefect of Studies and an English professor of controversy and 'cases' (casuistry)—subjects which had to be taught in an English context. William Weston and Michael Higgins, who lectured in these subjects at this time, were men of wide pastoral experience, and the former was a hero of the English mission. Students were able to practise their controversial skills in the 'conversations' held with Protestant prisoners or visitors in the college hall. The high standard of teaching in the humanities is evident from the successes obtained by students in local poetry contests. The mention of instruction in music and liturgy is interesting. William Davis (ECS 1595-1600) went on to become the director of music at the English College in Rome. In 1599 an organ costing 120 ducats was installed in the college chapel by John Pickford, sometime organist of the chapel royal in Lisbon and later English consul at Sanlúcar.[50] He was one of several Cornish brothers from St Germans who spent their lives in the service of the Spanish crown.

In the second decade of the 17th century a more organised pattern emerged, with the regular despatch from St Omer of students who had completed their studies of humanities and came to Seville to start their philosophy. In 1616 a decision was taken that the philosophers should go to Valladolid and the theologians to Seville,[51] but this arrangement did not work out, for the Annual Letters continue to record the arrival of students at St Gregory's to begin philosophy. On matters of study as well as discipline the Rector of St Gregory's was instructed by the General to take advice from the Rector of the English College in Rome. In 1630 the Rector was told not to admit students unless they came from St Omer, in view of the poor standard of knowledge shown by those recently taken from elsewhere.[52]

Paradoxically, those alumni of St Gregory's who achieved distinction in later life as theologians or controversialists were noted for their opposition to the Jesuits and tended towards Gallicanism. Their erudition, however, is a tribute to the training they received at St Hermenegild's. Paul Green and Henry Mailer were contemporaries at St Gregory's between about 1599 and 1602, when Richard Smith, the future titular Bishop of Chalcedon, was a lecturer there. Thirty years later, Mailer, as a doctor of the theological faculty of Paris, was an active promotor of Smith's cause in his dispute with the Jesuits, and collaborated with Green, then in Dublin, in securing the condemnation of the 'Irish propositions' by the Sorbonne.[53] Two other prominent figures in the anti-Jesuit party, Thomas White, *alias* Blacklow, and Mark Harrington, *alias* Drury, were contemporaries at St Gregory's between 1612 and 1614. The most curious of this crop of theologian alumni was John Salkeld, a contemporary of Green and Mailer, who left the college to become a Jesuit in Andalusia in 1602 and remained there until 1608. Returning to England, he conformed to the Church of England and was presented to the living of Wellington, Somerset, by James I. In 1613 he published *A Treatise of Angels: of the nature, essence, place, power, science, will, apparitions, grace, sinne and all other proprieties of angels: collected out of the holy scriptures, ancient fathers and schoole-divines.* In his 'epistle dedicatorie' to the King he wrote that the angels had 'touched' him 'long since by ministeriall motion and illustration to search those things which of myselfe it was impossible for mee to attaine unto, about the Romish abuses, errors, tyrannies and usurpations. But what had all this beene, if the splendour of your Majesties beames, the force of your Majesties reasons, the evidence of your demonstrations, had not so manifestly convinced, so forcibly perswaded me . . . loosing the fetters wherewith I was tied, bringing mee out of the Dungeon to which I was condemned? *Nunc scio vere quod misit angelum suum et eripuit me de manu Herodis, Papae, Hispanicae Inquisitionis, omnique expectatione Jesuitarum'*. In 1617 Salkeld followed this up with an equally learned and curious work, *A Treatise of Paradise and the principall contents thereof*, dedicated to Sir Francis Bacon. This unlikely disciple of Suárez, transplanted from Andalusia to a West Country rectory, lived on through the Civil War to die in the year of the Restoration.[54]

As the number of students and of English Jesuits at St Gregory's declined, so did the standard of theological studies. St Hermenegild's never recovered its prestige after the bankruptcy scandal of 1649. By then, theological studies throughout Spain were moribund, and in the following century sterile disputations displaced the study of the scriptures and the fathers. It became the routine for students to proceed to 'doctorates'—which St Gregory's claimed to award, according to the terms of Clement VIII's bull of foundation, on a par with the universities of Oxford and Cambridge—but they were valueless.[55]

Fiestas and Justas

When St Teresa inaugurated her convent at Seville in 1576, she reluctantly gave way to her advisers who recommended that instead of the private ceremony she would have preferred, she should, in the interests of public relations, attract public attention with a spectacular *fiesta* marked by flowers, music, fireworks and the discharge of cannon. The enthusiasm of the crowd almost caused a disaster when a stray rocket set off a blaze in the cloister, threatening to set fire to the silk hangings with which they were adorned. Seville lived for the *fiesta*, and the Jesuits adroitly harnessed this passion, refining it by means of sacred art and rhetoric to create a unique form of devotional spectacle.

The most dazzling of these events was that staged in 1610 to celebrate the beatification of Ignatius Loyola. The octave of festivities began with a cavalcade of the students of St Hermenegild's College, three hundred and fifty in number, who paraded through the city to the accompaniment of trumpets and drums, the lay students magnificently attired and mounted on horses and mules, while bells rang out all over the city. The event coincided with the royal decree ordering the deportation of the *moriscos*, and the authorities must have welcomed it as a providential distraction at a time of major social upheaval. It was also the time of year when the fleet of the Indies was due to depart, so the city was more than usually crowded. The celebrations reached their climax on the Sunday, when at the stroke of midnight the bells of the Giralda began a peal which was taken up by every

belfry in the city, accompanied by a blaze of pyrotechnics. The cloisters of
St Hermenegild's were hung with decorated scrolls bearing mottos,
emblems, hieroglyphs and enigmas, and 'between it and the English College,
a little distance away, there was a wire along which many varied and
ingenious rockets sped to and fro. On the last day of the octave the students
of the English College sang the solemn mass in the chapel'.[56]

The frenetic atmosphere of such occasions, added to the normal cycle of
Sevillan street festivals, must have been a heady experience for English
seminarians reared in a less exotic religious climate. In the years that
followed, St Gregory's was caught up in the excitement of the so-called
'Marian Wars', in which the Society of Jesus played a leading part. The
hostilities were sparked off in 1613, when a Dominican friar preached a
sermon offensive to devotees of the Immaculate Conception, which had
long been an object of special piety in Seville, a city which takes pride in its
Marian fervour and in believing today what Rome defines tomorrow. One
of the factors which endeared the English students to the populace was their
devotion to Mary, and it is significant that Persons and his successors made
much of the tradition of England's prerogative as the dowry of Mary.

Henceforward the Dominicans fought an unequal battle against popular
fervour supported by Jesuit preaching and organisation. Mariology took to
the streets, where small boys taunted Dominicans and chanted the popular
quatrain composed by the poet Miguel Cid:

> Todo el mundo en general
> a voces, Reina escogida,
> diga que sois concebida
> sin pecado original

('let all the world proclaim aloud, chosen Queen, that you are conceived
without original sin').[57] The protagonists in this conflict were closely
connected with St Gregory's. The leading Jesuit Mariologist, Juan de
Pineda, had preached at the dedication of the college chapel in 1598, and
delivered the panegyric for Doña Luisa de Carvajal there in 1614. Miguel
Cid, who more than any other fired Seville for Mary without spot, left a
bequest to the college in his will.[58] Students from St Gregory's took part in
poetry contests held in honour of the Inmaculada by local confraternities,
and later participated in the explosion of rejoicing which in 1617 followed
Paul V's decree forbidding public assertion either for or against the
doctrine. Only in Seville could such a non-committal ruling have been hailed
as a victory for the *opinión pía*. Reporting the celebrations, Pineda
described how a crowd attacked the house of a Portuguese merchant,
denouncing him as a 'Thomist dog'. Others strung up a grotesque effigy
representing 'Original Sin', and such was the blaze of illuminations that the
price of wax rose from three to four reales. Contemporary accounts, with
their descriptions of cavalcades and street theatre, convey an atmosphere of
collective mariomania. There was another wave of rejoicing in 1622 when
Gregory XV shifted ground a little further by imposing a stricter ban on
expression of the Thomist view. A contemporary witness recorded the
progress of the victory procession. A sumptuous silver altar was erected in

the Calle de las Armas opposite the entrance of St Gregory's, where the street was spanned by a castellated arch flying the standards of England and Spain, its battlements manned by students of the college in military costume, armed with muskets which they fired as each statue passed beneath, to a flourish of trumpets.[59]

Like their counterparts at other Jesuit colleges, the English students publicly took the *voto sanguinario*, whereby they pledged themselves to defend the doctrine of the Immaculate Conception, even unto death. The profession of this oath was attended with much solemnity.[60]

It had become fashionable in Seville to mark festive occasions with poetical jousts (*justas*), or contests, judged by persons of social or ecclesiastical eminence, who awarded rich prizes in various categories. The contests attracted a large popular audience, drawn by the element of gladiatorial combat which prevailed. Jesuit showmanship turned what might otherwise have been an academic exercise into a spectacle. In several such contests the English swept the board of prizes for Latin verse. The *justa* held to mark the beatification of Ignatius Loyola in 1610 attracted entries in the vernacular from the finest poets of the day: Luis de Góngora, Juan de Jáuregui, Francisco Pacheco, Rodrigo Caro and Juan de Robles. But alongside their names appeared those of Henry Ballinger, Robert Smith, Edward Hopton, Henry Salkeld, William Morris, Andrew Barnes, William Aston, Thomas Pigott, Richard Curtis and Nicholas Harrington who put on a dazzling dislay of baroque Latinity in the form of epigrams, elegiacs, hexameters, palindromes, acrostics, hendecasyllables, alcaics and sapphics, all ingeniously connected with events in the life of Ignatius or based on Ignatian anagrams.[61]

Another 'joust' was organised by a priestly confraternity in 1615 to honour the Immaculate Conception, when popular fervour was at its height. Here too English students carried off prizes: a purse richly embroidered with silk and gold, a silver toothpick and a gold ring—odd gifts, it might be thought for clerical students.[62] In 1623 the Basque community at Seville held a further competition to celebrate the canonisation of their countrymen Ss.Ignatius and Francis Xavier. In awarding the first prize for Latin verse to two English students, William Philips and Robert Barret, the adjudicator praised the first as 'a great English poet' who could bear comparison with Horace. On this occasion the prizes were more appropriate: a breviary in a gold-tooled binding, and a Plantin bible.[63]

The Jesuits in Seville had succeeded in capitalising on the passion for the theatre which pervaded all classes of society . The *Tragedy of St Hermenegild* staged at the inauguration of their new college in 1580 was nicely calculated to appeal to a popular audience. Though sections of the play were in Latin, it was mainly in the vernacular and contained broadly comic scenes which satirised the pedantry of the scholastic traditionalists of the *colegios mayores*. The play was later revived at the English college, which suggests that it had a lasting popularity.[64] The plays at St Gregory's attracted a fashionable and aristocratic audience. In 1595 the feast of St Hyacinth was marked by an exhibition of poetry and by a Latin play devised by Robert

Persons and written by one of the students, *Anglia Lapsa Resurgens*, described as 'a history of the principal events in England in the reign of Queen Elizabeth'. According to the *Annuae Litterae*, the first domestic performance was so successful that two further performances were put on for the Cardinal Archbishop, the Inquisitor, the Asistente and the Regent.[65] Another topical 'tragicomedy', *Cicilius ἄθεos, non Anglicanus*, was given three performances in 1598 and attended by such distinguished figures as the Duke of Alcalá and the Marquess of Tarifa.[66] In 1619 the college put on an acclaimed performance of a tragedy entitled *Rex Isauricus*, presumably on the theme of the Byzantine emperor Leo III, 'Isauricus', whose edicts against image worship provoked the iconoclastic controversy.[67] The production of this play at Seville came only five years after the production at St Omer of *Arsenius*, the first example of any play based on Byzantine history and the forerunner of a long series of Byzantine tragedies written and staged at St Omer. *Zeno*, another play by the author of *Arsenius*, Joseph Simons (*vere* Emmanuel Lobb), the English Jesuit, was performed at Seville between 1631 and 1634.[68] Earlier, according to James Wadsworth, the adventures of the twelve unfortunate travellers from St Omer to Seville in 1622 were made the subject of 'a tragical comedy, whereby they [the Jesuits] got much money and honour'.[69]

St Gregory's benefited from the close contacts which the Society of Jesus established with leading figures in the cultural as well as the social life of Seville. Among its early benefactors was the poet and classical scholar Juan de Arguijo, famous for his munificent patronage of the arts, and the distinguished Latinist Canon Francisco Pacheco whose 'academy' or salon was attended by the leading poets and painters of the day.[70] The visual arts, too, came within the Jesuit orbit. To adorn the high altar of St Gregory's chapel, admired for its 'great beauty and rare contriving', a painting was commissioned in 1608 from the most eminent artist in the city, Juan de Roelas. His *retablo*, or reredos, described by Fr John Price as 'one of the best and most curious in Seville', was calculated to emphasise the ancient links between the churches of England and Seville. It portrayed St Gregory, the apostle of England, in a group which included the local hero St Hermenegild; St Gregory's friend and correspondent St Leander, the bishop of Seville who converted the Visigoths from Arianism to orthodoxy; and ten bishop saints who belonged to St Leander's 'school': Isidore of Seville, Fulgentius of Cartagena, Ss.Helladius, Eugene I, Eugene II, Ildephonsus and Julian of Toledo and Ss.John, Braulius and Tagus of Saragossa. Though these were all saints who followed the rule of St Benedict, they were represented by the painter not in the Benedictine habit but in the choir dress of canons regular. Perhaps, as Dom Romanus Ríos has suggested, the fathers who commissioned the painting instructed the artist not to stress the Benedictine connection, in view of recent defections to that order from the English seminaries in Spain. Another painting which Roelas executed for the Jesuits, a *retablo* of the circumcision for the Casa Profesa, was certainly carried out to a precise iconographical brief.[71]

Though the great age of Seville printing had come to an end by the late

16th century, as the old humanism fell victim to the Inquisition and the Index, Seville remained a centre of printing and the chief exporter of books to America. The earliest printer to the college was Clemente Hidalgo, a native of Cadiz. Francisco de Lyra, who printed for the college between 1623 and 1625 and was a poet in his own right—famous for his edition of the *Rimas* of Juan de Jáuregui—had premises in the alley leading to St Gregory's from the Calle de las Armas. News-sheets based on intelligence received at the college were distributed through the network of Jesuit houses in Andalusia and even in America. College account books record the despatch of *impresos* about English Catholic affairs to Lima and Mexico on several occasions between 1595 and 1601[72]. Among those sent to Peru in 1595 were 170 copies of Creswell's *Martirio que padeció el P.Henrique Walpolo*. The cause of St Gregory's was promoted in America by Rodrigo de Cabredo, the first Rector of St Alban's Valladolid and a close friend of Francisco de Peralta, who was Provincial in Peru from 1599 to 1609 and in Mexico from 1610 to 1616. This may explain why Peralta's letter to Cabredo on the death of Luisa de Carvajal, printed in Seville in 1614, was reprinted in Lima later.[73]

If the *relaciones* and *cartas* were written for an educated readership, popular ballads or *coplas* celebrated the English martyrs in the street. In 1598 Canon Pacheco was asked to give his imprimatur to such a ballad on 'the life and martyrdom of Father Walpole', and in 1615 the Jesuit Martín de Luna published at Cuenca a verse *romance* based on a report of the suffering of imprisoned English Catholics published at Seville and Granada the same year.[74]

One book at least is known to have been printed in English at Seville for use by Jesuit fathers working among prisoners and seafarers in the Andalusian ports. This was the catechism, *A Briefe Instruction*, written by William Warford S.J, under the pseudonym George Doulie and published in 1600. It was still being used in Andalusia nearly forty years later, as is shown by a letter written from Cadiz in 1638 by the English Jesuit William Johnson, acknowledging receipt of copies from St Omer (where it was reprinted in 1616) and ordering 300 more.[75]

In 1623 there was a plethora of news-sheets at Seville reporting every detail of the Prince of Wales' visit to Madrid, based on information received at St Gregory's from the Rector of St George's College in the capital. After that there was a falling-off of publications emanating from St Gregory's, as interest shifted away from English affairs.

Temporalities

For all his initial success at Seville, Robert Persons left St Gregory's two legacies which amounted to a *damnosa hereditas*. The first was a disadvantage common to the entire English Catholic community in Spain, namely that as clients of the King of Spain they could be represented by their enemies as collaborators. The second handicap was peculiar to St Gregory's: its lack of an adequate endowment, which made it dependent on Spanish charity. The college relied mainly on its annual grants of six hundred ducats from the city and a hundred ducats from the cathedral chapter. Other contributions from the public were bound to fluctuate according to circumstances and mood. In the early years fashion favoured the college. Two of its influential patrons, Juan de Arguijo and Miguel de Jáuregui, among others, donated the annual salary due to them as city councillors, and as at Valladolid, so at Seville rich nobles volunteered to sponsor one or two students each year.[76] But the college lacked the normal rents from property which would have provided more lasting security. In 1600 the King had to make a secret grant of a thousand ducats, and a similar subsidy of 1500 ducats was paid in 1608.[77] That St Gregory's survived during these years was largely due to Creswell, whose business acumen, as Persons once remarked, was 'greater perhaps' than his talent 'for dealing with young men in a college'.[78] His appeals for funds made much of the martyrs, using the argument, still adduced as late as 1644, that 'anyone who supports these seminaries is supporting martyrs'.[79] This was a strategy which had much success in the years of persecution but which paid fewer and fewer dividends as time went on.

The conclusion of a peace treaty between England and Spain in 1604 made it necessary for Creswell to shift his ground. When the city's grant to St Gregory's came up for renewal that year, there was some opposition to it among the councillors, on the grounds that they had more pressing debts to honour and more urgent calls on their charity at home. In arguing the case for continued charity, Creswell appealed to motives of piety, of 'Christian nobility' and of 'temporal advantage'. As long as heresy prevailed in England, he maintained, there would be no lasting peace or prosperity for Spain. The rebellion in the Spanish Netherlands, the raids on Spain's American territories, the disruption of her Atlantic trade—all these problems were caused by England and would continue as long as England was Protestant and therefore hostile. No city had felt the effects of English aggression more acutely than Seville, and no city had more to gain from peace, but the key to peace was the conversion of England. In continuing to support St Gregory's, therefore, the city fathers would not simply be doing their Christian duty, they would be helping to train a spiritual army which would convert England not by force of arms—for the failure of the armadas had shown that this was not in accordance with God's will—but by apostolic preaching. That was the only lasting means of making Spanish harbours secure again, thus reducing the sums spent on protecting the Atlantic fleet.[80]

These were ingenious arguments, calculated to appeal to the economic self-interest of the Seville merchant class, and they were effective, for the council renewed its grant—not before consulting a panel of theologians, who ruled that the debtor (in this case the city council) was not exempt from the general obligation of almsgiving.

Creswell had some novel ideas for raising funds. In 1612 he put to the King a proposal that he should lift the ban on the cultivation of tobacco in the Windward Islands (Islas de Barlovento) and that a proportion of the resulting proceeds should go to support the English and Irish colleges at

Seville. America was an important source of funds. Rodrigo de Cabredo, the first Rector of the English College at Valladolid and a close friend of Francisco de Peralta, was active in raising funds for St Gregory's in Peru and Mexico. In 1613, for instance, he obtained a donation of 225 pesos from the Bishop of Tlaxcala. Permission to seek alms in America was rarely given, but in 1620 the King sent an official instruction to all the Viceroys, prelates and governors in his dominions there to raise funds for this pious end, and in January 1621 the Father General followed this up with a letter to the Provincials of Mexico and Peru, asking for their help in collecting money 'for the English seminaries in Spain and Flanders'. The Seville college was particularly well placed in this regard. The Procurator of the Indies resided at St Hermenegild's College, and Jesuit missionaries awaiting passage for America were lodged there, so that useful contacts could be made.[81]

In questing for alms at home, St Gregory's came into competition with the Professed House at Seville, and the issue was to become a lasting cause of contention and bad feeling. As early as 1596 the Superior of the Professed House successfully obtained from Rome a ruling that alms collectors from St Gregory's had to be accompanied on their rounds by two students from the college, to make it explicitly clear that they were seeking donations not for the Society (thereby infringing on the territory of the local Province) but specifically for the English college. The Father General was still having to remind the Rector of St Gregory's of this ruling nearly thirty years later.[82]. At least one and often two English Jesuit laybrothers resided at the college until about 1650 with the title of *eleemosynarius*, and are listed as such in the triennial catalogues. The students, it appears, were not always keen to accompany them on their rounds. When the Rector reported this reluctance to the Father General in 1623. the latter wanted them to be reminded that this was normal practice in Rome, where 'for many years English students have gone out collecting alms not only in this city and the surrounding district but throughout the Kingdom of Naples, causing great edification by their modesty and the excellent example they have given everywhere'. Nevertheless, he added, they should not be forced to go out begging— though two English laybrothers would have to go out together instead.[83]

A glimpse of this practice—and of the fund-raising methods used—is afforded in the otherwise tendentious account of St Gregory's by Lewis Owen, in his *Running Register*: 'They have an English youth that walks up and down the city in a gown, and a box in his hand, all the day long, and begs from door to door for the English College; and yet he comes to one place but once a week; for the city is great and spacious, and they have many good benefactors that bestow upon them a certain set pension or stipend monthly or weekly; some in money, and some in bread, wine or oil; and this their young collector has a catalogue of all their names, where they dwell, and how much they usually give. They have also a great box in every ship that sails either from Seville, Sanlúcar or Cadiz to the West India, with the picture of St Thomas Becket upon it, with this superscription, *Sancte Thoma Cantuariensis, ora pro nobis*; St Thomas of Canterbury, pray for us; which box is tied with a great chain unto the mainmast of the ship, and in the lid there is a hole, for people to put their devotion into. The Rector of the English College has the key of this box, and promises to have a world of masses said for the prosperous and safe return of the ship and the passengers'.[84]

Occasionally the methods of fund-raising at the college drew a rebuke from Rome. In 1622 the General was disturbed to hear that the Procurator had taken to sitting at the church door with a plate, soliciting donations—something 'unheard of in the Society'— and demanded that he should be publicly reprimanded. On a number of occasions the college was in such financial straits that the Rector had to write to St Omer asking them to send no students that year. It was normal practice for St Omer to pay two-thirds of the students' travelling expenses, while St Gregory's covered the other third—following the precedent set by the English College at Rome.[85]

At an early date it became customary for the King to pay a *viático* of 50 ducats to each priest travelling back to the mission—the sum being claimed from the Casa de la Contratación in Seville by the college. The grant payment was made in silver—even after Spanish missionaries travelling to the Indies began to be paid in debased *vellón*. An additional *viático* was frequently given by the cathedral chapter, and the college itself provided 12 ducats. Some of this money would have been spent on clothes for the journey.[86]

Shortage of money, therefore, was a source of never-ending preoccupation and successive Rectors devoted a disproportionate amount of their time to the problem of survival. It is not surprising, then, that the foundation of an Irish College at Seville in 1611 caused the Society some alarm at the prospect of further competition for charity. In January 1614 the Father General wrote asking for information about a house of Irish youths in the city under the charge of a secular priest.[87] In 1619 the Society solved the problem by taking over the foundation itself. The number of students was kept to a minimum, so that it posed no financial threat. Like St Gregory's it was subject to the Andalusian Provincial of the Society, but was allowed to have an Irish Jesuit Rector, at least until 1687.

Towards the middle of the 17th century it became ever more difficult for the college to obtain its annual grant from the city, as repeated petitions show. The grant was reduced in 1645, when the King allowed it to claim the proceeds of a duty of two *maravedís* (a third of a *reál*) on every pound of fleshmeat sold at the city slaughterhouse.[88] Another source of income was the boarding fees of Spanish *porcionistas*, lay student lodgers studying at St Hermenegild's. Nevertheless the grants from the city and Cathedral chapter continued to be paid, albeit reluctantly, right up to the suppression of the college, and in the 19th century they were claimed by St Alban's College, Valladolid, as the legal heir of St Gregory's.

St Gregory's and the Society of Jesus

An examination of the alumni list and the lists of English Jesuits recorded in Andalusia show that St Gregory's had closer ties with the Society of Jesus than any other English seminary on the continent. Of all the students recorded in the alumni list, just under a fifth went on to join the Society. Most of these proceeded to Flanders for their novitiate, but some joined in Spain. In April 1602 the Father General wrote to the Andalusian Provincial urging him to receive Englishmen into the Society on the grounds that it would be a source 'of general edification and of comfort to the seminaries as proof of our love and esteem'. In 1610 he urged all four of the Spanish Provincials to accept two or three, and preferably more, English novices a year whenever possible, and in 1618 he extended the request to include one Irishman a year. There were financial advantages involved in this practice, since the recruitment of two students a year by the Society meant two less mouths for St Gregory's to feed—a consideration which is made explicitly in a letter of the General to Francisco de Peralta in May 1619.[89] Most of the alumni of St Gregory's who joined the Society in Spain went to the Andalusian novitiate at Montilla (later transferred to Seville), but some went to other provinces. In 1614, for instance, Richard Curtis and Edmund Campion entered the novitiate of the Province of Castille, at Villagarcía. The archives of other provinces may contain other names, still to be discovered.

II. THE IRISH YEARS, 1710–1767

For nearly twenty years, from 1693, St Gregory's took no students from the British Isles, though it continued to be called the 'English' College. According to Bishop Challoner, writing in 1754, the Andalusian Province was finally stirred to action by an attempt on the part of the Irish Dominicans to have the college transferred to them. There had long been an Irish Dominican presence at Seville, based at the monastery of San Pablo. When St Gregory's reopened as a college about 1710 it took in Irish students, with only the occasional Englishman.

The Irish College of St Patrick, which as a Jesuit foundation dated back to 1619, was even less well endowed than its English neighbour.[90] Its premises, in the calle de las Palmas, near the Alameda de Hércules, were small, and the foundation could only support about five students at any one time, though in the 18th century that number increased to a dozen. Although subject to the Andalusian province, it was until 1687 governed by an Irish Rector, but there were frequent disagreements between the latter and his Spanish confrères, and discontent among the students broke out on several occasions into open rebellion.[91] From 1687 it was administered by Andalusian Rectors, who found their subjects intractable. However, unlike St Gregory's in the late 17th century, it had no trouble in recruiting students and so it was natural that when the supply of Englishmen dried up, the places at St Gregory's should have been made available to Irish candidates. The distinction between Irish, English and Scots was one which most Spaniards regarded as immaterial, and the confusion is evident in the way that students of St Gregory's continued to be recorded as 'English'. From 1710, therefore, until its closure in 1767, St Gregory's was *de facto* an Irish college. There were never more than about six students there at any one time, often less, and in many cases they were ordained soon after arrival (or even before), in order that they could earn the stipends attached to masses which the college was obliged to have said to meet the terms of endowments. One Bartholomew Boylan, for instance, entered the college in 1738, was ordained the following year, and left in 1744 after taking his doctorate. The majority of students came from the archdiocese of Dublin, and from the counties of Dublin and Meath, which were the recruiting grounds of the Irish College also. Though these students continued to take the oath to return 'to England' when the Rector 'saw fit', in fact some of them remained in Spain for as long as ten years. There were reasons for this. At the beginning of the 18th century the English merchant colony at Seville withdrew, and its place was taken by a large number of Irish, most of them from Waterford, who established themselves in Seville, Cadiz, Huelva and Malaga. There was pastoral work to be done among these exiles. Few priests remained permanently in Spain. Most returned to Ireland, some to England. The Spanish chapel in London was staffed for much of the century by a succession of priests from St Gregory's.

The English link, meanwhile, was all but broken. Writing to Bishop Stonor in May 1737, James Dodd observed that 'the college at Seville has been totally neglected of late by the English Jesuits, so far that the Spanish Rector, to maintain himself and companions by charity, upon the account of its primitive institution for English clergy, admits of Irish or any he can pick up of the three kingdoms'.[92] For the moment the English vicars apostolic were content to let sleeping dogs lie. In 1753, as a result of complaints from the Irish merchant community in Andalusia, who wanted St Patrick's College at Seville to be put under the authority of Irish Jesuits, Propaganda ordered an investigation into the two colleges by the arch-diocesan authorities and by the nuncio. The coadministrator at Seville reported that the state of both colleges was satisfactory, though the students were often 'rough and wild characters who take badly to discipline'. There were currently eight students at each college, he reported, though he was less well informed about St Gregory's than about St Patrick's.[93]

In August 1754 Richard Challoner addressed a long memorandum to Propaganda in which he outlined a plan for the revival of St Gregory's. He reminded the Roman authorities of the decline in the number of priests working in England: a hundred years ago there had been only 40, and even including the Irish there were currently only 140. This situation would be improved if the two Spanish colleges were to be revivified, but it was important that the choice of students should lie with the Vicars Apostolic, not with the Jesuits, who would if left to themselves send their cast-offs ('quisquiliae') from St Omer, keeping their most promising students for the Society. He suggested that younger boys also should be sent to Spain for education in the humanities, since the lack of such provision for Catholic youth in England meant that seminary candidates were inadequately prepared to begin their studies of philosophy. One or two English priests, he suggested, should remain in the colleges to teach these younger boys. However it was important that the students should be properly fed (food being 'the major cause of complaint against the Seville college') and that the curriculum should have a practical orientation towards the apostolate, with an emphasis on scripture and on polemical and moral theology.[94]

It was fortunate for Challoner and for the Church that his proposals were not acted upon. It can only be supposed that his schemes were based on complete ignorance of the financial situation of the Seville college. His distrust of the Jesuits may be explained by the fact that an alarming number of students from Valladolid were joining the Society rather than returning to England. For more than sixty years, he declared, St. Alban's had not sent a secular priest of any note to England. There were currently only two alumni of the college serving as priests in England, and one of them, in London, 'because of his crass ignorance and dissolute morals is considered unfit to be entrusted with the administration of the sacraments'. Perhaps as a result of Challoner's representations, and on the initiative of the Nuncio in Spain, the Father General forbade students from Valladolid to be admitted to the Society until after they had served a term as priests in England. They had to take an oath to this effect, but in 1766 five students of the college wrote to the Cardinal Protector at Rome asking for exemption.[95]

The future of the Spanish colleges was soon to be determined by other factors, political rather than ecclesiastical. The enemies of the Society in Spain were awaiting their opportunity to strike. By 1767 it was under attack from a variety of interested parties: from a regalist government which wanted to break its hold on education and to carry through a programme of ecclesiastical and educational centralisation; from the secular clergy and other religious orders who were jealous of its power; from 'Jansenist' reformers who denounced the laxity of its moral theology; from a Bourbon king who wanted a Church which would be under his control, not that of the Pope. Added to this was a more general but none the less powerful resentment fed by stories of the Society's fabulous wealth, its political intrigues and condoning of regicide. A series of popular riots in Madrid in 1766 was alleged to have been fomented by the Jesuits and became the pretext for the final act of suppression.[96]

The details of the operation were planned with a precision and efficiency more often associated with Teutonic Germany than with Latin Spain. Secrecy and surprise were essential, and were observed with total success. The order for the suppression was approved by the royal council on 29 January 1767, and signed by the King on 20 February. Sealed orders were despatched to every city in the kingdom, with instructions that they were not to be opened until 2 April. In Seville the Teniente Mayor opened his envelope on the appointed day and at 11 p.m. briefed his forces on the details of the operation. At 3 a.m. on 3 April, on a night of pouring rain, every Jesuit house in the city was picketed by an armed guard, which moved in at dawn. The entire contents of every establishment were seized, and in due course inventoried. (Among the monies found at St Hermenegild's were rents collected at Carmona for Henry, Cardinal Duke of York, who was Archdeacon of Carmona and a Canon of Seville Cathedral.) The fathers themselves, together with those novices who opted to share their fate, were given nine days to prepare for departure and were allowed to take with them only the bare necessities. At midnight on 10 April the entire Jesuit population of Seville was conducted to the quayside to begin the journey down river to Sanlúcar, from where they went on by land to Jerez to join their confrères from the other towns in the province. The entire company, thus rounded up, was then taken to Puerto de S. María to embark for Italy and exile. They reached Civitavecchia on 30 May. The deportation process, so catastrophic for the Society, was an organisational coup of a kind not seen in Spain before or since.[97]

At the suppression, the handful of students remaining at the English and Irish colleges were transferred to a third institution confiscated from the Society, the Colegio de las Becas, and there the three colleges were amalgamated and placed under the Rectorship of a secular priest, Manuel de Cevallos. For their theology the students now attended the Dominican college of Santo Tomás. By the end of 1768 Cevallos was reporting to Madrid on the improvement in discipline and studies that had resulted from the transfer.[98] One of the students who passed from St Gregory's to the Colegio de las Becas was the Irishman Thomas Hussey, who left Seville in 1769 with a doctorate of divinity and was appointed to the Spanish Chapel in London the following year. The expenses of his education were paid by the Spanish crown, and he was to repay the debt by a lifetime of service to Spain in the field of diplomacy and espionage. The last, but by no means the least, of the alumni of St Gregory's, he returned to his native Ireland only at the end of his career to become the founder and first President of Maynooth (1795) and Bishop of Waterford and Lismore. There is some irony in the fact that it was he, a European and a Gallican to his fingertips, who in creating Maynooth set Irish Catholicism on a course which in the next century was to make it at once more insular and more ultramontane.[99]

The date of the suppression of the Jesuits coincided with the arrival in Seville of the most radical reformer of the Spanish enlightenment, Pablo de Olavide. As Asistente of Seville, Olavide set about a programme of modernisation which included an ambitious plan for educational reorganisation. His main objective was to free the university from the monopoly of theology, and to this end theological studies were to be separated and centralised in one seminary, under state control. Small independent colleges such as St Gregory's had no place in this scheme of things. They were, Olavide declared, difficult to supervise and lax in discipline, and their administrators tended to use their revenues to feather their own nests. As far as St Gregory's was concerned, this was not altogether fair. It was not the fault of the Andalusian province that they had no English students, and they had at least put the building to educational use by taking in student convictors. Olavide's strictures were far more applicable to the Irish College at Salamanca, which for years had been a thorn in the side of the Spanish authorities but nevertheless escaped reform.

Under Olavide's plan at Seville the buildings of the English college were earmarked as an élite institution for the education of boys of noble birth. In designing the curriculum Olavide took more than one leaf from the Jesuits' book. It was to be a school for the future leaders of society, with an emphasis on moral education and an important role allotted to declamation and drama. But all these ambitious plans came to nothing, and they were consigned to final oblivion when Olavide was brought down by the Inquisition in 1775. The Jesuit schools had been destroyed, but nothing took their place. The next generation of young men such as Blanco White (b.1775) were left to educate themselves.[100]

Under a royal decree of September 1767, the three English colleges in Spain were formally united in one establishment, that of St Alban's, Valladolid. Legally, therefore, the Seville property now belonged to St Alban's. In 1771, however, the Medical Society of Seville, which lacked a permanent home, successfully petitioned the King to grant them the use of the building. The contents were exempted from this arrangement. Some of the books from the library, like those of other Jesuit colleges, were donated by the crown to the University. The Rector of St Alban's, Philip Perry, obtained official permission to take seven large chestloads of effects to Valladolid, and these included the large painting of St Gregory by Roelas which had formed the *retablo* of the college chapel.[101] Later, after the War of Independence, the then Vice-Rector of St Alban's, Thomas Sherburne, took the painting with him to England as security for a loan to the college, and installed it in his church at Kirkham, Lancs, whence it eventually passed to Ushaw College. Another fine painting, that of St Thomas of Canterbury by Herrera the Elder, disappeared entirely, either at this time or later, but other works of art were acquired by the Society of Medicine. These include the historic painting of Our Lady with four English seminarians which goes back to the very beginnings of the college and which Robert Persons described in *Newes from Spayne* as hanging above the inner door of the college.[102]

Though Philip Perry successfully established the legal right of St Alban's to the Seville property and even secured the transference to Valladolid of the yearly alms paid to St Gregory's by the city council and cathedral chapter of Seville (payments which were continued well into the nineteenth century), it proved difficult to maintain legal rights at such a distance and through third parties. The War of Independence put an end to any thoughts of pursuing the claim. The Society of Medicine had the advantage of occupation, and as the years passed, they looked more like proprietors than tenants, and the English connection had in any case long ago faded from folk memory. The chapel was closed and the fabric deteriorated until in 1867 it was leased to one of the Holy Week brotherhoods, the Hermandad del Sacro Entierro. At last, however, in 1908 an enterprising Procurator of St Alban's revived the legal claim to restitution, thereby beginning a process which was to last for fifty years. Meanwhile the Medical Society moved to another site and in 1932 the old college buildings were demolished, to be replaced ten years later by the present Escuela de Estudios Hispano-Americanos. In 1940 the adjoining chapel of San Gregorio, now altered beyond recognition and retaining no trace of its origins other than its dedication to the Apostle of England, was entrusted by Cardinal Segura, the Archbishop of Seville, to the Mercedarian order. The legal dispute came to an end in 1965 with the announcement that St Alban's, as the rightful claimant to the Seville property, was to be indemnified for its expropriation two centuries earlier.[103]

Notes

1. The chief sources for the early history of St Gregory's are as follows:
   (i) *Annales Seminarii seu Collegii Anglorum Hispalensis*, in CRS 14, pp.1-24. This chronicle was written by Persons in Rome in 1610, with the aid of information sent from Seville by John Price, S. J. Price's letter to Persons of 1 March 1610 (Stonyhurst Anglia A.iii.9) is reprinted in T.-D.2, Appendix 376.
   (ii) *Newes from Spayne and Holland*, Antwerp 1593 (facsimile edition by Scolar Press, London, 1977). This was almost certainly written by Persons in collaboration with Henry Walpole. See W. F. Rea, 'The Authorship of *Newes from Spayne and Holland* and its bearings on the genuineness of the confession of the Blessed Henry Walpole, S.J.', in BS 1 (1951), pp.220-30.
   (iii) 'Como se começo otro colegio para los ingleses catolicos en la ciudad de Sevilla', in D.de Yepes, *Historia particular de la persecucion de Inglaterra*, Madrid 1599 (facsimile edition, London 1971), pp.764-67. In his introduction to the facsimile edition, Dr D. M. Rogers shows that most of Yepes' material was supplied, if not written, by Joseph Creswell.

The only modern accounts are by Leo Hicks, S.J., in *The Month*, 157-8 (1931) and G. M. Murphy, 'Los comienzos del colegio inglés de San Gregorio de Sevilla', *Archivo Hispalense* 204 (Sevilla 1984), pp.3-24.

2. J. Alban Fraser, *Spain and the West Country*, 1935, pp.108-17; Gordon Connell-Smith, *Forerunners of Drake*, 1954, *passim*; Pauline Croft, *The Spanish Company*, London Record Society 9 (1973), pp.vii-xxxviii.

3. Pauline Croft, 'Trading with the Enemy, 1585-1604', *Historical Journal* 32 (1989), pp.281-302.

4. Francisco Morales Padrón, *Historia de Sevilla: La ciudad del quinientos*, 2a edición, Sevilla 1987; Ruth Pike, 'Seville in the 16th Century', *Hispanic-American Historical Review* 41 (1961), pp.1-30; Henry Kamen, 'The Mediterranean and the Expulsion of Spanish Jews in 1492', *Past and Present* 119 (1988), pp.30-55.

5. *Complete Works of St Teresa*, ed. E. Allison Peers, vol.3, 1946, p.129 (*Book of the Foundations*, chapters 33-36). Cf.*The Letters of St Teresa*, ed. E. Allison Peers, vol.1, 1951, pp.181, 229, 279.

6. Paul Hauben, 'Spanish Calvinists in London, 1559-1565', CH 34 (1965), pp.50-56; idem, 'Spanish Heretics during the Wars of Religion', *Historical Journal* 9 (1966), pp.275-85.

7. Juan Suárez to Francisco de Borja, 31 May 1570, in *Monumenta Paedagogica Societatis Jesu*, ed. L. Lukacs, Rome 1965, III, Sect.IV, pp.479, 482.

8. Ibid., p.511.

9. Lucette Elyane Roux, 'Le théâtre dans les collèges des Jésuites en Espagne', in *Dramaturgie et société*, ed. Jean Jacquot, Paris 1968, 2, p.503.

10. See pp.131-34.

11. William Weston: *The Autobiography of an Elizabethan*, ed. P. Caraman, 1955, p.xxvi.

12. A.Astraín, *Historia de la Compañia de Jesús en España*, Madrid 1909, tom.3, lib.2, pp.247-49, 476-83.

13. *Informacion que da el P. Roberto Personio de nacion inglesa de la compañia de Jesus acerca de la institucion del seminario que por orden de su Magestad se ha hecho en Valladolid*, Valladolid 1589 (Palau 119283).

14. Pauline Croft, *The Spanish Company*, 1973, p.30; M. E. Williams, *St Alban's College, Valladolid*, 1986, pp.269-70; A. J. Loomie, 'Thomas James, the English Consul of Andalusia, 1556-c.1613', RH 11 (1972), pp.165-79.

15. Text in Diego Ortíz de la Zuñiga, *Anales eclesiásticos y seculares de la muy noble y muy leal ciudad de Sevilla*, Madrid 1796, 4, pp.152.

16. John Price, S.J., writing to Persons in 1610, names among these early benefactors the Inquisitors DD. Francisco Blanco, Juan Zapata and Juan de Valdes; Canons Bernardino Rodríguez, Alonso Coloma (later Bishop of Barcelona) and Francisco de Ribera; Doctors Bahamonde, Pacheco, Santander and Asoca; 'the secular gentlemen of the cabildo' Juan Vicentelo, Juan de Arguijo, Juan Antonio del Alcázar and Miguel de Jáuregui. See M. A. Tierney, *Dodd's Church History of England*, 2 (1839), pp.ccclxxvi-viii. Another important benefactor was Antonio de la Raya, Bishop of Cuzco and Inquisitor Apostolic of the Kingdom of Granada, who made the college a bequest of 4000 ducats (FG 1606/6/III, no.3).

17. *Newes from Spayne*, pp.4-13.

18. Baet.3 I, ff.85, 168.

19. Quoted in A. Astraín, op.cit., 3, p.256.

20. See the lengthy dossier on the lawsuit brought by Don Geronimo de Mallea in 1665 (FG Tit.X/786). For the Espinosas, see Appendix, p.199.

21. See p.158.

22. 'La muerte de Roberto Gaulero y Tomas Egerton', in Yepes, pp.852-4. For a discussion, see M. E. Williams, 'The Ascetic Tradition and the English College at Valladolid', SCH 22 (1985), pp.275-83.

23. SP 94/6, ff.212-13.

24 'La vida y martirio de tres padres priores de la Cartuxa D. Joan Houthon, D. Roberto Laurens, Don Augustin Vuebiter . . . por el Pe Don Alonso de la Torre', SU 333-170; Fernando de Herrera, *Tomas Moro*, Sevilla 1592 (ARCR 831); Juan de Godoy, *Relacion verdadera que trata como de catolico don Iacob rey de Inglaterra trae a sus vassallos al conocimiento de la santa fe*, Sevilla: C. Hidalgo, 1606; *Relacion muy verdadera del recebimiento y fiestas que se le hizieron en Inglaterra a Don Juan de Tassis*, Sevilla: Bartolomé Gomez, 1603. See pp.115-16.

25. See p.180.

26. ALSJ of 1602, 1605, 1606, 1608.

27. A. J. Loomie in CHR 50 (1965), pp.27-51; Pauline Croft, 'Englishmen and the Spanish Inquisition, 1558-1625', EHR 87 (1972), pp.249-68. When the Scottish traveller William Lithgow was imprisoned by the Inquisition at Malaga in 1620, his papers were translated by an English priest

there. See W. Lithgow, *The Totall Discourse of the Rare Adventures and Painefull Peregrinations*, Glasgow 1906, p.407.

28. SP 12/262, f.86.

29. SP 14/16, f.99. In 1604 Adam King reported on his conversations with Creswell at Seville (SP 14/61, f.23).

30. M[artin] A[ray], *The Discoverie and Confutation of a Tragical Fiction*, 1599, 6r.

31. See Francis Edwards, 'The Case of the Poisoned Pommel', AHSJ 56 (1987), pp.1–82, for full documentation.

32. SP 94/12, ff.90, 104.

33. See pp.163–67.

34. The charges are summarised in Creswell's rejoinder, 'Respuesta a las razones escritas en la margen y apologia en defensa de los Padres y Alumnos Ingleses' (Simancas E 2858, f.46). See also 'Las razones que sean propuesto contra los rectores ingles [sic] y su respuesta', RAH PJ 182/30.

35. Letter of 9 October 1612, in Simancas E 2858.

36. In a letter to the Provincial of Castille, 27 April 1613, the Father General requested that he should negotiate with Anthony Hoskins the transfer of St Alban's to Palencia, Avila or Arévalo (ARSI Hisp.70, f.82r).

37. The narrative of the account of this journey by William Atkins, S.J. (see p.50) was published in abbreviated form by Joseph Stevenson in *The Month* XVIII–XX (December 1879, January and July 1880). For an alternative account, see James Wadsworth, *The English Spanishe Pilgrime*, 1629 (1979).

38. A. J. Loomie, 'Olivares, the English Catholics and the Peace of 1630', RBPH 47.2 (1969), pp.1154–66. See also RH 18 (1987), pp.402–17.

39. *Relacion del grandioso recebimiento y hospedaje que . . . se hizo en la ciudad de Sevilla a su Exca el Sr D. Francisco Continton* [Sevilla 1630]. See p.121. Cottington was later to declare himself a Catholic in 1651, when he retired to Valladolid, dying there the following year.

40. Bl. Thomas Green (1642), Bl. Ralph Corby (1644), Bl. Edward Bamber (1646).

41. Baet.6 I, ff.254–255v.

42. ARSI Hisp.Epp.Gen.86, f.69.

43. Baet.6 II, f.222.

44. A. Astraín, op.cit,5, pp.40–47. There are claims by creditors in AAW A 37/76 and S leg.1.

45. For their petitions to the city council, see AMS Siglo XVII, Seccion IVa, tom.20.

46. Henry More, *Historia Missionis Anglicanae Societatis Jesu*, St Omer 1660, 5, p.4.

47. Jonathan Brown, *Images and Ideas in 17th century Spanish Painting*, Princeton 1978, pp.21–43.

48. CRS 58, p.256. Verstegan also supplied books for the library at ECS. See his letter to Persons of 2 October 1593, ibid., Letter 43. It is of interest that these included Holinshed's Chronicle as well as works of controversy.

49. *Algunos motivos y razones que ay para favorecer los seminarios*

ingleses [Sevilla c.1604]. ARCR 1062.

50. Receipt for the organ in S I. On Pickford's consulship, see A. J. Loomie, RH 11 (1971–2), p.172.

51. Acquaviva to the Spanish Provincials, 7 August 1616, ARSI Hisp.Epp.Gen.86, f.102.

52. Baet.4 I, ff.39, 51; 5 II, f.168.

53. See A. F. Allison in RH 18 (1987), pp.361–2, 367.

54. For Salkeld, see p.93. The entry on him in the DNB is unreliable, being based on the doubtful evidence of Anthony Wood. In *A Treatise of Angels* Salkeld claimed to have been 'assistant in studies' to Francisco Suárez and Miguel Vázquez. Suárez taught at Coimbra between 1597 and 1603. Miguel (not the better known Gabriel) Vázquez taught at Cordoba from 1603 to 1606. Salkeld's writings contain a number of curious references to Spanish customs.

55. Printed degree certificates of the 18th century in S XXIX (copy in the Bodleian). See also *Summa privilegiorum concessorum Collegio Anglicano Hispalensi a Clemente VIII*, ECV Misc.Ser.II 1/21.

56. Francisco Luque Fajardo, *Relacion de la fiesta que se hizo en Sevilla a la beatificacion del glorioso S.Ignacio*, Sevilla: Luis Estupiñan, 1610 (ARCR 1073), p.25.

57. See T. D. Kendrick, *St James in Spain*, 1960, pp.88–103; Stanko Vranich, 'Carta de un ciudadano de Sevilla. La guerra mariana en Sevilla en el siglo XVII', AH 44–45 (1966), nos.137–8.

58. Stanko Vranich, *Ensayos sevillanos del siglo de oro*, Valencia 1981, pp.123, 133.

59. J. Alenda de Mira, *Relaciones de solemnidades y fiestas publicas de España*, Madrid 1903, no.686; Manuel Serrano y Ortega, *Glorias sevillanas*, Sevilla 1893, p.508.

60. *Formula iurisiurandi ac voti quod publice in honorem intemeratae Conceptionis BVM nuncupatum est [apud] Collegium Hispalense D. Hermenegildi S.J., Collegium eiusdem B.M.conceptae sine labe, Seminarium Anglicum et Hibernum eiusdem Societatis*. Sevilla: Ignacio de Lyra, 1653. I was unable to locate the copy listed by M. Serrano y Ortega (see n.59) as in AMS.

61. F. Luque Fajardo, *Relacion de la fiesta* &c, 1610 (see n.56), pp.23–48.

62. F. Luque Fajardo, *Relacion de las fiestas que la cofradia de sacerdotes de San Pedro de Vincula celebro en su paroquial yglesia de Sevilla a la Purisima Concepcion de la Virgen Maria nuestra Señora*, Sevilla: A. Rodríguez Gamarra, 1616. The English prizewinners were Thomas Wharton, *vere* Foster, and William Fransam. See p.40.

63. Juan Antonio de Ibarra, *Encomio de los ingenios sevillanos en la fiesta de los santos Iñacio de Loyola i Francisco Xavier*, Sevilla: Francisco de Lyra, 1623 (facsimile edition, Valencia 1950), pp.20–22v.

64. *Tragedia de San Hermenegildo rey y martir que se represento en el colegio anglico de Sevilla*, n.d. (copy in the library of the Hispanic Society of America). On the play, see Justo García Soriano, 'El teatro de colegio en España', BRAE XIV, 1927, p.540.

65. ALSJ 1594–5 (Naples 1604), pp.570–73.

66. Litterae Annuae, Baet.19 I (see p.123).

67. Annual Letter of 1619, in GU, Papeles de Jesuitas, caja A-40. In April 1615 the Father General wrote to Peralta congratulating him on the performance by the students of a play about King Henry VIII, and expressing the hope that the distinguished audience would be moved to donate money. The connection between the plays and fund-raising is clear (Baet.4 I, f.150v).

68. See William H. MacCabe, 'The Playlist of the English College at St Omers', *Revue de Littérature Comparée* 17 (1937), pp.355–75; *An Introduction to the Jesuit Theatre*, St Louis 1983, p.117. On *Zeno* at Seville, see ARCR 947n.

69. J. Wadsworth, *The English Spanishe Pilgrime*, 1629, p.47.

70. See Jonathan Brown, op.cit. (n.47), pp.21–43. Arguijo donated his year's salary as *regidor* to the ECS. See F. Rodriguez Marín, *Nuevos datos biográficos para las biografías de cien escritores de los siglos XVI y XVII*, Madrid 1923, p.356. Pacheco was a close friend of the humanist Benito Arias Montano, who spent the last ten years of his life (1588–98) on his estate near Seville.

71. Romanus Rios, O.S.B., in *The Ushaw Magazine*, July 1965, pp.72–74. See also Diego Angulo Iñíguez, 'El cuadro de San Gregorio de Roelas', *Boletín del Seminario de Arte de Valladolid*, 1935–36, pp.51–58. A catalogue of the paintings formerly belonging to St Gregory's and now the property of the Real Academia de Medicina de Sevilla was compiled by Isabel López Garrido for a licentiate thesis at the University of Seville in 1984. The painting of St Thomas of Canterbury by Francisco de Herrera (see p.29) has been lost. On Roelas and his Jesuit patrons at Seville, see Jonathan Brown, op. cit. (n.47). The Academy of Medicine also inherited from St Gregory's a curious painting of Christ dressed as a Jesuit, of the late 17th c.

72. S 7, pp.237–237v; S 24, pp.19v–20.

73. ARCR 1066 (see p.116).

74. F. Rodríguez Marín, op.cit. (see n.70), p.400. For Martín de Luna, see ARCR 1068.

75. Martin Murphy, 'The Cadiz Letters of William Johnson *vere* Purnell, S.J.', RH 21 (May, 1992).

76. F. Rodríguez Marín, op.cit. (see n.70), p.356.

77. *Consulta* of 23 February 1600, Simancas E 185; *real cédula* of 1 May 1608, AI Contaduría 220.

78. ARSI, Cast.136, f.138.

79. *Breve proposicion de algunos de los motivos que ay para favorecer los seminarios ingleses y en particular este de San Gregorio de Sevilla* [c.1644], ARCR 1071.1.

80. *Algunos de los motivos que ay para favorecer los seminarios ingleses* [1604], ARCR 1062; [Joseph Creswell], *Informacion a la ciudad de Sevilla por parte del colegio ingles*, Sevilla: Clemente Hidalgo, 1604 (ARCR 279).

81. Tobacco proposal in Creswell's letter of March 1613, Simancas E 2858; rejected in royal *consulta* of 31 December 1614, AI Indiferente 751.

Indult to quest for alms in America in *cédula reál* of 20 September 1620, S XVII/14; letter of Father General to Provincials of Mexico and Peru, 20 January 1621, ARSI Hisp.Epp.Gen.86, f.120; records of bequests to St Gregory's from Panama, Potosí and Lima, in S XIX.

82. Acquaviva to Persons, 29 July 1596, Baet.3 I, f.278; re-statement in 1622, Baet.5 I, f.110.

83. Baet.5 I, f.1, f.129.

84. Lewis Owen, *The Running Register*, 1626, pp.67-73.

85. Baet.5 I, f.113v. Financial arrangement with St Omer, Baet.5 II, f.218r.

86. AI Contaduría 246 (ruling of 31 August 1635); Baet.5 I, f.124.

87. Baet.4 I, ff.75, 86; 4 II, f.51. Evidently there had been a tacit agreement that Irish and English Colleges should not be founded in the same towns.

88. *Memorial por parte del colegio ingles* [c.1644]. See p.121.

89. Baet.3 I, f.554; Hisp.Epp.Gen.86, f.69; Baet.4 II, f.171; Hisp.Epp.Gen.86, f.112v (the Irishman).

90. John J. Silke, 'The Irish College, Seville', *Archivium Hibernicum* 24 (1961), pp.103-47.

91. Francis Finegan, S.J., 'Irish Rectors at Seville', IER 5th series 106 (1966), pp.45-63; *Wadding Papers*, ed. B. Jennings, Dublin 1953, pp.352-3; Bodleian MS, Arch.Seld.A subt.4(11).

92. AAW, A series, 40/128.

93. AP Serie II, vol.65 (Collegi Vari), letter of 8 May 1753 from Irish merchants in Andalusia; report of Seville coadministrator, 22 May 1753.

94. AP Serie II, Vol.65, memoriale of 8 August 1754.

95. ibid., letter of 18 January 1766 to Cardinal Lante from John Buller, James Parker, Richard Morgan, John Mattingly and Joseph Addis, all of ECV.

96. Teófanes Egido, 'La expulsión de los jesuitas de España, in *Historia de la Iglesia en España*, ed. R. García-Villoslada, III-2o, BAC, Madrid 1980, pp.745-92.

97. Account by the Teniente Mayor of Seville, Archivo Municipal de Sevilla, Conde del Aguila libros en 4to, Sección 11, vol.12, no.32. This volume also contains an account by a Jesuit father of the events of 3 April 1767 (no.33); *Archivo Teológico Granadino* 54 (1991), pp.44-50.

98. Cevallos to Campomanes, 11 December 1768, in Biblioteca Colombina, Seville, 63-9-87, f.19.

99. See G. M. Murphy, 'Cloak without Dagger: Dr Thomas Hussey, 1746-1803', in RH 19 (May 1988), pp.80-94.

100. F. Aguilar Piñal, *La universidad de Sevilla en el siglo XVIII*, Sevilla 1969, pp.185-221, 375.

101. M. E. Williams, *St Alban's College, Valladolid*, 1986, pp.72-3. See also the same author's article, 'Philip Perry, Rector of the English College, Valladolid', RH 17 (May 1984), pp.54-5.

102. On the removal of the Roelas painting to Kirkham, see F. J. Singleton, *Mowbreck Hall and the Willows*, Kirkham 1983, p.31.

There is an inventory of the contents of St Gregory's and of its country house at Dos Hermanas, dated 21 December 1768, and an inventory of the library dated 20 April 1772, in the Seville archive at ECV (S XXI).

103. The history of the litigation is summarised in M. E. Williams, op.cit., pp.266-68. For correspondence between the Rectors of ECV and their agents in Seville, 1767-1829, see S leg.2.

38

2. SOURCES AND ABBREVIATIONS

1. *General*

AAW	Archives of the Archdiocese of Westminster.
ACS	Archivo Capitular, Sevilla. Minutes of the meetings of the Seville Cathedral chapter. These note grants to students to cover travelling expenses to the mission (*viáticos*).
AHN	Archivo Histórico Nacional, Madrid.
AHSJ	*Archivum Historicum Societatis Jesu.*
AI	Archivo de Indias, Sevilla.
AL	Annals of Lisbon (MS at Ushaw College, Durham).
ALSJ	*Annuae Litterae Societatis Jesu* (published volumes).
AMS	Archivo Municipal, Sevilla.
Ang.	'Anglia' series, ARSI (copy at Stonyhurst College).
Ans.	G. Anstruther, *The Seminary Priests*, 4 vols, 1968–77.
AP	Archives of Propaganda, Rome.
A&R	A. F. Allison & D. M. Rogers, *A Catalogue of Catholic Books in English printed abroad or secretly in England, 1558-1640*, Bognor Regis, 1956.
Aray	*The Discoverie and Confutation of a Tragical Fiction . . . by M[artin] A[ray] preest*, 1599 (facsimile edition 1971).
Arch.Hib.	*Archivium Hibernicum* (Catholic Record Society of Ireland, Maynooth).
ARCR 1	A. F. Allison & D. M. Rogers, *The Contemporary Printed Literature of the English Counter-Reformation between 1558 and 1640*. Vol.1. Works in languages other than English. Aldershot, 1989.
ARSI	Archivum Romanum Societatis Jesu.
Atkins	[William Atkins, S.J.], 'A relation of the journey of twelve students from . . . St Omers . . . to . . . Seville in Spain, A.D. 1622', Stonyhurst College Ms E.LLL.1.
Ave.1	J. C. H. Aveling, *Northern Catholics*, 1966.
Ave.2	J. C. H. Aveling, *The Catholic Recusants of the West Riding of Yorks*, 1963.
Ave.3	J. C. H. Aveling, *Catholic Recusancy in the City of York* (CRS Monograph 2), 1970.
Baet.	'Baetica' series (Andalusian Province), ARSI.
BCC	Biblioteca Colombina y Capitular, Sevilla.
Belg.	'Belgica' series, ARSI.
Bell.	Dominic Bellenger, *English and Welsh Priests 1558–1800*, 1984.
Birt	Norbert Birt, *Obit Book of the English Benedictines*, 1913.
BL	British Library
BRAE	*Boletín de la Real Academia Española* (Madrid).
BS	*Biographical Studies*. See RH.
Cast.	'Castilla' series, ARSI.

Chall.	Richard Challoner, *Memoirs of Missionary Priests*, 1924.
Chamb.	N. E. McClure, ed., *The Letters of John Chamberlain*, Philadelphia 1939.
CHR	*Catholic Historical Review.*
Copia	F. de Peralta, *Copia de una carta . . . en que se da cuenta de . . . doña Luisa de Carvajal.* Sevilla, 1614.
CRS	Catholic Record Society, Records Series. Volumes:

    5. Unpublished Documents relating to the English Martyrs, 1584–1603.

    10–11. Douay College Diaries, 1598–1654.

    14. Annals of the English College, Seville, 1610 (pp.1–24).

    29. The English College at Madrid, 1611–1767.

    30. The English College at Valladolid, 1589–1862.

    37. Liber Ruber of the English College, Rome, 1579–1630.

    40. Liber Ruber of the English College, Rome, 1631–1783.

    52. Letters and Despatches of Richard Verstegan, c.1550–1640.

    54–5. Responsa Scholarum, English College, Rome, 1598–1685.

    69. St Omers and Bruges Colleges. A Biographical Dictionary.

    70. The English Jesuits, 1650–1829. A Biographical Dictionary.

    72. Lisbon College Register, 1628–1813.

D	T. F. Knox, *The First and Second Diaries of the English College, Douay*, 1878.
Dockery	J. B. Dockery, *Christopher Davenport, Friar and Diplomat*, 1960.
de León	Pedro de León's narrative of his ministry in the Seville prison, 1578–1616, in Pedro Herrera Puga, *Grandeza y miseria en Andalucía*, Granada, 1981.
de Roa	Martín de Roa, 'Historia de la provincia de Andalucía de la Compañía de Jesús'. Ms [before 1637] in Seville University Library (331–23).
Díaz	José Simón Díaz, *Bibliografía de la Literatura Hispánica.*
DNB	Dictionary of National Biography
Dodd	Charles Dodd [*vere* Hugh Tootell], *Church History of England*, 3 vols, 1737–42.
Downshire	Downshire MSS, Berks Record Office.
DR	*Downside Review*
ECD	English College, Douai.
ECL	English College, Lisbon.
ECM	English College, Madrid.
EC	English College, Rome.
ECS	English College, Seville.
ECV	English College, Valladolid.
EHR	*English Historical Review.*

ER   *Essex Recusant.*
FG   Fondo Gesuitico, ARSI.
Fo   H. Foley, *Records of the English Province, S.J. 8 vols*, 1877–83.
Foster   J. Foster, *Alumni Oxonienses.*
Gee   John Gee, *The Foot out of the Snare*, 1624.
Gill.   J. Gillow, *A Bibliographical Dictionary of the English Catholics.*
GU   Granada, University Library.
Ham.   W. Hamilton, *The Chronicle of the English Augustinian Canonesses . . . Louvain* 1904–06.
HHY   G. Anstruther, *A Hundred Homeless Years: English Dominicans 1588–1658.* 1958.
Hisp.   'Hispania' series, ARSI.
H.-L.   E. Henson and A. J. Loomie, 'A Register of Students of St Gregory's College at Seville, 1591–1605', RH 9 (1967–8), pp.163–75.
HMC   Historical Manuscripts Commission.
HS   Harleian Society
Ibarra   Juan Antonio de Ibarra, *Encomio de los ingenios sevillanos en la fiesta de los santos Iñacio de Loyola i Francisco Xavier*, Sevilla 1623 (facsimile edition, Valencia 1950). (Díaz 12, no.214).
ICS   Irish College, Seville.
IGI   International Genealogical Index (Mormon microfiche).
IER   *Irish Ecclesiastical Record.*
JEH   *Journal of Ecclesiastical History.*
LF 1   Francisco de Luque Fajardo, *Relacion de la fiesta que se hizo en Sevilla a la beatificacion del glorioso San Ignacio &c*, Sevilla, 1610. (ARCR 1073).
LF 2   Francisco de Luque Fajardo, *Relacion de las fiestas que la cofradia de sacerdotes de San Pedro de Vincula celebro . . . a la Purisima Concepcion de la Virgen Maria.* Sevilla: A. Rodriguez Gamarra, 1616. (Biblioteca de la Facultad de Filosofía y Letras, Sevilla, Ra 293).
Litt.Ann.   Litterae Annuae Provinciae Baeticae, ARSI Baet.19 I–II.
Lunn   David Lunn, *The English Benedictines 1540–1688*, 1980.
Lus.   'Lusitania' series, ARSI.
m.o.   minor orders.
Newes   [Robert Persons] *Newes from Spain and Holland*, Antwerp 1593 (London 1977).
OB   Archives of the Old Brotherhood, AAW.
ORS   Ordination Registers of the archdiocese of Seville. The registers, kept in the archives of the Archbishop's palace, cover the years 1610–20 (incompletely) and 1632–1767. There are no records of the years 1592–1610, when num-

bers at ECS were at their highest, nor of the period
1620–32.

Peralta [Francisco de Peralta], *Summa de algunas razones* &c, 1604.
See pp.142–62.

RAH Real Academia de la Historia, Madrid. Its collection of
Papeles de Jesuitas (PJ) contains much printed and MS
material relevant to ECS.

RPBH *Revue Belge de Philologie et de l'Histoire.*

Relacion *Relacion . . . de los dos sacerdotes* [T.Benstead, T.Sprott],
Sevilla, 1600. See p.115.

RH *Recusant History.*

RN *Reportorium Novum* (Archdiocese of Dublin).

S. Archives of St Gregory's College, Seville, now at ECV (see
pp.43–7)

Salis. Calendar of Salisbury MSS at Hatfield House, HMC.

SCH *Studies in Church History.*

San-   Juan Santibañez, *Historia de la Provincia de Andalucía de*
tibañez *la Compañía de Jesús* [1640]. 19th c. transcript in the
Archivo SJ, Granada, of the original MS, now lost. Parte
2 Libro 3, contains a lengthy section on the early years of
ECS, much of it derived from de Róa (q.v.).

Silke John J. Silke, 'The Irish College, Seville', in *Archivium
Hibernicum* 24 (1961).

Sim.1 Archivo de Simancas, Estado leg.1771. Petition to Philip
III, 25 March 1613, signed by 32 priests and students of
ECS.

Sim.2 Archivo de Simancas, Secretería y Superintendencia de
Hacienda, leg.966. Royal *viáticos* to departing Irish and
English priests, 1730–1758.

SO St Omer.

SP State Papers, Public Records Office.

St G. Liber Graduum of St Gregory's, Douai, now Downside
Abbey.

SU Seville, University Library.

T-D. M. A. Tierney, *Dodd's Church History of England.*

Tha. Fr Thaddeus, *The Franciscans in England, 1600–1850*, 1898.

TL *The Tanner Letters*, ed. C. MacNeill, Dublin 1943.

Tol. 'Toletana' (Toledo Province) series, ARSI.

UM *The Ushaw Magazine.*

Varones Juan de Santibañez, 'Varones ilustres de la Provincia de
Andalucía', Centurias 1–3. MS copy in the Jesuit archive
at Granada.

Vat. Vatican Library.

Wads. James Wadsworth, *The English Spanishe Pilgrime*, 1629
(1979).

Whatmore L. E. Whatmore, *Recusancy in Kent*, 1974.

WJ William Jessopp. An alumnus of ECS (1595–1600), who

under examination in October 1600 gave the names of 33 past and present members of ECS (Salisbury MSS. HMC, vol.10, 1904, pp.340–42).

WP   *Wadding Papers*, ed. B. Jennings, O.F.M., Dublin 1953.

WR   *Worcestershire Recusant*.

Yepes   Diego de Yepes, *Historia particular de la persecucion de Inglaterra*, Madrid 1599 (London 1971).

3. THE ARCHIVES OF ST GREGORY'S

The archives of the college were removed to Valladolid soon after the suppression in 1767. They fall into two main categories:

(a) Documents collected by Mgr Henson in 30 folio volumes bound in blue leather, mainly relating to college property (S I-XXX)

(b) 24 vellum-bound books (S 1-24) mainly relating to college administration. Unfortunately these do not include a *Liber Alumnorum* or a *Liber Primi Examinis* of the kind which survives in the case of the English colleges at Valladolid, Rome and Douai.

A. *BOUND VOLUMES* (S I-XXX)

The Spanish titles which follow are those assigned by Mgr Henson:

I. 'Capilla Mayor y Pleito del Patronato.' Deeds and documents relating to the foundation of the chapel. They include a receipt signed by Juan de Roelas for the sum due to him for his painting of St Gregory commissioned for the *retablo* of the high altar (1608). Another receipt for 120 ducats is signed by the organ-maker John Pickford.

II. 'Casas Principales y Acesorias. Mayorazgo de Ortíz'. Deeds relating to the college site bought from Doña María Ortiz y Sandoval.

III. 'Casas Principales y Acesorias. Mayorazgo de Ortíz. Convento de las Victorias de Triana.'

IV. 'Casas del Convento de San Gerónimo. Hospital del Cardenál. La Catedrál. Convento de Santa María de Gracia'.

V. 'Escrituras (Deeds) Segundas Copias'. These include the deed of gift by the college benefactress Doña Ana de Espinosa, October 1595, which carries the signatures of a number of the students then at the college.

VI. 'Escrituras. Copias Simples.'

VII. 'Agua de las Casas. Renta para Estudiantes Pobres. Discordia con el Colegio de las Becas.'

VIII. 'Limosnas del Cardenal y de la Ciudad'. These relate to the annual subsidy paid to the college by the city council (cabildo) and by the Cardinal of Seville. They include several printed and MS documents relating to the college's efforts to forestall a possible reduction or discontinuation of this subsidy by citing expert theological opinion to support the view that the city's debt did not cancel its obligation to continue its charity. These documents include:

(i) 4 copies of J. Creswell, *Informacion a la ciudad de Sevilla*. Sevilla: Clemente Hidalgo, 1604, with MS endorsements by various Seville theologians. See p.116.

(ii) *Copia de una relacion hecha en el cabildo de la ciudad de Sevilla que mando imprimir el Assistente della . . . sobre un caso, si la ciudad . . . podia continuar la [limosna] que hazia al seminario de los Ingleses*. Sevilla: Clemente Hidalgo, 1604. See p.116.

(iii) MS 'Resolucion y parecer de varios teologos que dicen que puede y

debe Sevilla dar a este colegio la limosna solicitada' [1643].
(iv) Successive petitions by the ECS to the city *cabildo* for payment of the annual *limosna*.
IX. 'Varios Tributos y Legados.'
X. 'Varios Censos y Legados.' (leaseholds and bequests).
XI-XIV. 'Legado de Luis Téllez.'
XV. 'Miscelánea.'
These include:
   (i) Documents relating to the will of Joseph Gilbert, of Norwich, clerk in the firm of Anthony Hutton and Company of Seville, signed on 17 June 1664. The legator was to be buried in the chapel of the college, which was a beneficiary of the will.
   (ii) The will of Richard Richardson, signed at Guadalcanal 13 July 1730 (see pp.187–92).
   (iii) *Memorial por parte del colegio ingles sobre la pretension que tiene de que la ciudad de Sevilla le continue la limosna que desde su fundacion le ha Señalado.* n.p. [1648]. See p.121.
XVI. 'Huerta de la Cruz del Campo y tierras contiguas.'
XVII. 'Miscelánea.'
These include:
   (i) *Cédula Reál* of Philip III granting the three Spanish colleges (ECV, ECS, ECM) a 4-year licence to beg for alms in Spanish territories overseas, 20 September 1620.
   (ii) 'Informacion de los yngleses que estan en este colegio de Sevilla'. An MS information sheet about the college and its work, for use by preachers in appealing for funds.
   (iii) 'Estilo y practica que en el colegio ingles de Sevilla se a observado con espacio de 32 años, en que a asistido en dicho colegio el Padre Antonio Araoz de la Compañía de Jesus hasta este año 1662'. A brief statement of the (very meagre) provision for academic studies in the college at that date.
   (iv) [F. de Peralta], 'Summa de algunas razones' [1604]. See pp.142–62.
   (v) A ruling of 1613, signed by several Seville theologians, stating that student priests had the obligation to say 6 masses a week on the college foundation in return for their keep.
   (vi) A *Cédula Reál* of the Queen Regent dated 4 September 1675 granting the college 28,000 reales for the rebuilding of the college buildings and chapel, to be paid out of the proceeds of French property seized at Seville.
   (vii) A copy of Cardinal Allen's letter of appointment as Prefect of the missions of England and Ireland, 1591.
   (viii) Rules for the Prefect of the Mission, 1598, 1604.
   (ix) Correspondence and certificates relating to the provision of students to ECS from St Omer, or to the payment of *viáticos* to departing students by the Casa de la Contratación in Seville on behalf of the King.
   (x) Autograph copies of the mission oath, most of them dated, signed

by individual students, classified with the common number B/67.

(xi) An undated MS set of house rules for *convictores* resident in the college (18th c).

XVIII. 'Obligaciones y cartas de pago.'

XIX. 'Miscelánea.' These include documents relating to bequests made to the college by benefactors in Panama, Lima and Potosí.

XX. 'Miscelánea.' These include a transcript of chapter 101 of M. de Roa's MS history of the Andalusian province SJ, relating to the foundation of ECS (see p.39).

XXI. 'Inventario y cuentas,' an inventory of the contents of the college and its country house at Dos Hermanas, dated 21 December 1768. 'Relacion autentica del menaje y demas efectos', a later inventory of 1779 made by Pedro de Cuerva y Medina. 'Relacion de los libros', an inventory of the college books still on the premises 20 April 1772.

XXII. 'Censos redimidos.'

XXIII. 'Miscelánea.'

XXIV. 'Extraordinario. Autos de Juan Pache 1627-1639.'

XXV. 'Autos de Juan Bazán 1641-1669, capellán de Isabel de Lugo.'

XXVI. 'Libro de misas que entran en este colegio ingles de San Gregorio desde primo de otubre de 1627 en adelante.'

XXVII. 'Recibos.'

XXVIII. 'Miscelánea.'
These include:
(i) Reglas de los Cardenales Protectores para evitar discordias entre los monjes benedictinos y regulares de la Compañia de Jesus residentes en Inglaterra año de 1608. MS.
(ii) 'Libro de las alajas de la sacristía,' dated 1 January 1737.

XXIX. 'Miscelánea'.
These include:
(i) A certificate of the degree of licentiate, baccalaureate and master of theology conferred on Dominic de Burgo, 1716.
(ii) Blank forms of the degree certificate and of certificate of faculties, 18th c.

XXX. *Catalogi Provinciae Boeticae S.J.,* 1752-1764.

B. *VELLUM-BOUND COLLEGE BOOKS* (S 1-24)
These have been numbered or lettered differently over the years. The current numbering dates from 1987, but the previous coding (by letter) is given in brackets.

1. 'Constitutiones Collegii Anglorum Hispalensis', 1600. MS.
2. 'Exercitia Spiritualia per annum in usum Collegii Anglici Hispalensis', n.d. MS.
3. (A). 'Protocolo de las escrituras en pro i en contra deste Colegio Yngles'. A register of the property and capital of the college from its foundation up to June 1767.
4. (M) 'Libro de Censos y Cargos'. An account of the perpetual rents paid

by the college, and of interest on borrowed money, 1650-1766.

5. (T) 'Entrada y Cumplimiento de Misas de Abril 1644 a 1678'. A book of Mass stipends received and complied with during the period.

6. (C) 'Misas. Limosnas al Colegio y Cuentas con particulares'. A register of mass stipends and alms received, and accounts with individuals, January 1595 to November 1606.

7. (B) A register of receipts from 2 November 1592 to 12 March 1606, and of money handed to the bursar between 1 December 1592 and 1 March 1607. Also included are details of *viáticos* paid between 1600 and 1612, and (from p.237r) details of consignments of books relating to the English martyrs, etc, sent by the bursar of ECS to Jesuit missions in America, 1600-01.

8. (N) 'Cuentas mensuales del Procurador de 1640 a 1655'. Bursar's monthly accounts of income and expenditure.

9. (O) 'Procuraduría de 1655 a 1672'. Bursar's account books.

10. (P) 'Libro del Procurador agosto de 1672 a 1692'. Bursar's account books.

11. (Q) 'Libro Procurador de 1692 a 1730'. Bursar's account books.

12. (R) 'Libro del Procurador desde 1 de septembre de 1730 a 1766'. Bursar's account books. They are monthly until the end of May 1733, when they begin to be kept every two months or more, until from June 1757 they are kept yearly.

13. (H) 'Manual'. Accounts of expenditure from April 1663 to March 1666 (ff1-45). The rest of the book contains accounts of the vineyard, farm, clothing, alms, building and repairs, sacristy and lawsuits, from 1663 to 1701.

14. (I) 'Manual entre 1698 y 1741'. Separate accounts of clothing, church expenses, building and repairs, lawsuits, alms collected and distributed, and farm produce.

15. (J) 'Manual San Gregorio de Sevilla 1740 a 1767'. Accounts of expenditure on the church, clothing, building and repairs, servants' wages etc.

16. (U) 'Libro principalmente para las obligaciones de misas que tiene este colegio por los patronos del Colegio Mayor'. A record of masses said by priests at the college, 1723-1768, in fulfilment of obligations to founders and benefactors.

17. (D) 'Varias Cuentas'. Accounts of the Rectorship of Fr Alonso Díaz, 12 March 1607 to 17 November 1612. From f.25r is an inventory of clothes, linen, foodstuff, and contents of the sacristy and church made during the same rectorship. From f.34v to 140r and 166r to 183r are accounts dating from 1607-12 and 1628-32.

18. (E) 'Cuentas con varios particulares'. Accounts with individuals from September 1646 to May 1651.

19. (F) 'Quentas con particulares desde 1632'. Accounts with individuals, 1631-53.

20. (G) 'Libro de Particulares'. Accounts with individuals, 1663-1759.

21. (L) 'Libro de Alimentos de Comunidad'. Accounts of expenditure on

food from March 1721 to March 1767.
22. (S) 'Libro de Visitas de los Padres Provinciales'. Register of the official visitations by the Andalusian Provincial S.J., from 1 April 1677 to 8 March 1766.
23. (K) 'Apuntamientos de gasto ordinario'. Rough notebook of expenditure from August 1652 to August 1656.
24. (V) 'Alajas que an dado a la sacristía en el Rectorado del P. Bernal'. A register of additions to the vestments and linen, etc, of the sacristy during the rectorship of Fr Bernal. On ff.19v–20, in a much earlier hand, are notes of consignments of books (on the English martyrs etc) despatched from ECS to Lima and other places in America c. 1596.

C. *LEGAJOS*
Loose files containing miscellaneous *impresos* and mss, not all related to the college.
1. (i) *Orden que ha de tener el informante que ha de hazer las pruebas de que pretende beca en el Colegio de la Purísima Concepción de Nuestra Señora de la Compañía de Jesus que fundó en Sevilla el Ilustrísimo Señor Don Gonzalo de Campo Arcediano de Niebla.* [c.1759]. Relates to ICS.
   (ii) MS 'Memorial que el P.Provincial de la Paraguay presentó al Sr Comisario Marqués de Valdelirios en que le suplica que suspenda las disposiziones de guerra contra los Indios de las Misiones'.
   (iii) 'Traslado de una petición de querella que por parte del Colegio de San Hermenegildo de la ciudad de Sevilla está presentada en el pleito de acreedores contra Andrés de Villar'. Incomplete.
   (iv) *Compendio apologético y jurídico de los títulos y privilegios en que se funda la graduación del Colegio Mayor de Sevilla con omnímoda igualdad a los demás Colegios Mayores.* n.d. (20pp).
   (v) Blank forms of certificates of D.D. and faculties granted by the college.
   (vi) Assorted printed theses or theological conclusions defended by students at the College of St Hermenegild, 1736, 1753.
   (vii) *Jubileo pleníssimo concedido por N. Smo P. Clemente XII para la Iglesia del Gran Padre S. Gregorio Magno . . . de los católicos ingleses . . . en la calle de las Armas de esta ciudad.* n.d.
2. Correspondence from Seville lawyers in charge of ECS property, 1767–1829.

4. ALUMNI OF ST GREGORY'S, 1592-1767

Preliminary note

The following list includes the names of all those English and Irish students or priests known to have been members of the college between 1592 and 1767. The names in square brackets are those of men who were not strictly speaking *alumni*—for instance the companions of Robert Persons who passed through Seville in 1591, the year before the foundation of the college.

Not all the students listed below were ordained priest, but I have recorded evidence of such ordination where it exists. The list includes English and Irish convictors (student lodgers who were not seminarians) but not Spanish convictors, of whom there were many in the late 17th and 18th centuries. The use of aliases was practised more commonly at ECS than elsewhere (see p.10), and this has made the compilation of the list unusually difficult. The hispanised versions of English surnames (given in brackets) has presented an additional complication. In the most intractable cases I have ventured an educated guess, but the identities of such as Carlos Anglicano may never be known.

To avoid the proliferation of references, I have generally not included those already listed by Anstruther but have cited sources which he overlooked. Very full information on those students who were alumni of St Omer is available in CRS vol. 69.

ADDEY, (Aden), Richard [1631-32]

SO before 1629-1631 (CRS 69/15). From ECS to England 1632 (S 18), presumably not a priest.

AINSWORTH (Ansur), *alias* SKEVINGTON, John [c.1605-07]

b.London 1577. B.A., Christ's College, Cambridge, 1599. To ECD 1601. To ECV Oct. 1603. Tried vocation with O.S.B. 1604, but left for ECS, where he was ordained. Left ECS in May 1607, but was captured by an English pirate off the Spanish coast and taken to Alarache (see p.124). Released, he set out again for England via Douai, 1608. In Newgate 1608-10. Banished 1610, but returned soon after. In Newgate 1613-15, Wisbech 1615-18. Banished 1618, but in Warwicks 1632. (Ans.2/2-3).

ALFORD, Michael See GRIFFITH

ALLEN (Alano), Peter [1612, or before,—1617]

m.o.at ECS, Dec. 1612. Signs petition, March 1613, as student Petrus Alanus (Sim.1). Priest, March 1617 (ORS). (Ans.2/4).

ALLEN (Alano), William [c.1608]

Signs deed at ECS, May 1608, as student (S V).

ALLERTON, Matthew, [1672–78]

Mission oath, Dec. 1672 (S XVII). Priest, April 1677 (ORS). Received viaticum, May 1678 (S 10). (Ans.3/2).

ALMOND (Alman), Henry [Between 1595 and 1600]

Studied philosophy at ECS during this period (WJ). Received alms at ECR, 1616. (Fo 6/596; Ans.1/6; Pollen, *Acts of the English Martyrs,* p.173).

[ALMOND (Alman), Oliver]

b.Oxford 1561. Matric. Brasenose College, Oxford, 1578. To Rheims 1581. To ECR 1582. Priest 1587. To England via Seville 1591. Active in Oxon. d.before June 1625. (Ans.1/6–7; listed in H-L, but not a student).]

ANDERSON See RICHARDSON, William

ANDERTON, *alias* RIGBY (Ribe), Gray, Laurence [1597–1602]

Christened at Chorley, Lancs, 12 Aug. 1575, son of Thomas A. (IGI). B.A., Christ's College, Cambridge, 1597. To ECS 1597. To England as priest c.1602 (S 7). S.J. 1604. Worked in Lancs and London. (RH, May 1982, May 1983). To ECS 1632, when the Andalusian Provincial sent him back to Flanders as unsuitable for a post there (Baet. 6/1/49).

ANDERTON, Thomas [1680–86]

m.o. at ECS 1680 (ORS). Lic. Theol. and priest 1686 (S 10). To be distinguished from the Thos Anderton (2) of Ans.3/5.

ANDOE, Thomas [1732–39]

Arrived Dec. 1732 (S 20). m.o. 1733 (ORS). Left, Oct. 1739 (S 20) with viaticum (ACS). Probably Irish, in which case the name may be a Hispanisation of (Mac)Endoe or (Mac)Adoo.

ANGELINO, Thomas See DARCY

ANGLICANO, Charles [Before 1712–c.1716]

Collected viaticum, 1712 (ACS). Perhaps the Spanish registrar could not decipher his real name and so fell back on this. Or perhaps his name was English (a surname found in Co. Limerick).

ANTHONY, Peter [c.1644]

b.Sanlucar 1620, son of the English consul. SO 1636-42. ECR 1642-43, 1645. Studied philosophy at ECS as a convictor. (Fo 6/358,624; CRS 55/477, 69/20).

APPLEBY, *alias* ROBINSON, Peter [1622-28]

b.Yorks 1591. SO ?-1622. From SO to ECS 1622 (Wad., Atkins). Viaticum 1628 (S 17). S.J., Watten 1629 (Ang.10). To England 1631. Active in London district. d.July 1671. (Ans.2/7; Fo 7/14; CRS 69).

ARCHER, Robert [Before 1616]

Subdeacon 1616 (ORS).

ARTON, William [1596-98]

b.Wisbech c.1576. A servant in Wisbech gaol, where he was converted. SO 1593-96 (CRS 69/21). To ECS 1596. To ECV 1598. To England, in ill-health, 1600. ECD 1603-04. Priest 1603. To England 1604. Deported 1606. In S. Wales 1610. (Ans.2/9. H-L wrongly gives his Christian name as Robert).

ASHE, *alias* FEZARD, Edward [?-1604]

Left ECS 1604 to enter O.S.B. at Obarenes, Spain. Imprisoned in England 1612. At Chelles 1613. To England 1614. At Midhurst, Sussex, 1627-29, and died there. (CRS 10/58, 33/218; Lunn 228, 235).

ASPINALL. See SMITH, Edward

ASTON, William [c.1610-c.1613]

Poetry contestant 1610 (LF 1). Signs petition 1613 as priest Gulielmus Astonus (Sim.1). Viaticum c.1613 (S 7).

ATKINS, William [1622-28]

b.Cambs 1601. From SO to ECS 1622 (Wads.). For his account of the journey, see *The Month* 18 (1879), pp.534-49; 19, pp.44-58, 392-410; 20 (1880), pp.395-412. Collected viaticum as a priest, 1628 (S XVII). S.J., Watten, 1629 (Ang.10). In England by 1631. Active for fifty years in the Staffs district. Condemned to death at Stafford Assizes, 1679, but was reprieved. Died in Stafford gaol, 1681 (Ans.2/10; CRS 69/23).

ATKINS (Aquino) [-Before 1637]

Died at ECS after ordination, c.1637 (S 19).

ATKINSON (Achinson) William [c.1593]

b.Richmond, Yorks. To Rheims 1589. To ECV 1592. Priest. To ECS c.1593 (CRS 30/20). To England before 1595, so he may only have passed through Seville, without studying there. A government spy by 1602, and still active as such in Feb. 1618. Reconciled and living in Flanders 1622 (Downshire 36/81). (Ans.1/13; Fo 6/xix, 160, 192).

BAAL, Joachim, *alias* **BASSET, Anthony** [1608-11]

b.Hadleigh, Suffolk, c.1587. SO 1604-08 (CRS 69/24). Studied logic and philosophy at ECS 1608-11. ECR 1611-12. d.Padua 1612. (CRS 37/164, 54/248-50; Fo 5/523).

BABTHORPE, *alias* **SMYTHE, Robert** [?-1605]

b.Babthorpe, ER Yorks, c.1584. To ECD, Jan.1606, to continue philosophy begun at ECS. Dismissed and returned to England 1608. Entered O.S.B (as Dom Mellitus) at Rheims for Dieulouard 1608. To St Malo 1611. To England (N.Province) 1619. d.c.1654. (Birt 34-5; CRS 10/71, 33/226-8).

BALLINGER (Valinger), Henry [c.1608-11]

Signed a deed at ECS in May 1608 (S V). Poetry contestant 1610 (LF 1). Deacon, June 1610 (ORS). Viaticum March 1611 (S 17).

BALL, William [1593-4]

Of Chester dioc. To ECV June 1591. To ECS Jan.1593. Priest. d.at ECS April 1594. (Ans.1/19).

BALSON, Francis [?-1627]

Left ECS in 1627, not yet a priest, and was given an advance for the journey by Francis Felton S.J. at Sanlúcar (S 17).

BAMBER, Edward, *alias* **READING, HELMES, Leonard** [1621-26]

Son of Richard Bamber, of The Moor, Great Carleton, Poulton-le-Fylde, Lancs. b.c.1602. SO 1618-21 (CRS 69/27). To ECS 1621. Ordained priest at Cadiz, July 1626. Arrested at Plymouth 1626. Pardoned in March 1627 after conforming. Resumed apostolate in Lancs from 1632. Captured 1643 and imprisoned for three years in Lancaster Castle. Executed at Lancaster, Aug.1646. Beatified 1987. (Ans.2/13; CRS 1/113; 6/182-3; 15/313).

BANISTER (Vanistero), *alias* **PUDSEY, Thomas** [Before 1642-1645]

m.o. and subdeacon 1642 (ORS). Collected viaticum as a priest, 1645 (S 19). Residing at Sanlúcar 1647. (Ans.2/17 *sub* Barrister; CRS 10/291, 295; Fo 5/767).

BARKER, Thomas, *alias* CLARENCE, Peter [Before 1631]

Studied at ECS (CRS 72/31). In England (Cambs and Essex), a priest, 1631. President of ECL 1638. Returned to England 1642. In London district 1649. In Berks 1660, d. June 1673. (Ans.2/16; CRS 72/31).

BARLEY (Barle), John [1597-1602]

b.Hathersage, Derbys, 1577. To Valladolid 1596, but was not admitted to ECV and left, 1597. A priest when he collected viaticum at ECS in March 1602 (S 7). (CRS 30/43, 71/15).

BARNARD, James [1756-7]

b.Shoreditch, 1733. Educ. Christ's Hospital 1742-47. Received into the Church as a clerk at Seville. Admitted to ECS 1756. Ordained at Cadiz, July 1757 (S 20). To ECL 1758. To England 1761. Worked at Cowdray and in London. President ECL 1776-82. Later, V.G. of London district. d.Kentish Town 1803. (Ans.4/18-20; CRS 72/7; Gill.1/136-7).

BARNES, Andrew [c.1609-13]

At ECS by July 1609 (S VII). Poetry contestant 1610 (LF 1), m.o.1610 (ORS). Signed petition March 1613 as Andreas Varnesius, priest (Sim.1). Not to be confused with Richard Trim, *alias* Andrew Barnes, at ECV 1610-12, who was not ordained at ECS until Dec.1613.

BARNES, Richard See TRIM

BARRET, Robert [c.1623-?]

Poetry contestant 1623 (Ibarra).

BARRISTER See BANISTER

BARROWS, *alias* HARDING (Gardingus), Christopher [1616-18]

Of Winchester dioc. After military service, converted at SO (CRS 69/28-9). To ECS 1616 as Christopher Harding. m.o.Dec.1617 (ORS). To Dieulouard to try O.S.B. vocation, thence to ECD. Priest 1621. To England 1623. Still active in 1634. (Ans.2/18).

BARTON, James [Before 1636-c.1640]

SO c.1631-2 (CRS 69/29). m.o. at ECS 1636 (ORS). In April 1640 the General gave permission for him to be sent to Rome to join the S.J. (Baet.6/1/321).

BARTON, Robert See BRADSHAW

BARTON, Thomas See FORSTER

BASSET, Anthony See BAAL, Joachim

BATH (Batt), Edward [c.1606–08]

A priest when he left ECS in May 1608 (S 17). The same month a priest named Edward arrived at ECD in ill-health, having studied theology at ECS for a year or more. (CRS 10/92).

BECKET (Bequeto, Becher), Thomas [Before 1633–1634]

Priest by 1633. Received viaticum 1634 (S 19).

BEDINGFIELD, Edmund [c.1640–c.1644]

b.1615, 3rd son of Sir Henry B., of Oxborough Hall, Norfolk, by his third wife Elizabeth, daughter of Peter Houghton, of Leyland, Lancs, Sheriff of London. SO 1627-33 (CRS 69/31). Studied philosophy at Liège, but was not a Jesuit and is said to have been ordained at ECS c.1644. Chaplain to English Carmelite nuns at Antwerp and Lierre from 1648. d.at Lierre, Sept.1680. (Ans.2/20; Fo 5/573-5, 6/626).

BEDINGFIELD, *alias* DE MENDOZA, **Thomas** [?–c.1635]

b.dioc.London c.1609. S.J. at Seville 1634, after one year of theology, so he probably studied at ECS (Baet.9/162,208). A priest, in fourth year of theology, at St Hermenegild's, Seville, 1639. In Lincs 1642-9. (Fo 7/46).

BEDINGTON, John See BERINGTON

BEESLEY, *alias* NELSON (Nessono), **John.** [1617–c.1621]

b.c.1593, son of Edward B. (CRS 6/183-4). SO ?-1613 (CRS 69/32). To ECV 1613 (CRS 30/115). To ECS Feb.1617, and ordained there as John Nelson, Dec.1620 (ORS). S.J. at Liège, 1622, as John Nelson. In Hants district 1629-36. d. in Derbys district 1670. (Ans.2/21; Ang.10).

BENNETT, William [c.1710–?]

m.o.1710 (ORS).

BENSON, Francis See THOROLD

BENSTEAD, *alias* HUNT, CANFIELD, **Thomas.** [1593–9]

b.Norfolk 1574. To ECV May 1592. Arrived ECS Feb.1593 (CRS 14/17). Priest. To England 1599, via Sanlúcar and France. In the Clink, Dec.1599. Escaped from Wisbech, March 1600. Arrested at Lincoln in June 1600 with Thomas Sprott, and executed there, 11 July. Beatified 1987 (Ans.1/33; *Relación*).

BENTLEY (Vencleo), Hugh ([1593–6]

b.Cheshire. M.A., Oxon 1587 (Foster 1/110). Rheims 1591-2. ECV 1592-3. Priest. To ECS Nov.1593. Signed deed there Oct.1595 (S V). Viaticum 1596 (S 6). (CRS 30/19, 5/267).

BERINGTON (Berindon), John [1593–5]

Of Dinmore, Herefords. To ECV 1592. To ECS Jan. 1593. Priest. To England after Oct.1595. Working in Worcs/Herefords area c.1600 (CRS 30/21). There is no firm evidence to identify him with the John Bernard Berington who was professed O.S.B. at Oña, Spain, 1607, was Prior of St Edmund's, Paris, 1616-18, and d. at Paris 1639. (CRS 5/267, 30/21, 33/211,218; Birt 20; WJ).

BERRY, Anthony See BURY

BESTON, John [?–1637]

Received viaticum as priest, 1637 (S 19).

BIRTWISTLE, John [?–1594]

Of Lancs. To ECV from ECS Nov.1594. To England Oct.1600. At Croxteth 1610. d.Feb.1620, buried at Little Crosby, Lancs. Possibly O.S.B. late in life. (Ans.1/36; CRS 6/150; 30/31; Lunn 227).

BLACKLOW, Thomas See WHITE

BLAKE, James, *alias* CROSS (de la Cruz). c.1669–1675

b.London 1649. At ECS by 1669 (S 13). Priest 1673 (ORS). Left March 1675 (S 10). S.J., Watten, July 1675. Liège 1676. At ECM 1677-83. To England 1685. Provincial 1701. Chaplain at Bromley Hall, Colchester from 1720. d.1728. (CRS 29/158; 70/34; Fo 7/64, 968).

BLANCHEVILLE, John [1766–67]

Irish. b.1738. Took oath July 1766. Went home at closure of college 1767. (Silke 122).

BLANCO, Juan See WHITE, John

BLISS (Blis) Nicholas [Before 1599–1606]

At ECS before 1599 (WJ). Viaticum 1606 (S 7).

BLOFIELD See IPSLEY

BLOMER, George. [1592–93]

b.Oxon c.1572. From ECV to ECS 1592. Dismissed 1593. (CRS 14/17;30/18).

[BLUNT (Blondo), Richard] [1591]

b.Leics 1563. Balliol College, Oxford 1581-83 (Foster). At Rheims 1583. ECR 1584-89. Priest 1589. To ECV 1589. At Seville en route for England 1591, before the college was established. S.J. 1596. Provincial 1623-38. Spent many years at Scotney Castle, Sussex. d.1638, buried in chapel at Somerset House. (Ans.1/41; CRS 14/15; Yepes 640-41; Fo 7/64-5.)

BOLD, Thomas [Before 1646-1650]

m.o.1646 (ORS). Priest by 1650 (S 5). Died at Sanlúcar 1650 (S 22), probably as a result of the plague.

BOND (Bun), John [?-1600]

Viaticum September 1600 (S 7). Named by WJ as student after 1595. (Ans.1/43).

BOSCO, George See BURSCOUGH

BOYLAN, Bartholomew [1738-c.1744]

Irish. Entered Oct.1738 (S 20). Priest by 1739 (S 16). Left, a D.D.,1744 (S 20; ACS).

BOYLAN, Matthew [1760-67]

Irish. Of Stamullen, Co.Meath. Entered 1760. Priest 1764 (ORS). Viaticum 1767 (Sim.2). Possibly the Fr Matthew Boylan, P.P.of Drogheda, who d.1773. (Silke 123).

BOYLAN, Nicholas [1766-70]

Irish. Of Dublin. Mission oath 1766 (S XVII). Priest Feb. 1767 (ORS). Transferred to Irish College, Salamanca, 1770. Viaticum 1771 (Sim.2; Silke 124).

BRADSHAW, or BRADSHAIGH, *alias* BARTON, Robert [1611-13]

b.Lancs 1589, son of Robert Bradshaigh, of the Haigh, Wigan. SO 1602-06 (CRS 69/45). ECV 1606-09. ECV 1609-11. Signed petition at ECS in March 1613 as priest Robert Barton. S.J. Louvain 1614 (Belg.). d.Liège 1617. (Ans.2/34; CRS 10/96.109).

BRENAN, Luke [Before 1722-1723]

Irish. All orders 1722 (ORS). Viaticum Dec.1723 (ACS). (Silke 124, where 1722 is misprinted 1772).

BRIANT [1595-97]

Two brothers of this name died at ECS in 1597 (ALSJ), having spent two years at the college.

BRIANT, Edward [1646-53]

m.o.1646. Priest 1652 (ORS). To England 1653 (S 23).

BRIERLY (Breile), Anthony [c.1688-c.1693]

Clothing bought for him, 1688 (S 10). Took the oath at Lisbon College, July 1693. After ordination at ECS he returned to Spain (? Sanlúcar) and died there before 1719. (Ans.3/28; CRS 72/24,37).

BRINKLOW See CHAPPERLIN

BRITTON, Richard, *alias* JACKSON, Bonaventure. Before 1609-1610.

Of West Bretton, Sandal Magna, WR Yorks. b.c.1586. SO 1599 (CRS 69/47-8). ECD 1599-? At ECS by July 1609 when he signed deed (S V). Viaticum April 1610 (S 17). ECD 1610-12. In England 1612-13. O.F.M. at Mechlin by 1616. First Praeses of St Bonaventure's, Douai, 1618. Confessor at the English Franciscan (Third Order) convent, Brussels, 1622. First Guardian of St Bonaventure's, 1624, but resigned and is listed by John Gee as resident in London after that year. In Newgate 1633. Still in London 1635. Definitor O.F.M. 1630,1634. (Ans.2/36; Dockery 22,26-29,41,117; BS 3/17; Tha.105,256).

BROWN (Bruno), John [Before 1656-1660]

m.o. and subdeacon 1656 (ORS). Viaticum applied for in August 1657, but it was spent by the college in 1660 (S XVII/9), which may mean that he died.

[BRUSHFORD, John] [1590-91]

b.Cornwall 1559. ECR 1581-85. In England 1585-c.1590. In Seville 1590-91. Again to England 1591, but was arrested off the Cornish coast and died in a London prison before March 1593. (Ans.1/56-57; CRS 14/16n; de Roa).

BRYERLY See BRIERLY

BULLER or BUTLER (Bulero), Thomas [?-1629]

Left ECS for S.J. novitiate in Watten, Oct.1629 (S 17), but not recorded there.

BURGO, Dominic de [1709-1716]

Irish, of dioc. Kilmacduagh. Priest 1711 (S 11). Graduated as bachelor, licentiate and master of theology, Jan.1716, having studied at the college for 7 years (S XXIX). Viaticum Jan.1716 (ACS).

BURKE, John [1748-54]

Irish. Of Dublin. Entered Oct.1748 (S 20). Deacon Dec.1753. Viaticum 1754 (ACS and Sim.2). (Silke 123).

BURKE, William [1745-51]

Irish. Of Dublin. Entered Dec.1745 (S 20). Priest Jan.1751 (ORS). (Silke 123).

BURON (*anglice?***Bourne** or **Byrom**), **James** [?-before 1646]

Viaticum collected between 1643 and 1646 (S 19).

BURROUGHS. See BARROWS

BURSCOUGH (Borsco), William [?-c.1669]

Licentiate by 1669 (S 13).

BURSCOUGH (Bosco), George [c.1646-?]

m.o.1646 (ORS). Possibly a victim of the Seville plague of 1649.

BURY (Berri), Anthony [Before 1611-1613]

Deacon 1611 (ORS). Signs petition March 1613 as priest Antonius Berius (Sim.1). Clothed O.S.B. at St Gregory's Douai, 1614, but left the same year. (Ans.2/38; St. Gregory's profession book).

BUXTON, John. After 1636-before 1646.

SO c.1633-36 (CRS 69/55). Viaticum collected at ECS before 1646 (S 19).

BYRNE, Thomas [1748-54]

Irish. Of Dublin. Entered Oct.1748 (S 20). Priest 1750 (ORS). Viaticum 1754 (Sim.2). (Silke 126).

CALLAGHAN, *alias* **DODD, Peter** [1746-53]

Irish. Of Dublin. Entered 1746 (S 15). Priest 1750 (ORS). At ECS till Oct.1753 (S 12). Probably the Fr Peter C. of James Street Chapel, Dublin, who d.1770 (Silke 126).

CALLAGHAN, Richard [1747-c.1753]

Irish. b.Dublin 1728. Entered 1747 (S 20). Priest Nov.1752 (ORS). SJ. Missioner in Philippines from 1753. To Ireland 1771. d.Dublin 1807. (Silke 126; Oliver, *Collections* . . . 1845, p.239; Fo 7/110).

CAMPBELL, Andrew [1732-36]

Irish. Entered Oct.1732 (S 20). m.o.1733. Priest 1735 (ORS). At ECS till 1736 (S 12). Completed studies at Irish College, Alcalá de Henares. Bishop of Kilmore 1753-1769. (Silke, 127, mistakes place of ordination).

CAMPION, Edmund [Before 1611-after 1613]

b.1594. m.o.c.1611 (ORS). Signs petition March 1613 as student Edmundus Campianus (Sim.1). S.J. at Villagarcía 1614 (Cast.).

CAMPION, Francis [1660-66]

m.o.1660, son of John Campion and Mary Gifford, dioc.Canterbury (ORS). Priest by 1663 (S 20). To England 1666 (S 9). Possibly identical with Francis Gifford, at SO 1655-60 (CRS 69/115).

CAMPION, Thomas [?-1630]

Viaticum collected June 1629, and paid to him March 1630 (S 17).

CANDALO, John See CONDALL

CANNON, Edmund [1595-1602]

b.Essex 1578. Matric. Douai University 1592. TO ECS June 1595. Priest by May 1602 (S 6). Viaticum 1602 (S 7). In Oxon district Aug.1610 (OB 1/26). In the Clink 1618, 1622-26, and from 1632 (SP 14/97/95; 14/128/71). Condemned to death 1641, reprieved at intercession of French ambassador. d. in Newgate before 1649. (WJ; Ans.1/62).

CARROLL, James [1709-15]

Irish. At ECS by April 1709. Priest Nov.1713 (ORS). Viaticum June 1715 (ACS). (Silke 127).

CAR(E)Y (Careo), Francis [After 1636-1646]

b.Devon c.1610. SO 1632-36 (CRS 69/5). m.o. and subdeacon 1642 (ORS). Left April 1646 (S 8). S.J. 1647. In Flanders 1649-59. To England 1659. Worked in Hants and Oxon districts. d.London 1665. (Ans.2/48; Fo 7/120).

CAR(E)Y (Careo) *alias* STAVELEY, Ignatius [c.1646-?]

SO 1642, or earlier, to 1643, or later (CRS 69/250). m.o. at ECS 1646 (ORS). Perhaps a victim of the Seville plague of 1649.

CA(R)EY, William [c.1654-1657]

At ECS by April 1654 (S 8). Subdeacon Sept.1656 (ORS). d. at ECS July 1657 (S 9). (Silke, 127, incorrectly makes him Irish).

CAR(E)Y See CRISP

CASULLO (*anglice* ?Cassily), **John** [1757-63]

Priest at ECS from June 1757 (S 16) until at least April 1763 (S XXIX). Probably Irish.

CATTERICK, George [?1641-1647]

SO c.1639-40 (CRS 69/60). His viaticum was claimed by ECS in 1645, and he left via Cadiz, Oct.1647 (S 19). Possibly a Catterick of Hornby Hall, Brougham, Westmorland.

CHAMBERLAIN, George [1592-97]

b.Ghent 1576, of the family of Shirburn Castle, Oxon. To ECV 1591. Founder member of ECS, Nov.1592 (CRS 14/16). To England for health reasons 1597. To ECR 1599. Priest 1600. To Belgium. Dean of St Bavan's, Ghent, and Bishop of Ypres 1628. d.1634. (Ans.1/69; BS 2/84; Fo 6/213).

CHAMPION, George [1622-?]

To ECS from SO 1622 (Atkins).

CHAPPERLIN, *alias* BRINKLOW, John [1606-?]

b.Cirencester, Glos, c.1584. ECR 1604-06. To ECS Oct.1606 (S 7). (CRS 37/136).

CHARNOCK, George See WORTHINGTON, Laurence.

CHATTERTON (Chatelthorn, Chatelton), Thomas [Before 1611-After 1613]

m.o. c.1611 (ORS). Signed petition March 1613 at ECS as priest Thomas Chetelt^us (Sim.1).

CLARENCE, Peter See BARKER, Thomas.

CLARK, Francis [?-1632]

From ECS to S.J. novitiate, Watten, July 1632 (S 19), but not recorded there.

CLARK, John [?-1630]

b.Essex c.1604. SO c.1623-25 (CRS 69/64). Viaticum at ECS April 1630 (S 17). S.J., Watten, 1632 (Ang.10). In Wales 1636, Suffolk 1638. At Watten 1649. Rector of Liège 1655. English Provincial at Brussels 1664. Rector of ECR and d. there 1672. (Ans.2/59).

CLAYTON, Henry See CLIFTON

CLIFFORD, - [1622-?]

To ECS from SO 1622 (Wads.).

CLIFTON, Henry [c.1596-7]

Christened at Kirkham, Lancs, 24 March 1580, son of Thos C. (IGI). Died at ECS in 1597 after six months there, having spent two years previously at SO. According to the Annual Letters, his father was 'Lencastrensis provinciae moderator' and 'oppidorum quattuor dominus legitimus'. The Annual Letters (Baet.19I) give his name as Clyfton. This was misprinted in ALSJ (1597) as Clyton and misinterpreted by Foley (7/xxxi) as Clayton.

CLUANE (*anglice* ?**MacClune), Richard** [1713-18]

Irish. Received viaticum in 1718 after five years at ECS (ACS).

COLEMAN, John [1722-34]

Irish. Entered Oct.1727 (S 11). Said masses for the college 1728-33 (S 16, 21). Viaticum 1734 (ACS).

COMERFORD, James [?-1722]

Irish. Viaticum 1722 (ACS).

CONDALL (Candalo, Condalo), John [1613 or later-1621]

SO 1612 or earlier-1613 or later (CRS 69/70). Subdeacon 1616, Priest Dec.1617 (ORS). In England by May 1622 (Baet.5 I,f.95).

CONIERS, George See PALMES

CONIERS, Thomas [1622-c.1623]

To ECS from SO 1622, but died shortly after arrival (Wads., Atkins). Perhaps of Sockburne, NR Yorks (CRS 13/103).

CONWAY (Conbeo), Thomas [?-1632]

To England, ill, 1632 (S 19).

CONYERS, James See MORGAN

COOPER (Coper), John 1594-97

Of Lincoln dioc. To Rheims 1590. Priest 1592. TO ECV 1593. To ECS Oct.1594. Signed deed there Sept.1595 (S V). He is probably the Joannes Ceperus who died at ECS in 1597 (ALSJ; Ans.1/86-7).

COOPER, William [?-1642]

A priest when his viaticum was collected 1642 (S 19).

CORBALLY, Robert [c.1722–27]

Irish. Convictor 1722 (S 11). All orders 1725 (ORS). At ECS till 1727 (S 14). (Ans.4/71; Silke 129).

CORBY, *alias* CORBINGTON, FLOWER (Floro), **Ralph** [1619–21]

b.Dublin 1598. SO 1613–19 (CRS 69/73). To ECS 1619. ECV 1621–25 (AAW A16/77). Priest. S. J. Watten 1625. In Yorks district 1632. In Durham district from 1634 (Ang.10). Martyred at London 1644, after arrest near Newcastle. Beatified 1929. (Ans.2/72).

CORBY, *alias* CORBINGTON, FLOWER (Floro), **Robert** [1617—after 1624]

b.Dublin 1596. SO 1612–16 (CRS 69/74). To ECV 1616. To ECS 1617. m.o.1620 (ORS). Priest c.1622 To England, but readmitted at ECS in 1623 (Baet.5/1/179). S. J. Watten 1626. At Liège and Ghent 1629–31 (Ang.10). Later English penitentiary at Rome and Loreto. d.in England c.1637. (Ans.2/72; Fo 3/66,96).

COSTELLO, John [?–1764]

Irish. Received viaticum March 1764 (ACS) as 'priest of the English College'.

COURTNEY (Cournei, Curni), George 1738–45.

Irish. Entered 1738. Priest 1743 (ORS). Viaticum 1744 (ACS; Sim.2). Left, a D.D., 1745 (S XXI). Probably the Rev.Mr C. of Bridge Street Chapel, Dublin, who died c.1780. (Silke 129).

COURTNEY, John [?–1747]

Viaticum 1747 (Sim.2).

COVERT, George [?–1608]

Received viaticum, a priest, 1608 (S 17).

CRANWISE, Richard [c.1597–1600]

b.Essex c.1577. To ECV 1596. To ECS c.1597. At ECV again 1600–01. Dismissed 1601. (CRS 10/32; 30/41; 69/77; Fo 6/584).

CRATHORNE (Catorno, Cratorno), Francis [c.1618–20]

b.Ness Hall, N.R. Yorks, before 1596. SO ?–1616 (CRS 69/77). ECV 1616–18 (AAW A16/77). m.o.at ECS 1618 (ORS). O.S.B. at Douai 1620. Priest. To England. d.1667 at Comberford Hall, Staffs. (Ans.2/75; Ham.2/ped.).

CRESWELL (Crisuelo), John [Before 1652-1655]
All orders at ECS 1652 (ORS). d.at college 1655 (S 23).

CRISP, Thomas [?-1599]
Left ECS, a priest, May 1599. In the Tower, August 1599. (Ans.1/92).

CRISP, *alias* CAREY, ?William [?-1628]
Received viaticum at ECS 1628 as Carey (S 17). Perhaps the Wm Krix at
Sanlúcar to whom the Fr General S.J.wrote in Nov.1628 (Baet.5/1/221v).
Married in London c.1630. (Ans.2/75-6, quoting John Southcott).

CROSS (Crucius), Aurelius. See WILLIAMS

CURRAN, John [1726-32]
Irish. Entered 1726 (S 11). Priest c.1727 (S 16). At ECS till 1732 (S 14).

CURTIS (Cortes), Richard [c.1610-1613]
b.1591. Poetry contestant 1610 (LF 1). Signs petition March 1613 as
student R.Cortesius (Sim.1). S.J. at Villagarcía, 1614, aged 23 (Cast.).

CURTIS, Thomas [1597-99]
b.Andover, Hants, 1576. ECR 1596-7. To ECS in ill-health 1597. To
ECD for the same reason 1599. Priest 1600. To England 1601. S.J. 1605.
Worked in Hants. Said by John Gee (1624) to be in London, where he
had a brother, a pewterer, in Tower Street. d.Liège 1657. (To references
in Ans.1/96, add Fo 7/191).

DALISON. See PRICE, Edward

DALLISON (de Alarson), Joseph or Edmund [c.1679-c.1681]
b.c.1658. SO c.1679. m.o.and subd.ECS 1680 (ORS). Viaticum 1681 (S
10). To ECR 1684. Joined service of Cardinal Howard c.1685. (Ans.3/45;
CRS 69/80; HMC 32/13).

DARCY, Anthony [c.1641-46]
SO c.1640-c.1641 (CRS 69/81). Subdeacon 1641-3 (S XVII). Viaticum
1646 (S 19).

DARCY, *alias* ANGELINO, Thomas [?-c.1645]
?Of Northants. Bro.of Arthur Darcy, *alias* Angelino, priest at ECR 1630
(Ans.2/81; CRS 69/81-2). Priest at ECS by 1645 (S 8). To England. Still
active there 1661. (Ans.2/371; Fo 6/345).

DAVENPORT, John [?-1601]

Received viaticum as priest 1601 (S 7).

DAVIES (Davisio), William [1595-1600]

b.Salop 1538. Musician. ECV 1593-5. Priest Nov. 1593. Admitted at ECS, May 1595 (CRS 14/18). Viaticum collected 1600 (S 7). At ECR as music master, 1601. To England 1603. Banished 1607. In Rome 1608-? (Ans.1/99).

DAWSON, William [?-1632]

Priest at ECS by 1631(S 24). To England 1632 (S 19).

DELANEY, Malachy [1748-56]

Irish, of Narraghmore, Co. Kildare. To ECS 1748 (S 20). Priest 1751. Viaticum 1754 (ACS and Sim.2), but still at ECS 1756 (S 16). (Silke 129).

DENNIS (Dionisio), John [Before 1630-1634]

At ECS by 1630 (S 17). Priest 1633 (ORS). Faculties 1634 (Lille A.N. Ser.H.18.h.13). In Sanlúcar 1637 (S 14).

DIAZ (*anglice?*Deas), Robert [c.1642-46]

m.o.1642 (ORS). Priest 1644 (S XIV;ORS). To England 1646 (S XIV).

DILLON, Richard [1737-44]

Irish, of Proudston, Co.Meath. To ECS 1737 (S 20). Priest 1742 (ORS). To England, D.D., 1744 (S 20). At Moorfields, London, 1744-80, and also signs Spanish Chapel register during that period. d.London 1780. (Ans.4/88; CRS 12/20, 50/117; Burton, *Challoner*, index).

DODD. See CALLAGHAN

DO(W)NING, John. See HAMELYN

DORAN, Nicholas [1748-52]

Irish. To ECS 1748 (S 20). Said masses at college 1748-52 (S 16). Viaticum 1752 (Sim.2).

DORINGTON, Robert [Before 1638-c.1641]

Priest at ECS 1638 (SP 94/40/63). Still there 1641 (S 24). Indicted as a priest in Middlesex 1653. (Ans.2/87).

DOWNING, John. See HAMELYN

DRAPER, *alias* TEMPLE, Thomas [1616–?]

b.Bucks c.1594. From SO to ECS, Sept.1616 (S XVII). m.o.as Thomas
Temple 1617 (ORS). After completing his studies he joined S.J. in 1621,
spent some years in England and was a tertian at Ghent in 1629 as Fr
Thomas Temple, aet. 35 (Ang. 10; Ans. 2/87, 315; CRS 69/88).

DRURY, Mark. See HARRINGTON

EDWARDS, *alias* PRESTON, Henry, *alias* HENRY, Edward [1660–9]

SO 1656, or earlier, to 1657, or later. m.o. at ECS 1660 as Edward
Henry. Subdeacon 1664, deacon and priest 1665 as Henry Preston (ORS).
Viaticum 1669 (S 9). According to ORS he was the son of William Henry
and Elizabeth Poyntz, of Canterbury dioc. (Ans.3/55,175; CRS 69/92).

EDWARDS, Peter. See EVELEIGH, Amesius

EGERTON, Thomas [1592–c.1595]

b.Cheshire c.1572. 'Of noble family' (ALSJ). Received into the church by
Richard Blunt S.J. To ECV 1592. To ECS Nov.1592 (CRS 14/16). d.at
ECS 1595. (CRS 30/15; ALSJ 1594–5; Yepes 853–4).

ELLIS, –. [c.1593]

Named by Henry Walpole as a priest at ECS by 1593 (CRS 5/267).

ELLIS, William, *alias* WILLIAMS, John [1613–?]

Page to Sir Everard Digby, and arrested with him in 1605 (DNB 5/957).
SO 1608–13. ECS 1613–14. S.J. laybrother 1614. (CRS 69/92; Fo 7/224).

ELLIS (Elisio), *alias* FLISK, William. [?–1623]

b.Bucks c.1590. A priest at ECS in Feb.1623 when the Fr General S.J.
approved his petition to be sent on the mission. (Baet 5/1/124) Novice
priest in London dist.1624–5 (Ang.10). Later active in Durham district.
d.1640 (Fo 3/100; 7/224).

EMERSON, Ralph [?–1633]

b.Holborn 1609. Deacon at ECS 1632 (ORS). To England via Madrid
1633. S.J. 1635. Priest novice S.J. at Watten 1636, in London district
1638 (Ang.10). d.Yorks 1684. (Ans.2/95).

ERRINGTON (Erinton), George [?–1637]

Collected viaticum as priest, 1637 (S 19).

EVANS, Edward [?–1605]

Collected viaticum as priest, 1605 (S 7).

EVANS, John [1595-?]

Of Caernarvonshire, b.1576. Entered ECS, May 1595 (CRS 14/18). No more known.

EVELEIGH, Amesius, *alias* EDWARDS, Peter [1622-27]

SO ?-1622. To ECS 1622 (Wad., Atkins). Priest. To ECV 1627, expelled 1631. To Madrid, where he fell ill. (CRS 29/152-3,217; 30/146; 69/94).

EVERARD, *alias* TALBOT (Talmoto, Talbato), William. [c.1611-c.1617]

b.Suffolk (?Little Linstead) 1590. m.o.c.1611 (ORS) Signed petition March 1613 as student Gul.Talbottus (Sim.1). Subdeacon 1614 (ORS). Professor at ECD 1618-33. To England 1633, still active there 1641. (Ans.2/96-7; Silke 146 wrongly takes him to be Irish).

EYRE, Anthony [1667-?]

Signed mission oath 1667 (S XVII). To be distinguished from the Anthony Eyre who was a licentiate in theology by March 1688 and received his viaticum in Feb.1689 (S 10).

EYRE, Vincent [?-1600]

b.Derbys 1578. SO 1595-6. To ECV 1596, and thence to ECS. Name listed, then deleted, as novice S.J. at Montilla 1600 (Baet.8) To ECD 1601. (CRS 10/32, 30/42, 69/95; Fo 7/1428).

EYSTON, Roger. See STONE

FAIRFAX, William [1622-?]

From SO to ECS 1622 (Atkins). Probably an *alias* of one of the three students named by Wadsworth as Hansby, Farmer and Clifford.

FALKNER, Stephen [After 1641-1647]

b.Kent 1621-2. SO c.1636-41. At ECS 1646 (S 8). Viaticum 1647 (S 19). S.J. 1650. At SO 1652. To England 1653. Active in Durham district 1654-64. Military chaplain in Ghent 1669. d. in England 1660. (Ans.2/100; CRS 69/97, 70/91).

FANÇONIO. See FRANSAM

FARMER or FERMOR, [-. 1622-?]

From SO to ECS 1622 (Wads.).

FARRELL, Patrick [1732-41]

Irish. To ECS 1732 (S 20). Priest by 1740 (S 16). d.August 1741 (S 20), (Silke 131).

FEARBURN or FAIRBURN (Ferber), George [?-1608]

Of Notts. SO c.1600. Received viaticum as priest at ECS 1608 (S 17). d.Newgate 1615. (Ans.2/98; CRS 69/99; *Algunos avisos,* 1615).

FELTON, Francis [1592-c.1603]

b.Valladolid 1577, of an English mother and Spanish father (in 1620 he signs himself 'Francisco Felton Durango'). To ECV 1591. To ECS Nov.1592 (CRS 14/17). Priest by May 1603 (S 6). Remained at Seville and Sanlúcar, where he was tutor to the sons of the Conde de Luna. In Oct.1627 he was dispensed from the age requirement for entry into S.J. (Baet.5/1/266). At ECS and Sanlúcar (not St George's) from 1631. Rector ECM 1635-6. d.Marchena 1647. (Ans.1/113; Baet. 9/1; 14/1; *Varones* 3.54).

FIELDING, Nicholas [Before 1609-1610]

At ECS by 1609 (S VII). To England, a priest, 1610 (S 17).

FINCH, Thomas [c.1600-1607]

Fourth son of Clement Finch, of Milton-next-Sittingbourne, Kent (Whatmore, pp.12, 14n.). SO ?-1598. Detained en route to Seville (HMC Salis. 10/144,229). Priest at ECS by 1605. To England 1607 (HMC Salis.20/170). Apostate and informer by 1609. (Ans.2/101; CRS 69/101).

FINN, John [1734-44]

Irish, of Stamullen, Co.Meath. Entered 1737 (S 20). Priest and D.D., 1744. Viaticum 1743 (ACS) and 1744 (Sim.2). (Silke 132).

FITZGERALD (Felix), Gerald [c.1728-1731]

Priest at ECS by 1728 (S 16). Viaticum 1730 (ACS). To mission 1731 (S 12).

FITZSIMONS, James [c.1718-23]

At ECS by 1718 (S 11). Priest 1723 (ORS). Viaticum 1723 (ACS). (Silke 132).

FITZSIMONS, Patrick (1) [c.1718]

All orders Dec.1718 (ORS). (Silke 132).

FITZSIMONS, Patrick (2) [c.1722]

m.o. and subdeacon 1722 (ORS). (Silke 132).

FITZSIMONS, Patrick (3) [1730–37]

Entered 1730. Priest 1735 (ORS). Viaticum 1737 (ACS). (Silke 132).

FLOWER, Charles. See WALDEGRAVE

FLOWER, Ralph and Robert. See CORBY

FLOYD, Henry [1592–3]

Of Cambs, born c.1563. At Rheims by 1588. ECV 1589–92. Priest. At ECS 1592–3 (CRS 14/16). To Lisbon 1593 (T-D 2/ccc/xxvii). To England 1597. S.J. 1599. Imprisoned and banished. In Lisbon again c.1603–c.1617 (Lus.). Superior of Suffolk mission 1621–3. On London mission 1624–38 (Ang. 10, 13). d. London 1641. (Ans. 1/120; RH 20, p.480).

FLYNN, Patrick [c.1721–6]

At ECS by 1721. Priest by 1725 (S XVII). Defended thesis 1726 (S 14).

FORCER, Francis [Before 1601–1603]

b.1583–4 at Eden, Easington, Co.Durham. Said by his brother John Forcer S.J. (Fo 3/106–7) to be studying in Spain by 1601. He joined the S.J. in Andalusia in 1603, so must have been a student at ECS. At Ecija 1606 (Baet.8/210). Subdeacon at Seville 1610 (ORS). At Cadiz c.1610–1616 (Baet.8; 4/1/195). At ECM from 1617 (Baet. 4/1/213) to 1627, when the Fr General ordered him under pain of excommunication to leave for Flanders (Baet.5/1/246; CRS 29/205–6, 214–5). In Durham district from c.1630 to his death in 1655. (Fo 3/107–8; 7/270).

FORTESCUE (Foseu), – [?–1603]

Viaticum Nov.1603 (S 7).

FOSTER, Henry [1636, or earlier, –1637]

m.o.1636 (ORS). Priest by Aug.1637 (S 24). Viaticum 1637 (S 19). Agent in England for ECD, still active in 1669. (Ans.2/115).

FO(R)STER, Thomas *alias* WHARTON (Barton), MOUNTAIN, John [1615–18]

b.Earswick (Erdswyke), NR Yorks, 1597. SO ?–1615. Poetry contestant at ECS in 1615 (LF 2). To ECR 1618. To Portugal 1620, not yet a priest. (CRS 37/188, 54/320–1; Fo 3/188, 6/287. Ans.2/116 confuses him with an elder brother. Cf.CRS 69/105–6).

FRANCIS (Francisco), Christopher [?–1605]

Viaticum Dec.1605 (S 7).

FRANSAM, William [c.1616]

A Guillermo Françonio was a prizewinner from ECS at a poetry contest in 1616 (LF 2). Probably the William Fransam who was at SO c.1611-12 (CRS 69/107).

FREKE, Thomas [c.1606]

A student of this name, 'of London', wrote from ECS in July 1606 to his uncle in Norfolk (SP 14/22/67).

FREVILLE, Thomas. See JENISON

FRIZELLE or FRISWELL, Francis [c.1650-c.1654]

SO c.1647-c.1650. All orders at ECS 1652 (ORS). Still there 1654 (S 23). (Ans.2/118; CRS 69/108).

FRIZELLE or FRISWELL, George [c.1648-c.1653]

SO c.1646-c.1648. All orders at ECS 1652 (ORS). Still there 1653 (S 23). (Ans.2/118; CRS 69/108).

FURLONG, Richard [1745-49]

Irish. Entered as priest 1745 (S 20). Viaticum 1749 (Sim.2 and ACS).

GALICANUS. See HALLING

GALLAGHER, John [1749-56]

Irish. Entered as a priest 1749 (S 20). Viaticum 1755 (Sim.2;ACS). Still at ECS 1756 (S 12).

GARNET, Charles [1659-63]

To ECS 1659 (S 9). All orders 1660 (ORS, which names him as son of Nathaniel Garnet and Mary Sutton, of Canterbury dioc.). Viaticum 1663 (S 13).

GARNET, James [1630-c.1633]

Nephew of George Garnet (see p.109).
Convictor 1630, alumnus 1631 (S 19). Priest by 1633 (S 19).

GARNET, William [1672-78]

Oath 1672 (S XVII). Priest 1676 (ORS). d.at ECS 1678 (S 10).

GAWEN, *alias* **GREEN, Edward.** [?-1615]

From ECS, a priest, to ECD 1615. (Ans.2/128).

GEORGE, Walter [1616-?]
?SO ?-1616. To ECS 1616 (S XVII).

GERANDO, James (Diego) [c.1646-?]
m.o. 1646 (ORS). He may have died in the Seville plague of 1649.

GERARD, - [1622-?]
Named by J.Wadsworth as one of the 12 students who travelled from St Omer to ECS in 1622.

GERARD, Henry [1692-3]
b.Lancs 1668. To ECR 1688, dismissed 1692 (CRS 40/106-7). To ECS Dec.1692, dismissed May 1693. (See pp.182-6).

GIBBONS, John, *alias* POLLARD, Augustine [?1673-76]
b.Exeter 1652. Converted by Henry Edwards (q.v.) at Seville. At ECS from c.1673. To ECR 1676. Priest 1677. To England. (Ans.3/64-5; CRS 40/9; Fo 5/910, 6/425).

GIBBONS, John [1756-63]
Irish. Entered 1756 (S 9). Priest 1763. Viaticum 1763 (ACS). (Silke 134).

GIFFORD, Francis. See CAMPION

GOLDSMITH. See MIDDLETON

GRACE, Patrick Thomas [1716-c.1725]
Irish. At ECS from 1716 (S 14). All orders 1722 (ORS). Defended thesis 1725 (S 11).

GRAVE (Gravi), John [c.1722]
Convictor 1722 (S 11).

GRAY (Grei), Thomas [c.1609]
Alumnus in 1609 (S XVII).

GRAY (Grayo), *alias* JENISON, William [c.1646-c.1649]
m.o. 1646 (ORS), subdeacon 1649. In that year Michael Jenison, *alias* Gray, of Heighington, Co.Durham, had a brother 'in collegio anglicano Hispaniae' which was not ECV (Ans.2/169). Possibly a victim of the Seville plague of 1649-50.

GREEN (Grino), Charles [?–1636]

Collected viaticum as priest 1635 (S 19). At Sanlúcar from c.1637 (S 19) to at least 1664 (S XV).

GREEN (Grino), Francis [c.1651–c.1656]

SO c.1646–51 (CRS 69/119). Probably one of the students sent from SO in 1651 to make up the numbers at ECS depleted by the plague (ALSJ 1651). At ECS in 1654 (S 8), subdeacon 1656 (ORS). Priest at Sanlúcar 1664–6 (S 20). Confessor to O.S.B. nuns at Ghent 1667–c.1712 (*Annals* 203). (Ans.2/137).

GREEN (Grino), John [1616–?]

To ECS from SO 1616 (S XVII). m.o.1617 (ORS). (Ans.2/138).

GREEN, *alias* HARRIS, WASHINGTON, Paul [?–1602]

b.Derbys c.1573. Collected viaticum at ECS 1602 (S 7). At ECD en route from Seville to England 1603 (CRS 10/51, which gives his real name as Green and alias as Washington). To Rome, 1609, where he was appointed chaplain to Robert Lord Shirley on his journey to Spain with the further prospect of a chaplaincy at Sanlúcar (ECV Sanlúcar MSS 2/35). To Ireland c.1615 (*Arctomastix*, A&R 380, p.119), where he was chaplain at Luttrellstown Castle, Co. Dublin, and was known as Paul Harris (WP p.505). Between 1624 and 1633 he engaged in controversy with Archbishop Ussher and with Provost Bedell of Trinity College, and between 1632 and 1635 published at Dublin under the pseudonym Paulus Veridicus a series of pamphlets (A & R 189, 380–6) against the regular clergy and Thomas Fleming O.F.M., Archbishop of Dublin, who suspended him. (Ans.1/137; DNB *sub* Harris; RH 18 (1987), p.367; SCH 25 (1989), pp.145–58; JEH 11 (1960), pp.202–12; RN 2 (1960), p.376; TL p.106).

GREEN, Richard [Before 1598]

At ECD and ECS before 1598, when he went to England. Imprisoned before 1606. (See letter of Andrew White S.J., in Fo 3/268–72).

GREEN, Richard. See WYLES

GREEN, *alias* REYNOLDS, Richard or Thomas [1601-after 1602]

b.Oxford 1579. To ECD c.1598. To ECS 1601. Priest 1602. Banished from England 1606. In England again by 1628, when he was condemned and reprieved. In Newgate 1632. Released 1634, but re-arrested. Executed at Tyburn, Jan. 1642. Beatified 1929. (Ans.1/138).

GRIFFITH(S), Lewis [1592-5]

b.Caernarvonshire 1571. To ECV 1591. To ECS Nov.1592 (CRS 14/17). Priest 1595. Signed deed at ECS Oct.1595 (S V). Left c.1598 (WJ). In S.Wales by 1610. (Ans.1/139; CRS 30/13; Salis.10/341).

GRIFFITH, *alias* ALFORD, **Michael** [After 1602-1606]

b.London c.1587. SO 1596-1602 (CRS 69/121). To ECV 1602. From ECS to ECD 1606. S.J. 1607. Priest. At Louvain 1607-11 (Belg.). To Naples as English chaplain. English penitentiary at St Peter's, Rome, 1615. In England (Leics district) by 1624. d.at SO 1652. (CRS 30/76; Fo 2/299-308;5/489;7/320).

HABARD, William. See HALLING

HALL (Gal), John [1595-9]

b.Norfolk 1574. To ECS via ECV 1595 (CRS 14/18). Signed deed at ECS Oct.1595 (S V). Priest at ECV. To England 1599. Banished 1606. (Ans.1/143; CRS 10/74,86;30/32).

HALLING (Galicano), John [c.1613-c.1618]

Signed petition in March 1613 as Joannes Gallicanus. Subdeacon 1617, priest 1618 (ORS). Perhaps an elder brother of the following.

HALLING, *alias* HABARD, **William** [1616-after 1617]

SO from 1612 (CRS 69/124). To ECS 1616 (S XVII). m.o. as Gulielmus Habardus, 1617 (ORS).

HAMELYN, *alias* DOWNING (Doningo), **John** [1639-45]

b.Sussex c.1618. SO 1631-38 (CRS 69/124). To ECS c.1639. Tonsure 1641, priest 1644 (ORS). Viaticum 1645 (S 19). ECD 1646-7. To Paris 1647. To England 1648. (Ans.2/87,142; CRS 11/456,459,468).

HAMMOND (Hamon, Amom), Lawrence [1592-c.1600]

b.Lichfield dioc.1575. To ECV 1591. At ECS 1592-c.1600 (WJ). Signed deed at ECS 1595 (S V). (Ans.1/145; CRS 14/17;30/14).

HANDS, *alias* JOHNSON, **Edward** [?-1606]

Of Lutterworth, Leics. From ECS to ECD in ill-health, 1606 (CRS 10/72). To England, a priest, 1612. Banished 1618. (Ans.2/143).

HANDS (Hannes), *alias* JOHNSON, **Robert** [?-1607]

From ECS to ECD 1606 with Edward Hands (q.v.). He is assigned to Lichfield diocese, so they were probably brothers. Priest 1607. To England. (Ans.2/143).

HANMER, Joseph [1687–c.1689]

Oath 1687 (S XVII). Lic.Theol. by 1689 (S 23). He cannot be the Joseph H. of CRS 69/110, who was at SO until 1694.

HANSBY, or HAUSBY, --

From SO to ECS 1622 (Wads.).

HANSON. See JANSON

HARDING, Christopher. See BARROWS

HARRINGTON, *alias* DRURY, METHAM, Mark [before 1611–1614]

b.Yorks 1592. m.o. c.1611 (ORS). Signed petition at ECS in March 1613 as student Marcus Drurius (Sim.1). At Louvain 1614–16. Priest at Arras, 1616. Professor at ECD 1622–24. In England 1624–26. Confessor at ECD 1626–28. Lecturer in theology at ECL 1628–33. To England. VG to Bishop Smith, resident in Kent. d.c.1657. (Ans.2/147; CRS 10/131 and *passim*; CRS 72/80-1; UM Dec.1976, pp.22–35).

HARRINGTON (Arintono), Nicholas [c.1610–13]

b.c.1586. SO c.1600 (CRS 69/126). Poetry contestant at ECS 1610 (LF 1). m.o.1610 (ORS). Signed petition in March 1613 as priest (Sim.1). Novice S.J. at Louvain, 1613 (Belg.). d.1614. (Ans.2/148; Fo 1/177–8).

HARRIS, Paul. See GREEN

HATTON (Haton), Francis [c.1620–?]

SO 1613–? (CRS 69/128). m.o. at ECS 1620 (ORS). (Ans.2/151).

HATTON, John [c.1611–c.1617]

m.o.c.1611 (ORS). Signed petition in March 1613 as student J.Hattonus (Sim.7). Priest 1617 (ORS). Is he the John Haughton, secular priest, at Garstang, Lancs, in 1639 (RH 4, pp.38–46)?

HAUSBY. See HANSBY

HAYWOOD. See HUNGERFORD

HEATH. See HOTHERSAL

HENRICKSON (Enriqueson), Anthony [?–1636]

Viaticum 1636 (S 19).

HENRY, Edward. See EDWARDS, Henry

HERNE, William. See WAFERER

HIDALGO, John. See WENTWORTH

HILARY, Francis [?-1600]
Viaticum as priest 1600 (S 7).

HILDESLEY. See MALLET

HILDRETH, *alias* SIMPSON, William [c.1612-?]
b.c.1585, in Durham dioc. SO 1605-09 (CRS 69/133). To ECV 1609. In ill-health to ECS via Madrid c.1612. Signed petition at ECS in March 1613 as Wm Symson, priest (Sim.1). (Ans.2/155; CRS 29/147;30/105).

HISHERAN, Gerard [c.1726-28]
Irish. Entered 1726 (S 11). Saying masses for college from 1727 (S XVII). Clothes bought for him 1728 (S 14).

HOLLAND (Olando), George [c.1618-?]
m.o.1618 (ORS).

HOLLAND (Olan), John [c.1620-?]
m.o.1620. Anstruther's suggested identification with St John Kemble (Ans.2/175) is unproved.

HOLMES, Matthew [1595-c.1597]
Of Kingston Lacy, Dorset. To ECS 1595. Priest. To ECV c.1597. To England c.1599 (Salisbury 10/340). In Dorset 1601-10 (Ans.1/173-4).

HOLMES (Horm), Richard [?-1594]
Of Chester dioc. From ECS to ECV, Nov.1594. Left ECV 1597 and died in the Basque country on his way home. (CRS 30/31).

HOLMES, Thomas [1595-?]
b.Lancs 1577. Reconciled to the Church by James Forth (Ans. 1/122). To ECV via Ireland, 1595. Entered ECS, May 1595 (CRS 14/18). A priest of this name was banished from York Castle in April 1630. (Ans.1/174).

HOPTON, Edward [c.1610-c.1613]
Poetry contestant 1610 (LF 1). Viaticum 1612 (S 7). Signs petition March 1613 as priest. (Sim.1).

HOTHERSAL, *alias* HEATH, George [1591-3]

b.1560, younger son of John Hothersal and Anne Talbot of Preston,
Lancs. Kinsman of John and Laurence Worthington (qqv.). To Rheims
1585. To ECV Dec. 1590. According to Santibañez and Yepes, he studied
and was ordained at ECS, though the ECV records say he was ordained
at Valladolid (CRS 30/11.Cf.CRS 6/161n). Arrested at Flushing 1594 en
route for England. In prison in London 1594-6 and 1599 (Santibañez). In
Lancs from 1603. Professed O.S.B. in England 1614. Still active in Lancs
1639 (RH4/40). (Ans.1/175-77; CRS 6/161; DR 1927, p.61; Santibañez
339; Yepes 777-8).

HOUGHTON (Auton), Luke [?-c.1657]

m.o.and subd.1656 (ORS). Viaticum 1657 (S XVII).

HOUSE OR HOWSE (Huseo), William [1592-5]

Christened at Bierton, Bucks, 13 Dec.1571 (IGI). For his probable
parents, see CRS 18/5. To ECS 1592 (CRS 14/17). Signs deed Oct.1595.
To England, a priest, c.1595 (Salisb.10/341). In Bucks 1610,1628.
(Ans.1/177; CRS 30/18).

HOWARD, Thomas [?-1628]

Viaticum Jan.1628. To Sanlúcar (S 17). Later in 1628 the college received
a legacy from a Fr Howard, which suggests that he died.

HOWSE, William. See HOUSE

HUDDLESTONE (Hundeston), Brian [1594- after 1595]

b.Seaton, Cumberland, 1577, son of Andrew H.of Leyland, Lancs. To
ECV 1593. To ECS 1594. Signs deed Oct.1595 (S V). (Ans.1/177; CRS
30/26).

HUDDLESTONE, William [1594-c.1600]

b.Seaton, Cumberland, 1578. To ECV 1593 with his brother Brian H.
(q.v.). At ECS 1594-c.1600 (WJ). Priest. At Farington Hall, Leyland,
Lancs, 1603-4. (Ans.1/177).

HUGHES, Edward [1593-1602]

b. St Asaph dioc., 1576. One of seven students who arrived at ECV in
June 1591, having travelled via Ireland and Fuenterrabía (CRS 30/14-15).
According to a letter of Robert Persons dated 24 June 1591 (RAH PJ
116/13) they carried a letter from Henry Garnett, S.J., who particularly
recommended the youngest, 'Edward', aged 15. He went on to ECS in
Jan.1593 and left for England, a priest, in 1602. He is not to be confused
with Edward Hughes (1) of Ans. 1/178, who was imprisoned at
Framlingham in 1603. (Ans.1/178 *sub* Edward Hughes (2); CRS 5/260).

HUMPHREY (Homfred), Richard [1595–?]

Of Cornwall. A Richard, son of John H., was christened at Camborne on 3 Dec.1577 (IGI). To ECS 1595. Signed deed Oct.1595 as Ricardo Sinfordo. (Ans.1/179).

HUNGERFORD, *alias* HAYWOOD, **Francis** [After 1613–c.1617]

To ECV 1613. Subdeacon at ECS, 1617, and died there (ORS; CRS 30/113).

HUNT. See BENSTEAD

HUSSEY, Thomas [1766–69]

b.Castlejordan, Co.Meath, 1746. To ECS 1766. Priest and viaticum 1769 (Sim.2; ACS). At Spanish Chapel, London, from 1770. FRS 1792. President of Maynooth 1795–8. Bishop of Waterford and Lismore 1797. d.1803. (RH May 1988, pp.80–94; Silke 135).

HUTTON, Edward [1595]

b.Co. Durham, 1577. To ECS 1595, and died there the same year. (CRS 14/18).

HUTTON, John [1597–8]

b.York c.1578, son of Wm Hutton, draper. SO 1594–7 (CRS 69/142). To ECS 1597. To ECV 1598. Priest. O.S.B. at San Martín, Compostela, 1599. To England c.1604. At Grosmont, Yorks, c.1614–1626. d.Yorks 1642. (CRS 30/50;33/198; Birt 25; Lunn 228; Ave.1/240).

HUTTON, Luke. See HOUGHTON

HUTTON, Peter [1594–5]

b.York 1573, elder brother of John H. (q.v.). To Rheims 1589. In prison 1590–2. At Eu 1592–3. To ECV 1593. To ECS 1594. Signed deed at ECS Oct.1595. (Ans.1/181; Ave.3/219).

HUYATH (*anglice* ?Yate, Wyatt, Hewett), **Edward** [?–1608]

Left ECS, a priest, 1608 (S 17). Possibly the Yate of CRS 13/130, n.517, and/or the Mr Yates who was in the Clink in 1618 (SP 14/95/95).

IPSLEY, *alias* BLOFIELD (Blofel), **Thomas** [?–1605]

b.Wilts 1580. Was he a brother of the Ferdinand Hippesley recorded at West Lavington in 1613–15 (IGI)? S.J. in Andalusia 1605. At Cordoba 1606 (Baet.8/205). Priest 1608 (Baet.3/2/1050). At Casa Profesa, Seville, 1611 (Baet.8/238). To England 1611 (Baet.4/1/48). In London district 1621–29 (Anglia 10). In Suffolk 1636. d.Ghent 1642. (Fo 7/393).

ISHAM, Francis [?-1600]

Theology student at ECS by 1600 (WJ). To ECD for health reasons, 1600. Left ECD 1601. (CRS 10/30,35).

JACKSON, Bonaventure. See BRITTON, Richard.

JEFFREYS (Walfridus), Owen, *alias* POLE, Thomas [?-c.1617]

b.1591, son of Griffin Jeffrey(s) (CRS 30/137), of Arllechwedd Isaf, Conway, Caernarvonshire (according to Hugh Owen, in his preface to *Dilyniad Crist*, 1684). To ECV 1614. Ordained priest at ECS as Thomas Polo, 1617 (ORS). S.J.1620. Resident in South Wales from 1621 as a member of the College of St Francis Xavier based at Llanrothal, Mon. He taught grammar and Greek at an unidentified school in this area, where he d.18 May 1654. (Ans.2/169; Fo 7/398,1446; CRS 29/149;30/116; Ang.10).

JENISON, *alias* FREVILLE (Frebillo), Thomas [1673-5]

b.Durham 1643. SO c.1660-3 (CRS 69/147). To ECS via ECV 1673 (S 10). S.J. 1664. Subdeacon 1673 (ORS). Priest 1674 (S 7). To S.J. college, Jerez, 1675 (S 20). In Ghent 1676-7, Brussels 1677-80, Loreto 1680-4, Paris 1685-9, SO 1691-2. In Suffolk district 1696. d.London 1701. (RH 3/8-9; Fo 7/401; CRS 30/170; 70/131).

JENISON, William. See GRAY

JENNINGS, John, *alias* NEWPORT, Maximilian [1631-7]

Of Great Dunmow, Essex. Convictor at ECS 1631 (S 17). Viaticum 1637 (S 19). Chaplain at West Grinstead. Archdeacon of Sussex 1657-67. Later chaplain at Ufton Nervet, Berks, where he d.1678. (Ans.2/171).

JENNINGS, *alias* NEWPORT, Richard [?-1636]

Of Great Dunmow, Essex. Viaticum 1636 (S 19). S.J. 1637. In Suffolk district 1638 (Anglia 10). d.Oxford district 1643. (Ans.2/172; Fo 7/399).

JESSOPP, William [1595-1600]

b.Checkwell (Chickerel), Dorset, c.1582. To ECS 1595. To England via ECV, in ill health, 1600 (HMC Salis. 10/340-2). For pedigree, see Hutchins, *History and Antiquities of the County of Dorset*, 2/494.

JOHNSON, George [c.1595]

b.1578. Travelling expenses paid by his uncle John Middleton, October 1594 (S XIX). d.at ECS 1595 (ALSJ 1594-5).

JOHNSON (Jonson), John [Before 1642-?]

m.o.1642 (ORS).

JOHNSON (Janson), Richard [?-1608]

Viaticum 1608 (S 17). At Sanlúcar 1626-30 (S 17,24). In 1630 he is said to have been Minister of the Sanlúcar Residence, which suggests that he was a Jesuit.

JOHNSON, Thomas [?-1605]

Died at Seville 1605 as a Jesuit novice (ALSJ), so is likely to have been at ECS previously. His sister entered the English Bridgettine convent at Lisbon the same year. (Fo 7/xxxiv,405; CRS 30/46n).

JOHNSON (Janson, Consonio), *vere* **PURNELL, William** [1617-19]

b.London 1597. Adopted as a boy by a Spanish couple at Malaga, he became a Catholic and attended the Jesuit college there. At ECS 1617-19. m.o.1617 (ORS). S.J. Seville May 1619. Studied at Seville, Cordoba and Granada (1621-25). Priest 1625. Minister at ECS by 1628, when he was transferred to Osuna. At Cadiz from 1631, carrying on a ministry among English-speaking visitors to the Andalusian ports and preaching missions at Puerto de S.María, Gibraltar, Vejer, Tarifa, Medina Sidonia, and in the N.African enclaves of Melilla and Peñon de Vélez. d.Cadiz 1642. (Obit.letter, Baet.26/90-92; RH 21 (May, 1992)).

KEMP, Richard [1666-c.1668]

Convictor 1666-7 (S 9). Licentiate by 1668 (S 13).

KENSINGTON, Thomas [?1622-29]

Viaticum collected for him at ECS in 1629 (account book). He may be identical with the Thomas Kensington whom Wm Atkins lists as one of the twelve students who sailed from St Omer to Seville in 1622, If so, he cannot (because of age) be the Thomas Gerard (q.v.) who became a Jesuit laybrother at Seville in 1628 aged 20. He may be the Thos Kensington of Lancs who joined the S.J. as a priest, aged 25, at Watten in 1628 and was still there in 1631 (Ang. 10; AAW 24/41). A Thomas Kensington was Minister at ECV in 1632 (CRS 30/xxvi-vii). The discrepancy in dates makes Anstruther's identification with Thos Killingham (Ans.2/177) untenable.

KENT. See NEAL

KEYNES, *alias* **LUTTRELL, NEWPORT, Maximilian** [1671-3]

b.London 1652. SO c.1667-70 (CRS 69/153). From ECV to ECS Dec.1671. Left ECS 1673 (S 10). S.J. Watten 1674. Liège 1676-83. Priest 1683. To England 1685. Active in E.Anglia. d.Watten 1720. (Fo 7/418; CRS 30/167n;70/137).

KIERNAN, Francis [1721–3]

Irish. At ECS by 1721 (S 14). Left in ill-health 1723 (S 11).

KIERNAN, William [1709–21]

At ECS 1709 (S 14). Signed oath as priest 1720 (S XVII). Viaticum 1721 (ACS).

KILLINGHAM, Thomas [c.1616]

Subdeacon May 1616 (ORS).

KING, John [1736–c.1740]

Irish. b.Co Meath 1715. To ECS 1736 (S 20). Priest 1739 (S 16). SJ 1741 (S 20). In Galway 1750–55. Rector of Irish College, Salamanca 1766–7. (Fo 7/419; Silke 136).

KING (Kin), William [1605–6]

A priest named King was at ECS 1605–6 (S 6–7). A William King was at Sanlúcar 1626–8 (S 17,24). (Ans.2/178).

KIRK (Cuerco, Quercus), James [?–c.1631]

Priest at ECS by 1631 (S 24). At Sanlúcar 1633 (S VI).

KNARESBOROUGH, Christopher [After 1595–c.1602]

Of Ferensby, Knaresborough, Yorks. Named by WJ as student of philosophy at ECS during this period. At ECV 1603 (CRS 30/xxi). Priest. To ECD and England 1604 (CRS 10/60). Returned to ECD 1608 (CRS 10/95). To England again 1610 (ibid.101). In Sussex 1610 (OB 1/26).

KNARESBOROUGH (Nasboro), Richard [1596–1603]

b.Ferensby 1579. SO 1594–6 (CRS 69/154). To ECS via ECV 1596. Priest. Viaticum 1603 (S 7). To England. Anstruther's identification of Richard with Christopher K. (Ans.1/200) is ruled out by the fact that WJ lists them separately as fellow-students between 1595 and 1600. (CRS 30/41).

KNARESBOROUGH, Robert [1597–8]

b.Ferensby 1582. SO 1593–7 (CRS 69/154–5). Student of rhetoric at ECS 1597–8. ECV 1598–9. Joined O.S.B. at San Martín, Compostela, 1599, but died before ordination. (CRS 30/49).

KNATCHBULL (Nasbul), *alias* **NORTON, John** [1594–1602]

b.Mersham Hatch, Kent, 1571, the son of Reginald K. and Elizabeth Copley. To ECS 1594 (CRS 14/12). Viaticum 1602 (S 7). At ECD 1605–16, from 1609 as Vice-President. S.J. Louvain 1618. At Ghent

1624-5, when his sister Dame Lucy founded the Benedictine convent there. Rector of ECM from 1625, Procurator of the English Province S.J. and royal confessor. d.Madrid 1630. (Ans.1/200; Fo 3/393; Gill.4/63-4; RBPH 47(1969), pp.1154-66). His younger brother Thomas was at ECS from 1594 (CRS 14/12) to Feb. 1596 (CRS 30/39).

LAITHWAITE (Latiud), *alias* KENSINGTON, Thomas or Adam [1601-04].

b. Wigan 1577. ECD 1599-1601. To ECS 1601. Priest. Viaticum 1604 (S 7). To England, arrested and imprisoned. To Rheims 1606. S.J. 1607. In London from c.1609 (Anglia 13). d.1655. (Ans.1/203-4; Fo 4/632-9).

LANGLEY (Langleo), John [1659-1663]

SO c.1656-58 (CRS 69/158). To ECS 1659 (S 9). All orders 1660 (ORS, where he is named as son of John Langley and Elizabeth Clare, of London diocese). Left 1663 (S XIX).

LANGON (Longon, Langonio), Nicholas [c.1613-c.1621]

SO 1611 or earlier-1613 (CRS 69/158). Subdeacon at ECS 1618 (ORS). In England, a priest, 1622 (Baet.5 I,f.95).

LAUGHTON, Matthew [1750-c.1754]

Irish. To ECS 1750. Saying masses for the college 1752-54 (S 16).

LAWLER (Logler), Matthew [1745-1751]

Irish. To ECS, already a priest, 1745 (S 20). Left 1751 (S 16).

LAYTON, LATHAM (Laton), John [c.1617]

Deacon 1617 (ORS).

LAYTON, John (?-1642]

SO 1633-36 (CRS 69/160). Viaticum as priest 1642 (S 19). (Ans.2/186).

LEA, Thomas [c.1615-17]

b.1594, 'of noble family'. To Rome, and thence to ECS for philosophy. m.o.March 1616 (ORS), S.J. at Seville 1617. d.1621 at St Hermenegild's, not yet a priest. (Baet.8, f.305v;26,f.16).

LEE, *alias* JOHNSON, Augustine [?-1603]

b.Mortlake, Surrey. Viaticum from ECS as a priest, 1603 (S 7). O.S.B. in England 1623. Active in Sussex. (Ans.2/187; Birt 21).

LEE, Edward. See SHELDON.

LEE, John Hyacinth [c.1663]
Lay convictor 1663 (S 9,20). Son of Abraham Lee, of Puerto de Santa María.

LENEGHAN, Nicholas [1736-42]
Irish. b.1716. To ECS 1736 (S 20). Priest 1739 (S 16). Left 1742 (S 20).
At St Mary's Chapel, Dublin, 1782 (Silke 137).

LESTER, Christopher [1600-c.1604]
Of Widnes, Lancs. SO 1598-1600 (CRS 69/162). To ECS 1600. Priest.
To England via ECD 1605. In Staffs 1627. (Ans.2/200;
Salisb.10/144,229).

LEVE (*anglice* ?**Levins**)**, Charles** [?-1734]
Irish. Viaticum 1734 (ACS).

LEVESON, Richard [1597-98]
Of Staffs, probably the Richard, son of Thos L., christened at St Peter's,
Wolverhampton, 8 June 1573 (IGI). B.A., Balliol College, Oxford, 10
October 1592 (Foster 3/904). To Rome, whence Persons sent him on to
ECS in 1597. d.1598. (Litt.Ann.1598; Fo 7/xxxii).

LEVINS, Philip [1747-53]
Irish. Of Drumcar, Co.Armagh. To ECS 1747 (S 20). Priest 1751 (S 16).
Viaticum 1753 (Sim.2). Parish priest of Ardee. Dean of Armagh 1781.
(Silke 137).

LEWIS (Luis), Edward [?-1602]
Viaticum as priest 1602 (S 7).

LEWIS (Ludovisio), Peter [1659-66]
To ECS 1659 (S 9). All orders 1660 (ORS, where he is named as son of
Peter Lewis and Frances Jones, of London diocese). Viaticum 1666
(S 13).

LEYBURN (Lighburn), John [1594-after 1595]
Of Westmorland. A convert. To ECV 1593. To ECS 1594. Signed deed,
Oct.1595. d.at Seville. (CRS 30/26).

LIGER (*anglice* ?**Legard**)**, Thomas** [Before 1606-1609]
At ECS by 1606 (S 7). Viaticum 1609 (S 17). Could he be the otherwise
unknown Fr Legard S.J., chaplain at Heaton and later at St Anthony's,

Newcastle-on-Tyne, c.1614-24 ? (Fo 5/717; 7/448; *Catholic Tyneside* 37-38).

LINGEN See LINGHAM.

LINGHAM (Lingamo), Richard [Before 1611-1612]

?Of Herefords (CRS 71/111;13/114). Deacon 1611 (ORS). Viaticum c.1612 (S 7). For pedigree, see Burke, 18th edn 1972, 3, pp.128-9.

LOCKYER (Loker), John [?-1604]

Viaticum as priest 1604 (S 7).

LONGON. See LANGON.

LONGUEVILLE (Longavilla), Henry [1617-?]

Son of Sir Henry Longueville, of Wolverton, Bucks. Brother of Thomas L. (CRS 54/311). SO ?-1617 (CRS 69/165). m.o.1617 (ORS). (Gill.4/328).

LOVE, *alias* DE MENDOZA, Christopher [1655-57]

b.London 1641. Convictor at ECS 1655-57 (S 9). S.J. in Spain, 1657. At Cordoba, 1664 (CRS 29/3/10). Procurator of the English Province at Madrid 1672. To Lancs 1675. (CRS 29 *passim*; Fo 7/501).

LOVELL, John [?-1629]

b.Norfolk 1605. Left ECS (S 17) to join S.J. at Watten 1629 (Ang.10). To England 1637. d.Oxford 1683. (Fo 4/601; 7/466).

LYNCH (Lise), Charles [1728-37]

Irish. To ECS 1728 (S XVII). Priest. Viaticum 1737 (Sim.2).

LYNN, Richard [?-1606]

Of Norfolk, probably the Richard, son of Thos L., christened at Norwich, 27 Jan. 1583 (IGI). His father was imprisoned as a recusant (CRS 60/56,84). From ECS to ECD 1606. Priest. To England 1607. (Ans.2/206).

MACDONALD (Maldonac), Augustine [1757-64]

Irish. To ECS, a priest, 1757 (S 16). Viaticum 1764 (ACS;Sim.2).

MADDOCK, John [c.1609-?]

b.Agden, Cheshire, 1590. SO 1606-08 (CRS 69/168). To ECV 1608. To ECS 1609. Priest. To England, where he was imprisoned. (Ans.2/207).

MAGRANE, John [c.1724-c.1728]

Irish. At ECS by 1724 (S 14) until c.1728 (S 11). Priest 1727 (S XVII).

MAGUIRE, Hugh [1728-c.1734]

Irish. To ECS 1728 (S 11). Priest (S 16). Viaticum 1734 (ACS).

MAILER, *alias* MAYNARD, Henry [c.1594-1606]

Of Bristol. Educated in Spain. To ECS before 1599 (WJ). Viaticum as priest 1606 (S 7). To England, where he was imprisoned and escaped, 1612. Professor at ECD 1613-17. To Paris, where he obtained a doctorate at the Sorbonne. In Madrid 1623, active in the royal marriage negotiations. Professor at ECL 1628-30. To France, 1630. In England 1636. (Ans.1/223; RH 18, pp.361-2; CRS 72/123-4; UM Dec.1975, June 1976, Dec.1976).

MAILER, Philip [c.1613]

Signed petition in March 1613 as student Philippus Mayler. A brother of the above?

MALBON, John [1680-85]

m.o.1680, subdeacon 1684 (ORS). Priest and D.D. by 1685 (S XVII). At Scarisbrick Hall, Lancs. 1688 (Fo 7/1404). Still active in 1698 (Kirk 158; Ans.3/140).

MALLEN (Maslen), James [?-1741]

Irish. Viaticum 1741 (ACS).

MALLET (Maleto), *alias* or *vere* HILDESLEY, Francis [Before 1616-1619]

Of Staffs. SO ?-1612 (CRS 69/170). Subdeacon 1616 (ORS). To ECD 1619. To England 1621. (Ans.2/208).

MANNOCK. See MONACIO.

MARKEY (Marchyn), Peter [1736-44]

Irish. At ECS 1736 (S 20). Priest 1742 (S 16). D.D. Viaticum 1744 (Sim.2;Silke 140).

MARSHALL (Marcial), *alias* TURNER, Peter [1611-?]

b.Derbys 1591. To ECD 1609. To ECS 1611. Priest. S.J. 1620 or 1623. Active in Worcs and Staffs from c.1625 to his death in 1655. (Ans.2/211).

MARSHALL (Marcial), Robert [Before 1620-1621]

m.o.1620 (ORS). Professed Bridgettine at Lisbon 1621 (BL Add.MSS 21203,f.52).

MARTIN (Myn), Gregory [1594-after 1595]

Of dioc.London. Son of a Catholic physician exiled in Flanders. To ECV 1592. To ECS 1594. Signed deed in Oct.1595 (S V). Brother of Peter Martin (CRS 30/21-2).

MARTIN, James [1735-42]

Irish. To ECS 1735 (S 12). Priest 1741. Left 1742 (S 20).

MARTIN, John [?-1611]

Viaticum 1611 (S 17).

MARTIN, John [c.1611-?]

m.o. c.1611 (ORS). Signed petition, March 1613, as student Joannes Martinus (Sim.1).

MARTIN (Martínez), John [Before 1633-1636]

Priest 1633 (ORS). Viaticum 1636 (S 19).

MARTIN (Martínez), Robert [1660-66]

m.o. 1660, son of Roberto Martínez and María Gondilga (?Golding) of Canterbury diocese (ORS). Viaticum 1666 (S 19).

MASSEY (Massi), James [After 1595-1602]

A contemporary of WJ, c.1595-1600. Viaticum 1602 (S 7), as a priest.

MATTHEWS (Matheo), Richard [1672-77]

Oath 1672 (S 7). m.o.1674, subdeacon 1675, deacon 1676 (ORS). Priested at Cadiz 1676. To England 1677 (S 10; Ans.3/144).

MAXEY, John [After1603-]

b.Chiswick. Apprenticed to a merchant at Lisbon, reconciled there by a Bridgettine priest. To ECV 1602. S.J. at Lisbon 1603. Sent to ECS, but left S.J. for health reasons. To Flanders as military chaplain. To London 1616, where he was betrayed by his father. d.in the Bridewell 1617. (See pp.176-7 and Ans.2/213-14).

MAXFIELD, William [1593-?]

Of York diocese. Sent to ECV with letter of recommendation from Robert Southwell, S.J. (RAH PJ 116/13/2). ECV 1591-3. To ECS, where he died after ordination. (Ans.1/222).

MAYHEW, Henry [1596–1600]

Of Dinton, Wilts. At Rheims 1583–89. To ECV 1592. Priest. At ECS from 1596 (S 6). Viaticum 1600 (S 6). Arrested in Wilts 1611, imprisoned in Newgate. Banished 1613. d.Douai 1616. (Ans.1/223; CRS 5/260; Gill.4/545).

MAYHEW (Mayu), John [?–1612]

Viaticum c.1612 (S 7).

MEDCALF (Mellent), William [1592–96]

b.Lancs 1569. To ECS Sept.1592 (CRS 14/17). Priest. To ECR 1596 (Aray). S.J., 1599. d. c.1600. (Ans.1/228; Fo 7/503; CRS 37/105).

MELLING (Meli), *alias* MORE, Thomas [c.1679–c.1681]

b.Lancs 1656. SO ?–1675 (CRS 69/183). S.J. 1675. At Watten 1678. To ECS. Subdeacon 1680 (ORS). Priest by 1681 (S 5). (Fo 7/501).

de MENDOZA, Christopher. See LOVE.

de MENDOZA, Thomas. See BEDINGFIELD.

METHAM (Mettam), William [c.1658]

Convictor 1658 (S 9).

MIDDLETON, John [1594–96]

b. Yorks, 1556. To ECS Dec. 1594 (CRS 14/18). Priest. To ECR 1596. Dismissed 1597. (Ans.1/229–30).

MIDDLETON (Mildentono), *alias* GOLDSMITH, Peter [1622–29]

b.Hants 1601. SO ?–1622 (CRS 69/180). To ECS 1622 (Wads., Atkins). Viaticum as priest 1629 (S 17). S.J. at Watten 1629 (Ang.10). To England 1631, Active in Lancs-Staffs district. d. c.1665. (Fo 7/507).

MILES, Thomas [c.1599–1603]

b.Hants 1582. SO 1593–99 (CRS 69/180). To ECS 1599. Priest. Viaticum 1603 (S 7). To England. (Ans.1.231).

MOLENS. See MULLINS.

MONACIO, John [c.1613–after 1614]

Signed petition, March 1613, as student Joannes Monaxius (Sim.1). Subdeacon 1614 as J.Monacio. Mannock seems the most plausible original. Is he the Fr Mannock, 'a friar', listed by John Gee as resident 'about London' in 1624?

MONSON, William [1599–1605]

At ECS by 1599 (WJ). Viaticum 1605 (S 7).

MORE, *alias* WEST, Thomas [1592–93]

b.Barnborough, W.R.Yorks, 1565. Great-grandson of St Thomas More. ECR 1587–c.1591. Priest. ECV 1591–92. ECS 1592–93. To England. At Battle Abbey 1594–1609. Agent for English clergy in Rome 1609–17. Agent for ECD in Madrid 1617–22. d.Rome 1625. (Ans.1/233–4; CRS 30/16;14/17).

MORGAN, *alias* or *vere* CONYERS, James [1671–72]

b.Llangattock-juxta-Caerleon, Mon.,1647, son of Captain John M. ECD 1661–71. At ECS 1671–72 (S XVII). ECD 1672–76. Priest. To England (Derbys) 1676. Some time after 1680 he returned to Douai, mentally ill. d.in France after 1721. (Ans.3/152; CRS 63 *passim*)

MORGAN, Roger [1632–35]

To ECS, already a priest, 1632 (S 24). Viaticum 1635 (S 18). In Sanlúcar 1637 (S 19)

MORGAN, William, *alias* WILLIAMS, Valentine [1597–1600]

b.?Tredunnock, Mon.1580 (cf.CRS 18/213–15). To ECS 1597, to study philosophy. To ECV 1600 and dismissed the same year. (CRS 30/58).

MORGAN, Walter [1593–c.1602]

b.Monmouthshire 1575. To ECS Feb. 1593 (CRS 14/18). Priest. S.J. at Seville 1603. At Trigueros 1606. d.ECV Nov.1608. (Baet.8/171,213; CRS 30/93–4).

MORLEY, Henry [?–1612]

Viaticum 1612 (S 17).

MORRIS (Moricio), Richard [c.1660–?]

Son of Thomas Morris and Anne Halsall, of London diocese. m.o.1660 (ORS).

MORSE or **MORRIS (Mauricio), William** [c.1609–after 1610]

Signed deed at ECS 1609 (S VII). Poetry contestant 1610 (LF 1). Possibly the W.M. of Warwicks who arrived at ECD in July 1607, recommended by William Bishop of Brailes, but returned to England in August because of lack of room (CRS 10/84)?

MORSLEY or **MAUDESLEY, Thomas** [c.1600]

A theology student some time between 1595 and 1600 (WJ).

MOTTRAM, John [1710–11]

Of Lincs. At Emmanuel College, Cambridge, 1703. Convert. To ECS 1710 (S 21). All orders 1711 (ORS). In prison for debt in London by 1713. Apostate by 1714. (Ans.3/154).

MOUNTFORD or **MUMFORD, Thomas** [c.1599–?]

b.Wereham, Norfolk, 1577. At Rheims 1597–98. To ECV 1598. To ECS c.1599. Priest. In Yorks 1604. In Oxon 1610. (Ans.1/233).

MOYSER. See PALMER, Thomas.

MULLINS (Molens), John [1612–after 1613]

Signed petition, March 1613, as priest Joannes Molens (Sim.1). (Ans.2/228).

MUMFORD. See MOUNTFORD.

NEAL, alias **KENT, Robert** [1622–29]

b.Lincs 1600. SO ?–1622 (CRS 69/189). To ECS 1622 (Wads.,Atkins). Priest at ECS by 1626 (S 24). Viaticum 1629 (S 17). SJ 1629. To England. Active in Lincs district from c.1631. d.1688. (Ans.2/230;Fo 7/537–38).

NELSON, John. See BEESLEY.

NELSON, John. [?–1630]

d.as a student 1630 (S 17).

NEWLIN (Nullino, Neulin), Robert [1678–83]

To ECS 1678 (S 13). m.o.1680. Priest 1683 (ORS). To Sanlúcar 1687, where he died 1696 (S 20).

NEWMAN (Numan), *alias* **SLYFIELD, William** [Before 1606–1609]

b.Staffs 1577. At ECD 1594 (CRS 58/303). Captured with St Anne Line 1601, but death sentence commuted to banishment. Priest at ECS by 1606 (S 6). Viaticum 1609 (S 17). To Lisbon 1609, where he laid the foundations of the English College. d.Lisbon 1640. (Ans.2/230–31; CRS 72/130–1; T-D 4/123–33, cclii–cclxvii; RH 20, pp.481–8).

NEWPORT, Maximilian [1631–37]. See JENNINGS, John.

NEWPORT, Maximilian [1671–73]. See KEYNES.

NEWPORT, Richard. See JENNINGS.

NICHOLS, Henry. [1654-56]
At ECS by 1654 (S 23). m.o.1656 (ORS).

NORRIS, John [?-1613]
Signed petition, March 1613, as priest J.Noricius (Sim.1). Viaticum after 1612 (S 7).

NORRIS, Richard [1659-63]
Entered 1659 (S 9). All orders 1660 (S 9). Viaticum 1663 (S 13).

NORTON, Henry [Before 1609-1610]
At ECS by 1609 (S VII). Viaticum 1610. Probably the H.N. who joined O.F.M. and was Procurator of the Poor Clares at Aire in 1632. d.1637, aged 51, on his way to the West Indies. (CRS 24/263; Thaddeus 279).

NORTON, John. See KNATCHBULL.

O'CONNOR, Patrick.
Irish. Of Ballymore Eustace, Co.Dublin. Entered 1750. Priest before March 1756. Left Dec.1756 with viaticum (ACS). (Silke 142).

OLDCORNE (Olcornius), George [c.1613-?]
Signed petition, March 1613, as student (Sim.1).

O'MEARA (Omeras), William [?-1722]
Viaticum 1722 (ACS). D.D.at Seville (*Arch.Hib.*16/97). Bishop of Ardfert 1743. Bishop of Killaloe 1753. (Silke 142).

OVERTON, Paul. See SNODE.

OWEN, *alias* HILL, COLLINS, John [1611-c.1614]
b.Godstow, Oxon, 1593, son of Richard Owen and Mary Chamberlain, and thus first cousin of George Chamberlain (q.v.). To Douai 1604. To England 1608. To ECS 1611. Priest. Arrested and condemned in London 1615 (HMC 75/464), pardoned 1618 (SP 14/97/129; 14/98/38) and banished. In Somerset 1631-32. (Ans.2/234; Chamb. 1/597. For his family, see CRS 13/102 and HS 5 (1871), pp.127-8).

OWEN (Adoeno), John [?-1630]
Viaticum 1630 as priest (S 17). Possibly the Dom John Owen of Birt 34, who was born at St Asaph's, professed O.S.B. in Spain and d.at Drury Lane in 1654. Birt states that he was at ECV, but there is no record of this.

PALMER, John. See PORTER.

PALMER, *alias* MOYSER [Before [1638–c.1642]

SO c.1636–37 (CRS 69/186). At ECS by 1638 (SP 94/40/63). Viaticum 1642 (S 19). (Ans.2/315 *sub* Taylor).

PALMES, alias PALMER, CONIERS, George [1639–42]

b.Naburn Castle, E.R.Yorks, 1618. SO 1632–37 (CRS 69/197). ECR 1637–39. To ECS 1639 (Baet.6 I, f.254). Subdeacon 1642 (ORS). Priest. O.S.B. Douai 1642. To Lamspring, Hildesheim, 1645. Confessor to O.S.B. nuns at Brussels and professor at St Gregory's, Douai, 1649. Prior of St Gregory's 1653–57. Procurator O.S.B. in Rome 1657. d.at Graz, Styria, 1663. (Ans.2/236; Fo 5/715).

PARKER (Parquero), James [1616–23]

b.Lancs 1597. SO ?–1616 (CRS 69/198). To ECS 1616 (S XVII). m.o.1617, priest 1620 (ORS). Left at Easter 1623 (Baet.5 I,f.176). S.J. Watten 1624. Professor at Liége. In England (Lancs) from 1631 (Ang.10). d.1657. (Ans.2/237).

PAULET, George [?–1652]

All orders 1652 (ORS).

PAULING, Thomas [?–1637]

Viaticum as priest 1637 (S 19). d.at Sanlúcar 1638 (S 24).

PEASLEY (Pesleo), Francis [1672–76]

To ECS 1672 (S XVII). m.o.1674, priest 1672 (ORS). Viaticum 1676 (S 5).

PENKETH, *alias* RIVERS (de Rivera), Charles [c.1680–84]

Of Lancs. m.o.1680, subdeacon 1684 (ORS). Priest. At Stonyhurst, Lancs, 1690–1721 (Ans.3/163).

PENTRETH, Richard [c1595–1600]

b.Cornwall c.1574. A contemporary of WJ at ECS. From ECS to ECV 1600. Priest. To England, in ill-health, Feb.1602. (CRS 10/33,38; 30/59).

PERCY (Pérez), Francis [Before 1647–after 1652]

Subdeacon 1649 (ORS). Still at ECS, a priest, in 1650. To Sanlúcar 1652, but later returned (S 5).

PERSONS, Robert [?–1613]

Signed petition, March 1613, as priest (Sim.1).

PETTINGER, John. See WENTWORTH

PHILLIPS, William [c.1623–28]
Poetry contestant 1623 (Ibarra). Viaticum as priest 1628 (S 17).

PHILPOT, William [1671–2]
To ECS to study philosophy, 1671. Returned to Flanders in ill-health, 1672 (S XVII).

PICKFORD, *alias* DANIELL, Thomas [c.1626–29]
Christened at St Germans, Cornwall, 17 March 1607, son of Richard P.(IGI). ECD 1625–6. To ECS 1626. S.J. at Watten 1629 (Ang.10). Priest by 1636, in Brussels. At ECS 1639–47 as Minister (Baet.9,14). To England 1652. Active in Hants, Oxon and S.Wales districts. d.Oxon 1676. (Fo 7/598; CRS 10/246; 69/205–6).

PIGOTT, Thomas [c.1609–12]
At ECS by 1609 (S 3). Poetry contestant 1610 (LF 1). Priest 1610 (ORS). Viaticum 1612 (S 17).

PLUNKET, James [1736–43]
Irish. Entered 1736 (S 20). Priest 1741. D.D. Left 1743. (S 20; Silke 142].

POLE, German [After 1599–1608]
b.Spinkhill, Derbys. 1578. SO c.1599 (CRS 69/210). Viaticum at ECS 1608 (S 17). In Derbys by 1610. S.J. 1619. d.Derbys 1648. (Ans.2/249; Fo 2/290).

POLE, John [c.1613]
Signed petition, March 1613, as student Jo.Polus (Sim.1).

POLE, Thomas (1) [1595–?]
b.in dioc.Chester, 1557, of Catholic parents. Sent to Spain via Ireland by Fr James Forth, *alias* Banke (Ans.1/122). Admitted to ECV in March 1595 but sent on to ECS (CRS 30/32).

POLE, Thomas (2). See JEFFREYS, Owen.

POLLARD, Augustine. See GIBBONS.

POLLARD, Henry. See POULTON.

POLLARD, James [?–1624]

At student of this name applied at ECS to join the novitiate S.J. at Watten in 1624. His application was approved (Baet.5 I,f.176) but there is no further record.

PORTER, Edward [1593–?]

Of Chester diocese. To ECV 1592. To ECS 1593 (CRS 30/19).

PORTER, *alias* **PALMER, John [c.1615–20]**

Of Worcester diocese. SO c.1613–14 (CRS 69/197). m.o.at ECS 1616 as Jo. Palmero (ORS). To ECD 1620. priest 1621. To England. (Ans.2/249).

POULTON, *alias* **POLLARD, Henry [1612–16]**

b.Northants c.1584. SO ?–1609 (CRS 69/213). ECV 1609–12. Signed petition at ECS, March 1613, as priest (Sim.1). S.J. Liège 1616. Minister, etc, at ECS c.1621–44 (Baet.8,9 I–II,14). d.at Seville 1644. (AHN SJ 56, obit.letter; Ans.2/250–51; CRS 29/152–55).

POULTON, *alias* **SACHEVERELL, SPENCER, William [c.1636]**

b.Irthlingborough, Northants, c.1615. m.o.at ECS 1636 as Guillermo Spensero (ORS). Left the college. Royalist officer in Civil War. At SO c.1645–50 (CRS 69/214). ECR 1652–57. Priest. To England. Chaplain in London to Lady Mary Somerset. d.London 1672. (Ans.2/252; CRS 3/100; Fo 1/155).

PRESTON, Henry. See EDWARDS.

PRICE, *alias* **ALISON, DALISON, Edward [?–1606]**

Left ECS 1606, in ill-health, for England. At ECD 1608–09 as convictor. To England 1609. (CRS 10/93–5).

PRICE (Pricio) *alias* **PRICHARD, John [1593–1600]**

b.Chester diocese (probably at Maelor Saeswyg, Flintshire), 1579. ECV 1592-3. To ECS Jan.1593. S.J. at Montilla 1600. At St Hermenegild's 1602 (Baet.8). Priest c.1604. Confessor and Minister at ECS c.1604–11. ECV 1613–15 (CRS 30/xxiii). Louvain 1617–18. Madrid 1621-2. To England 1622 as chaplain to Earl of Shrewsbury. In 1626-7 he kept a school at Greenfield Abbey, near Holywell (AAW A 19/111/391 and 20/83/295). Superior of Worcs district S.J. Died 1645. (Ans.1/282; Fo 7/xxviii,632; CRS 5/267, 29/150, 30/19; WR 32; pp.13–23; BS 2, p.108).

PRICE (Preis), John [1742-45]
Convictor 1742-3 (S 12). Alumnus 1744. Priest, August 1745 (S 16). Left Sept.1745 (S 5).

PRICE, Thomas [1593-4]
b.Chester diocese, 1571. Brother of John Price S.J. (q.v.). ECV 1592-3. To ECS 1593. ECV 1594-9. Priest. S.J. in England 1601. In Madrid 1611. In Lincs 1621, Hants 1622. d.London 1625. (Ans.1/283; CRS 5/267;29/241).

PURCELL, Philip [c.1747]
Irish. Entered 1747, but left soon afterwards (S 20).

PURNELL, William. See JOHNSON.

REYNER, *alias* DOUGELL, DOWGILL, DOUGLAS, Clement [c.1601-04]
b.Ripon, Yorks, 1582. ECD 1598-1601. To ECS 1601. To ECD 1604. Priest 1607 at Douai where he took the habit OSB as Dom Laurence. Dieulouard 1609-17. In England 1617-24. Prior of Dieulouard 1623-29, 1653-5. To Cambrai. Provincial of York 1649-53. President of English Congregation OSB 1655-57. d.1664. (CRS 10 *passim*, 33/228-9; Birt 42; Lunn, pp.231-3).

REYNOLDS, John [c.1595-1600]
A contemporary of WJ during this period.

REYNOLDS, Thomas [1601-] See GREEN.

REYNOLDS, Thomas [1727-41]
Irish. Entered 1727 (S 11). Priest 1729 (ORS). Viaticum 1741 (Sim.2).

RICHARDSON, *alias* ANDERSON, William [1594-1600]
b.Wales, W.R.Yorks, 1572. ECV 1592-4. ECS 1594-1600. Priest 1594. Viaticum 1600 (S 7). To London. Executed at Tyburn 1603. Beatified 1929. (Ans.1/288-9; RH 1983, p.317).

RIGBY, Laurence. See ANDERTON.

RIVERS, Charles [1680-84] See PENKETH.

RIVERS, Charles [1712-18]
Probably Irish. Entered 1712. Priest 1715. Viaticum 1718 (S 11).

ROBINSON, Gerard [1750-56]
Irish. b.Philipstown (now Daingean), Co.Offaly, 1729. Entered 1750
(S 20). Priest 1754. Viaticum 1756 (ACS). At the Spanish Chapel,
London, from 1757 to his death in 1799 (Registers). A relative of Thomas
Hussey (q.v.), with whom he lived in London. Buried in Old St Pancras
churchyard. (Ans.4/230; Silke 144; CRS 12/67;50 *passim*).

ROBINSON, John [1622-c.1627]
b.?Cumberland 1588. SO ?-1622 (CRS 69/223). To ECS 1622 (Wads.,
Atkins). Priest S.J. at Watten 1628. In England by 1633. Arrested at
London 1651, and acquitted. d.Watten 1669. (Ans.2/374; Fo 1/223-4).

ROBINSON, William. See APPLEBY.

ROCK, Nicholas [Between 1595 and 1600]
A priest at ECS at this time, contemporary with WJ.

ROFFE, Edward [Before 1613-c.1617]
b.Essex c.1585. SO ? = 1609 (CRS 69/226). To ECV 1609. Priest. Signed
petition at ECS, March 1613, as priest Odoardus Roffus (Sim.1). S.J.
1618. To England. In Wales 1625, London district 1629-33 (Ang.10). d.in
Hants district 1665. (Ans.2/272 *s.v.*Ross).

ROOTES, Henry [1672-74]
Oath 1672 (S 7). m.o.and subdeacon 1673 (ORS, where he is wrongly
listed as of the Irish College). Priest 1674 (ORS). d.London 1686.
(Ans.3/189).

ROSE (Rosio), George [?-1647]
Viaticum 1647 (S 19).

ROSS, Edward. A misreading of ROFFE.

ROWLAND, Robert [c.1666-c.1669]
SO c.1663-66 (CRS 69/226). At ECS 1668-9 (S 13).

ROWLE, Richard [?-1612]
b.Yorks. Left ECS 1612 for ECD and England. (CRS 10/115).

RUMBOLD, John Henry [1659-60]
Convictor (S 9).

RUSSELL, Anthony [1672–c.1677]

Oath 1672 (S 7). m.o. and subdeacon 1673, priest 1674 (ORS). Saying masses at ECS till 1677 (S 10).

RUSSELL, Thomas [c.1640–?]

m.o.and subdeacon 1642 (ORS). Possibly the Thomas R. who was at SO from 1638 or earlier to 1639 (CRS 69/227).

RUSSELL, William [?–1628]

Went, a priest, to the Bridgettines at Lisbon, 1628 (S 17). d.1646 (Bell.).

RYSDEN, Bartholomew [?–1603]

Left ECS for England in ill-health (CRS 10/50). Perhaps a Rysden of Bableigh, Bideford (Oliver, *Collections* . . . 1857, p.20).

SALKELD (Salquel), Henry [Before 1608–c.1610]

Younger brother of John Salkeld (q.v.) At ECS by 1608 (S 17). Poetry contestant 1610 (LF 1). Priest. To England. Conformed to C. of E., 1615. Rector of Weeke (Wyke) Without, Winchester, 1617–18 (Ans.2/276; Baigent, *History and Antiquities of the Parish Church of Wyke*, p.36).

SALKELD, *alias* DALSTON, John [Before 1600–02]

b.1579, fourth son of Edward Salkeld of Morland, Westmorland, second son of George Salkeld of Corby Castle, Carlisle. Theologian at ECS by 1600 (WJ). S.J. Montilla 1602 (Baet.8/179, which gives 'Westmer', i.e. Westmorland, as place of origin). Still at Montilla, now a priest, 1606 (Baet.8/208v). Sent to Flanders on Fr General's orders, April 1608 (Baet.3/2/1041). Viaticum 1608 (S 17). Conformed 1612 in England, when living with Sir William Godolphin. Later he lived in the house of Bishop King of London. His *Treatise of Angels* (1613) was dedicated to King James. Vicar of Wellington, Somerset, 1613. Rector of Churchstanton, dioc. Exeter, 1634. Deprived as a royalist, 1646. d.Uffculme, Devon, 1659. (DNB; Ans.2/276; Dodd 3/319; CRS 33/38, Fo 5/854). Anthony Wood (Ath.Oxon.2/315;3/487) claims that after a brief period at Oxford as a youth he was sent by his father to be educated with the Jesuits at Coimbra. In his *Treatise of Angels* he described himself as a 'Fellow' of the 'Jesuit Colleges in the Universities of Coimbra, Cordoba and Complutum [Alcalá].'

SANDER, Thomas [1594–after 1595]

Of Hereford dioc. To ECS via ECV 1594. Signed deed at ECS Oct.1595 (S V). (CRS 30/30).

SANDERS (Sandero), Nicholas [c.1620–?]
m.o. c.1620 (ORS).

SANDERS (Sangtero), Thomas [c.1633]
Subdeacon 1633 (ORS).

SAVAGE, *alias* or *vere* SWINBURNE, **Paul** [1687–93]
Of Derbys. Brother of John Swinburne S.J. (Fo 7/752). Oath 1687 (S 7).
STL 1688. Priest 1690. Still at ECS Jan.1693 (S 10–11). The letter in
Ans.3/197–8 is not his, but a forgery by Henry Gerard (*q.v.*)

SAVILLE, John (?–1618]
From ECS to ECV 1618 (AAW A16/77). Left ECV, not yet a priest,
1619.

SCAMMELL (Escamel), John [?–1609]
b.Tisbury, Wilts, 1584. Viaticum at ECS as a priest by 1609 (S 17). S.J.
Madrid 1609 (Tol.14). Active in Worcs district by 1621. d.1624.
(Ans.2/279; Fo 5/861/7/686; CRS 61/240).

SCOTT (Escoto), John (?–1603]
Viaticum as a priest 1603 (S 7).

SCOTT (Scoto), William [?–1603]
Viaticum as a priest 1603 (S 7).

SHANAHAN (Seneguen), Nicholas [?–1741]
Irish. Viaticum 1741 (ACS). Not in Silke.

SHARP, Robert [1659–67]
Entered 1659 (S 9). All orders 1664 (ORS). Viaticum 1667. His faculties,
signed and dated June 1668, remain in the archives, which suggests he
may have died at the college. However, a Fr Robert Sharp died in
London in 1684 (OB minute book 1667–93). (Ans.3/200).

SHAW (Chau), Gerard [1725–32]
Irish. Given a clothing grant by the cathedral chapter to enter ECS in
1725 (ACS). At College till 1732 (S 16). At Spanish Chapel, London, till
his death in 1780. Founded Bermondsey mission 1773. Brother of Patrick
Shaw and uncle of Thomas Hussey (*q.q.v.*). (Ans.4/239; CRS
12/20;42/112;50/142).

SHAW, Patrick [c.1731–38]

Brother of Gerard Shaw (q.v.). Entered 1731 (S 20) as a priest (S 16). D.D. Left 1738 (S 20). At Spanish Chapel, London, 1740–42 (Registers). d.1742. (Ans.4/241).

SHELDON, *alias* LEE (Leai), Edward [c.1611–after 1614]

Of Beoley, Worcs. m.o. c.1611 (ORS). Signed petition, March 1613, as student Edoardus Leus (Sim.1). Subdeacon 1614 (ORS). (Ans.2/187).

SHELLEY, William [1599–?]

b.West Mapledurham, Petersfield, Hants, 1583. SO 1594–99 (CRS 69/239). To ECS via ECV 1599. Later returned to ECV. Priest. To England c.1605. Active in Sussex. d.before 1643. (Ans.2/293; CRS 30/55–6; VCH Hants 3/88).

SHERBURN (Serbern), George [?–1608]

Viaticum 1608 (S 17).

SHERRAT, Henry [1593–95]

b.Lancs 1558. To ECV 1589. To ECS Feb. 1593 (CRS 14/18). Priest. To England 1595. d.in Ireland 1602. (Ans.1/310).

SHILTON (Sthileton), William [c.1620–?]

m.o.1620 (ORS).

SHIRLEY, *alias* GILMET, Henry [?–1633]

Of London. Priest at ECS by 1630. Left 1633 (S 17). Procurator at ECL 1634–36. To England 1636. (Ans.2/295; CRS 72/179–80; *Mount Carmel*. Spring 1977, pp.44–52).

SIDNEY, John [c.1613]

Signed petition, March 1613, as student Jo.Sidneius (Sim.1).

SIMPSON. See HILDRETH.

SKEVINGTON. See AINSWORTH.

SLYFIELD. See NEWMAN.

SMITH, Anthony [1616–after 1617]

To ECS c.Oct.1616 with letter of recommendation from SO (S XVII). m.o. Dec.1617 (ORS). Not the same as Anthony Pole, *alias* Smith, who was at Louvain 1615–18 (Belg.).

SMITH, alias ASPINALL, Edward [c.1613-c.1616]

b.Whalley, Lancs, 1585. To ECV Feb.1612, and signed petition there
c.March 1613 as student. To ECS, where he was ordained. O.S.B. at St
Gregory's, Douai, 1616 (Dom Benedict). At Midhurst, Sussex, as
chaplain and tutor in the household of Anthony, 2nd Viscount
Montague. Procurator O.S.B. at Madrid, where he d. 1637 (Ans.2/299;
Birt 19; St G.44).

[SMITH, Richard 1598-1602 (as professor)]

Of Welton, Lincs. b.1567. Educ. Trinity College, Oxford. ECR 1586-92.
Priest. Professor of philosophy ECV 1593-8, ECS 1598-1602. Viaticum
1602 (S 7). ECD 1602-3. At Battle Abbey 1603. Agent in Rome 1609-11.
Superior, Arras College, Paris, 1612-25. Bishop in England 1625-31. In
France from 1631. d.Paris 1655. (Ans.1/321-2; CRS 22/146; RH 18
(1987) pp.329-401, 19 (1989), pp.234-85)].

SMITH, Robert [c.1610]

Poetry contestant 1610 (LF 1).

SMITH, SMYTHE, Robert. See BABTHORPE.

SNODE, *alias* OVERTON, Paul [1616-c.1620]

b.Dorset 1595. SO 1612-15 (CRS 69/246). To ECS 1616. m.o. as Pablo
Oberton 1618 (ORS). At Dieulouard c.1620. ECD 1621-2. Priest. To
England. Still active in west country 1635. (Ans.2/302).

[SOUTHERNE, William].

b.Aycliffe, Co.Durham. 1579. At Jesuit college, Vilna, c.1589-c.1595. To
ECD 1596. To ECV Dec.1598. The ECV register states that he was
subsequently sent to ECS (CRS 30/51), but the Douai diaries record his
arrival at ECD in Nov.1599. There is no evidence that he was ever a
student at ECS, and he may only have used Seville as a port of exit.
Returned to ECV, where he was ordained c.1604. To England 1605.
Active in Northumberland and Durham. Executed at Newcastle-on-Tyne,
30 April 1618. Beatified 1987 (Ans.1/324-6; RH 4/205-6)]

SPARCHFORD, John [1593-5]

b.Salop 1567. Perhaps of Didlebury (CRS 18/272). To ECV 1591. To
ECS Feb. 1593, (CRS 14/17). Priest. Active in Seville 1594 (de León). To
England 1595. d. in prison. (Ans.1/328).

SPENSER (Espensero), John [?-1636]

Viaticum collected in 1635 and given to him in 1636 (S 19). He cannot
therefore be identified with John Spenser, *alias* Tyrwhitt, or Hatcliffe,
S.J., who was a tertian at Ghent in 1634 and a catechist at Watten in
1636 (Belg.).

SPENCER, William. See POULTON.

STAFFORD, William [?-1642]

SO c.1632-3 (CRS 69/247). Viaticum as priest at ECS 1642 (S 19). (Ans.2/308).

STANLEY (Estanleo), William [c.1660-63]

Son of Gregory Stanley and Anne Davenport, of dioc.Canterbury. m.o.1660 (ORS). Viaticum 1663 (S 7).

STAVELEY. See CARY, Ignatius.

STONE (Eston), Roger [?-c.1613]

Viaticum 1612 (S 7). Still at ECS in March 1613, when he signed petition as priest Rogerus Stonus (Sim.1). Ans. (2/97) follows Henson in wrongly transposing his name as Eyston.

STORY (Storio), Henry [1655-7]

Convictor 1655-7 (S 9).

STUKELY, Augustine [1593-after 1595]

b.Devon c.1575. To ECV 1592. To ECS Feb. 1593, (CRS 14/17). Signed deed in Oct.1595 as Agustín Citrelo (S V). (Ans.1/340; CRS 5/267).

STUKELEY, Thomas [1593]

Of Devon, brother of Augustine S. (q.v.). From ECV to ECS 1593. Expelled later that year. (CRS 14/17;30/17;5/267).

SUMMERHAYES, Thomas [1758-9]

Convictor 1758-9 (S 12). Son of Thomas Summerhayes, British vice-consul at Seville.

SWINBURNE. See SAVAGE, Paul.

TALBOT, John [Before 1633-c.1635]

Subdeacon 1633 (ORS). Priest 1635. Professed O.F.M. 1638 (Bell.). d.1668.

TALBOT, William. See EVERARD.

TARLETON, John [1672-4]

Oath 1672 (S 7). To England 1674 (S 10). Possibly the John T. returned at Brigg, Lincs, in 1680 as a recusant schoolmaster. (Ans.3/219).

TAYLOR (Tarlero, Talero), Francis [c.1636–38]

3rd son of Stephen Taylor, of Bickerton, Yorks, and Dulcibel Grinston; cousin of Henry Taylor, diplomat and Dean of Antwerp (RH 17, 1985, pp.234–5). m.o.1636 (ORS). To England, a priest, 1638 (S 24) but apprehended on arrival (RH 21, October 1992). Later chaplain in Vienna at the court of Ferdinand III and confessor to Leopold I. d.1665. (RH 17, p.235, quoting Dugdale and the Clarendon Papers).

TEMPLE, Thomas. See DRAPER.

TERRITT, TURRET or TYRWHITT, William [c.1638–46]

Clothes bought for him c.1643 (S 8). Viaticum collected between 1644 and 1646 (S 19). To England. A William Wood, *alias* Turret, wrote from ECS in June 1638, when he was already a priest, to his uncle Dr Simpson, of Easling, nr Ospringe, Kent whom he described to the bearer as 'something grummo and not so full of words' (SP 94/40/93). Perhaps he was a relative (? son) of Thomas Territt, listed as a recusant at Boughton Blean, Kent, in 1603 (Whatmore, p.2). Evidently he had been a physician before becoming a priest.

THOMPSON, John [?–1636]

Viaticum collected in 1635 and given to him in 1636 (S 19). Perhaps the Mr Wilks, *alias* Tomson, of Knaresborough, who d. in York Castle c.May 1642 (Chall. 416; Ans.2/318).

THOMPSON (Tonson), John [c.1640–46]

SO 1636–9 (CRS 69/262). Priest at ECS 1644 (ORS). Viaticum 1645 (S 19). To England 1646 (S 8). (Ans.2/318).

THOMPSON (Tonçon, Tacon), Thomas [c.1636–c.1642]

m.o.1636 (ORS). Clothing bought for him, then a priest, 1642 (S 8).

THORN (Torno), Richard [–1597]

Of London. To ECV 1589. Priest by 1593. At ECS before 1597. d.Sanlúcar 1597. (Ans.1/351–2; CRS 30/7,341; Santibañez; ALSJ 1597, p.403).

THOROLD, Clifton, *alias* BENSON, Francis [c.1635–38]

Christened at Grantham, 11 Sept.1614 (IGI), son of Anthony Thorold of Hough-on-the-Hill, Lincs (d.1624) by his wife Catherine Haslewood, and younger brother of Sir Robert T., 1st Baronet (HS 52/981). As Franciscus Menesio (= Benson) he received m.o. at ECS in Sept.1636 (ORS). To Lisbon, Feb.1638, after studying philosophy and one year of theology (CRS 72/197–8). To ECD later in 1638 where he took the oath as Clifton Thorold, *alias* Francis Benson. Priest. To England, where he was in prison 1641-3. Returned to Lisbon in 1643 to complete his studies, and became a Bridgettine there in 1646. He was the uncle, not the brother, of Anthony Thorold, O.F.M. (CRS 11/524, 69/262; Ans.2/318 needs correction).

THULES, Robert [1593-4]

Of Chester dioc. Relative of Ven.John Thules of Whalley, Upholland (Ans.1/354). ECV 1592-3. To ECS for humanities Jan.1593. Returned to ECV Nov.1594. Priest. To England. Imprisoned at Wisbech 1600, Framlingham 1601. d.1602. (Ans.1/355-6).

TICHBURN, Simon [?-1605]

Left ECS for ECD 1605. Not admitted at ECD, and went on to England. (CRS 10/67).

TIERNAN, Bernard [1722-7]

Irish. Convictor 1722 (S 11). Priest by 1725 (S XVII). Still at ECS 1727 (S 16).

TIGNEIO. See TILNEY.

TILNEY, John [c.1610-after 1613]

Signed petition March 1613 (Sim.1) as student Jo.Tylnicus. Perhaps he was the Joannes Tigneio whom the diocesan registrar recorded as receiving m.o. in June 1610 (ORS). A Fr Anthony Tilney was a Jesuit novice at Louvain 1613-4 (Belg.).

TINDALL, William [Before 1611-after 1613]

Of Yorks. m.o. c.1611 (ORS). Signed petition March 1613 as priest Gulielmus Tyndallus (Sim.1).

TORR, Charles. See ANGLICANUS.

TRAVERS (Treveris, de Treberis), *alias* SAVAGE, John [1639-c.1642]

b.Exeter 1616, son of Samuel Travers, Vicar of Thorverton 1616-46. Elder brother of Walter Travers, later Fr Bede of St Simon Stock, O.Carm. To ECS 1639 (see p.126). m.o. and subdeacon 1642 (ORS). Priest 1642 (S 8). S.J. Watten, 1642. Theology student at Liège 1644-7. Tertian at Watten 1647. By 1651 professor of philosophy at Liège. To England (E.Anglia) 1660. Rector of the College of the Holy Apostles (E.Anglia) 1668. Embezzled college funds and apostatised, 1671. Informer at the time of the Popish Plot 1678-80. Last heard of in 1686. (Ans.2/324; unpublished paper by T.McCoog S.J.).

TRAVERS, Thomas [c.1594–9]
? of Lancs. Contemporary of WJ at ECS.

TRIM, Richard, *alias* BARNES, Andrew [1612–14]
b.Wimborne, Dorset, 1590. Educated at Winchester. ECD 1609–10. ECV 1610–12. Signed petition at ECV, 1612, as Richardus Barnes. To ECS 1612 (CRS 30/xxiii), ordained Dec.1613 (ORS). (Ans.2/324; CRS 18/38).

TUNSTALL, Anthony [After 1630–1637]
SO c.1629–c.1630 (CRS 69/268). Priest at ECS by 1637. Viaticum 1637 (S 24). (Ans.2/324).

TUNSTALL (Tonstalo), George [c.1636–43]
SO c.1631–c.1632 (CRS 69/268). m.o.1636, subdeacon 1642 (ORS). Priest (S XVII). (Ans.2/324).

TUNSTALL, Laurence [After 1638–1646]
SO c.1637–c.1638 (CRS 69/268). Priest 1646 (S 8). Viaticum 1646 (S 19). (Ans.2/324).

TUNSTALL, Ralph [?–1638]
SO c.1629–c.1631 (CRS 69/268). Priest 1638 (SP 94/40/63). Viaticum collected in 1637 (S 19). (Ans.2/324).

TURNER, Francis [1597–9]
b.Devon 1577, of 'noble family'. Reconciled to the Church by John Gerard S.J. To ECV 1596. To ECS 1597 and died there 1599. (CRS 30/37).

TURNER, Peter. See MARSHALL.

TYLNICUS. See TILNEY.

TYRWHITT. See TERRITT.

URMESTON, Thomas [1592–3]
b.Lancs 1572. To ECS via ECV Nov. 1592 (CRS 14/17). d.at Seville 1593. (CRS 5/267;30/18). For the Urmestons of Horwich and Crosby Hall, see CRS 6 *passim*; 14/17;18/158,200; 71/178).

VAUGHAN (Bahano, Vahano, Baxano), William [1670–8]
b.c.1653. At ECS 1670 (S 13). Priest 1677 (S 10). m.o.1674, subdeacon 1676 (ORS). Priest 1677 (S 10). To England 1678 (S 5).

VINCENT, Thomas [?-1645]

To England from ECS, not yet a priest, 1645 (S 8).

VINCENT, William [1603]

b.Kent c.1578. SO c.1595 (RS 69/272). ECV 1596-1603. Priest. Viaticum 1603 (S 7). To England. Chaplain to O.S.B. nuns at Ghent 1624-60. d.Ghent 1660. (Ans.1/367).

WALDEGRAVE, *alias* FLOWER (Floro), Charles [1611-14]

b.Essex 1591. SO ?-1611 (CRS 69/274). m.o. 1611 (ORS). Signed petition in March 1613 as student C.Florus (Sim.1). To ECV 1614. SJ 1615. To Louvain 1616. Priest. In England (Oxon and Warwicks) 1629-51 (Anglia 10). d.London 1655. (Fo 5/382; 7/802-3; CRS 30/117).

WALKER (Gualquero), Richard [?-1609]

Viaticum as priest 1609 (S 7). In gaol at Bury St Edmunds 1627. In the Clink 1632-5. (Ans. 2/332).

WALLER (Gaulero), Robert [c.1592-3]

b.Kent, 1571, of Protestant family. Converted by Richard Blunt S.J. To ECV 1592, and in November 1592 to ECS where he d.,Sept.1593, not yet a priest. (ALSJ 1594-5; CRS 14/17,3//17; Yepes 852-3).

WALPOLE, *alias* or *vere* WARNER, Christopher [1616]

b.Docking, Norfolk, 1598. SO 1613-16 (CRS 69/277). ECS 1616 (Peralta). ECV 1616-17. ECR 1617-24. Priest. To England. S.J. 1625. SO 1630. Brussels 1631. SO 1632-3. In England (London district) from 1634. d.1664. (Ans.2/334; Fo 6/285).

WARNFORD, *alias* WEST, Peter [1602-c.1603]

b.Havant, Hants, c.1582. SO c.1597-1602 (CRS 69/277-8). To ECS 1602, but sent home in ill-health. ECD 1604-5. Became a soldier. ECV 1610-c.1613. Priest. In prison, Berks, 1626. In Sussex 1632. Took the habit O.S.B. for St Gregory's while in England c.1620, but was never professed. d.1657. (Ans.2/339-40; CRS 33/220;49/2; Weldon 1/387).

WARREN, John [?-c.1645]

Granted faculties at ECS in October 1645 as an alumnus of the college (S XVII).

WEEDON (Wideno), John [?-1669]

Licentiate and priest by 1668-9 (S 13). d.Kent 1694. Possibly a brother of Thomas Weedon, of Hanley Castle, Worcs (b.1637), who was at ECR 1658-63? (CRS 55/561-2;69/281). (Ans.3/245).

WENTWORTH, *alias* HIDALGO, PETTINGER, John [before 1624]

A John Hidalgo, *alias* Wentworth, alumnus of ECS, was chaplain to the French and Spanish ambassadors in London in 1624. Under the name John Hidalgo he published in London in 1636 a book entitled *A Catholique Cordiall*, which he withdrew in 1637 (hence no copies survive). According to Archbishop Laud, his real name was Pettinger. (Ans.2/242–3; CRS 9/120–21).

WEST. See MORE, Thomas; WARNFORD, Peter.

WESTON, Roger [c.1601–4]

b.London 1578. ECD c.1600. To Spain 1601. Viaticum at ECS as priest 1604 (S 7). In Yorks 1635. (Ans.2/345).

WHARTON (Barton), Thomas. See FOSTER.

WHITE, Andrew [1596–1604 and c.1612–c.1616]

b.London 1579. SO 1594–5 (CRS 69/285). To ECS 1596. Viaticum 1604 (S 7). Priest. To England. Banished 1606. S.J. Louvain 1607. In England 1609. ECV 1609–11 (Cast.15). At ECS 1611–15 (Baet. 4/1/71; 8). Louvain 1616–18 (Belg.44). In England (London district) by 1621, and in Hants 1632 (Ang.10). In Maryland c.1633–1645. d.Hants 1656. (Ans.2/347; Fo 3/334; 7/834–5,1146,1458).

WHITE, Francis [?–1632]

From ECS to Watten 1632, but died on the journey (S 19).

WHITE (Wbit), *alias* BLANCO, John [1730–37]

Irish. Entered ECS 1730 (S 20). All orders 1732 (ORS). Left, a D.D., 1737 (S 20).

WHITE, *alias* BLACKLOW, Thomas [1612–14]

b.Barking, Essex, 1593, second son of Richard White and Mary, daughter of Edmund Plowden. SO ?–1609 (CRS 69/285–6). ECV 1609–12. To ECS 1612. Signed petition in March 1613 as student Thomas Blacklow (Sim.1). Left with Mark Drury (q.v.) 1614 (CRS 29/148). At Louvain 1614–16 (CRS 10/131). Priest 1617. Lecturer at ECD 1617–23. Studying Canon Law in France, 1623. Agent in Rome for the English clergy by March 1626. President of ECL 1630–33. Vice-President of ECD 1634. His writings were condemned in 1655 by the Holy Office, to which he submitted in 1657. d.London 1676. (Ans.2/349–54; ER 7/78–85; 8/33–37,55–71; CRS 72/218–20).

WHITE (Vito), William [c.1600–1609]

Philosophy student by 1600 (WJ). Priest. Signed deed 1608 (S V). Viaticum 1609 (S 7) as Vito. In Sussex 1610 (WCA X/100). He may be

identical with Wm White, b.Wilts 1584, S.J. 1617, in Wales 1621-2
(Ang.13), in Yorks 1622-3 (Ang.10), d.1624. (Ans.2/354; Fo 7/838).

WILFORD, Hugh [1616-?]

SO ?-1616 (Ans.2/356). To ECS 1616 (S XVII).

WILFORD (Guildford, Vilford), William [c.1660-64]

Son of William Wilford and Elizabeth Sulyard, of Canterbury dioc. m.o.
1660 (ORS). Priest 1662 (S 9). Viaticum 1664 (S 20).

WILKINSON (Vilquinson), Henry [Before 1617-?]

b.Northants c.1594. m.o.May 1617 as S.J. (ORS). At Louvain 1617-21,
Ghent 1622-3, SO 1624. In Devon district 1625-6, Suffolk 1630-32,
Wales 1633, Lincoln 1634-6, Derbys from 1638 until his death in 1673.
(Fo 7/844; Ang.10, 13).

WILLIAMS, *alias* CROSS (Crucius), Aurelius [1671-2]

Of Llandaff dioc., possibly of Llanfoist, Mon. To ECS from Flanders
1671. Returned to Flanders 1672 (S XVII, B 654). ECD 1676-9. Priest
c.1679. Working in S.Wales 1707. (Ans.3/248).

WILLIAMS, Edward [Before 1600-1606]

Theologian at ECS by 1600 (WJ). Viaticum 1606 (S 7).

WILLIAMS, John. See ELLIS, William.

WILLIAMS (Guillermo), Stephen [?-1630]

Viaticum 1630 (S 17).

WILLIAMS, Valentine. See MORGAN, William.

WILSON (Guison), William [1592-after 1595]

b.Chester dioc., 1571. ECV 1591-2. To ECS Nov. 1592 (CRS 14/17).
Signed deed 1595 (S V). Priest. In England c.1597 and 'known to be a
spy' (CRS 25/246). In the Clink 1603. (Ans.1/383; CRS 30/15; 52/265
n.9).

WOOD, William. See TERRITT.

WOODSON, *alias* ROSS, ROSE, Leonard, or George [1605-12]

b.Hants c.1588. SO c.1600 (CRS 69/293). Probably the George
Woodson, *alias* Ross, sent to Spain from Douai in 1605 (CRS
10/64,66,70). According to his eulogy he was educated and ordained at
ECS (Fo 7/854,862). He went to England in 1612, was listed by John Gee
as in London in 1624, joined S.J. by 1630, and d.1651. (Ans.2/362).

WORSLEY, *alias* BROWN, Thomas [1593–1600]

Christened at Farnworth, Lancs, 13 Jan. 1571 (IGI). ECV 1592–3. To ECS Feb 1593 (CRS 14/18). Viaticum 1600 (S 7). To England. At Golborne, Lancs, 1604. Francis W. of Farnworth was suspected the same year of maintaining his brother, a priest. (CRS 53/148; Ans.1/386–7).

WORTHINGTON (Ordindin), John [1592–6]

b.Blainscough Hall, Lancs, 1573. At Rheims 1584–6, Eu 1586–9, ECV 1590–2. To ECS, Nov. 1592 (CRS 14/16), to ECR 1596 (Aray). Priest. S.J. 1598. To England. First Rector of Lancs district SJ, 1628. d.Lancs 1652. (Ans. 1/387).

WORTHINGTON (Vuordinton), Laurence, *alias* CHARNOCK, George [1596–99]

b.Lancs 1577, younger brother of John W. (q.v.). SO 1593–4 (CRS 69/294). ECV 1594–6. To ECS 1596. S.J. Montilla 1599. At ECV 1603 (CRS 30/xx), Cordoba 1603–6 (Baet.8). At ECS 1611 when he was sent to England, having unsuccessfully petitioned to go to Paraguay (Baet.4/1/47–8). Escaped arrest in London at the house of Doña Luisa de Carvajal, 1613 (*Copia*, 1614). Later active in Wales, Lancs and London districts. In Gatehouse prison 1615–18. Banished 1618. Professor at Louvain 1618 (Belg.). Later to Rome and Austria. d.Lorraine 1637. (Fo 2/95–132; 7/866,1459; CRS 25/100;30/29).

WRAY, John [c.1633)

Of Richmond, Yorks ? (CRS 13/104). Student c.1633 (Fo 4/667).

WYLES, *alias* GREEN, Richard [Before 1603]

At ECS and ECV before 1603, when he entered ECD as Richard Green, concealing his previous admission to, and dismissal from, both Spanish colleges (CRS 10/48). In 1604 he went back to Spain to join O.S.B., but returned to ECD where he was not admitted because of his earlier deception (ibid.58,65).

YATES. See HUYATH.

YORK, William [1599–1605]

b.Kempsford, Glos, 1581. SO 1594–99 (CRS 69/298). To ECS c.1599. Priest 1604. To England 1605. S.J. 1618. In Hants district 1621–2 (Anglia 13). d.Devon district c.1625. (Ans.2/369; Fo 7/876).

5. MARTYRED ALUMNI OF THE ENGLISH
COLLEGE, SEVILLE

Blessed Thomas Benstead, *alias* Hunt (ECS 1593–99)	d.1600
Blessed William Richardson (ECS 1594–1600)	d.1603
Blessed Thomas Green (ECS 1601–02)	d.1642
Blessed Ralph Corby (ECS 1619–21)	d.1644
Blessed Edward Bamber (ECS 1621–26)	d.1646

Dilatus

William Atkins, S. J. (ECS 1622–28)	d.1681

6. ENGLISH JESUITS IN ANDALUSIA, 1592–1660

English members of the Society of Jesus who resided at St Gregory's or at other houses in Andalusia are listed below. If they were themselves alumni of St Gregory's, there is a cross-reference to the alumni list. Spanish versions of surnames are given in brackets, though I have not been able to decode them in all cases (e.g. Christopher Wensonius, Thomas Ignatius).

Titles
Minister = Administrator of the college, subject to the Rector.
Procurator = Bursar
Praefectus Spiritus = Spiritual Director of the students.
Operarius = Missioner and preacher, engaged in pastoral work.
Temporal coadjutor = Laybrother.
Eleemosynarius = Collector of alms (usually an English laybrother).

Sources
Most of the information is based on the records of the Andalusian province (Provincia Baetica) in the Archivum Romanum S.J. (ARSI). I have also referred to catalogues of the provinces of Castille (Cast.), Toledo (Tol.) Belgium (Belg.) and England (Angl.). Otherwise the reader should refer to the list of sources and abbreviations on pp.38–42.

The main sources quoted below are as follows:
Baet.8. Catalogi triennales 1583–1622.
Baet.9/1. Catalogi triennales 1625–39.
Baet.9/2. Catalogi triennales 1640–51.
Baet. 14/1. Catalogi breves 1621–40.
Baet. 14/2. Catalogi breves 1641–99.
Baet. 3–6. Epistulae Generales.
Cast. 14/1. Catalogi triennales 1584–1600.
Cast. 27. Catalogi breves 1595–8.
Tolet. 21/1, Catalogi triennales 1584–97.
Belg. 43. Catalogi breves Provinciae Belgicae 1577–1615.
Belg. 44. Catalogi breves 1616–33.
Gall.-Belg. 24. Catalogi breves Provinciae Gallico-Belgicae 1613–39.

The triennial catalogues normally give the age of each subject, and his years in the Society, but often the figures are inconsistent from one entry to another. For that reason, some of the dates and ages given below have to be approximate. I have provided cross-references to entries in Anstruther, Foley and relevant CRS volumes, but there are some names below which are not found in these sources, and some of the data provided will require a correction of hitherto published entries on individual Jesuits.

Those Englishmen who joined the Society in Andalusia will have done their novitiate at the Casa Profesa, Seville, until about 1597, when the novitiate was moved to Montilla. About 1610 the novitiate returned to Seville, at San Luis.

Most of the Andalusian houses were called 'colleges', even though education was only one of the activities of the fathers resident there. Lesser houses were called 'missions' or 'residences' (such as the one at Sanlúcar).

A further source of information has been the *cartas edificatorias* written on the death of a member of the Society by the Rector of the college where he resided. Several such letters relating to English Jesuits are to be found in the Archivo Histórico Nacional (AHN), Madrid (Sección de Jesuitas, leg.56). Five Englishmen (Michael Higgins, Stephen Chapman, Francis Felton, William Johnson and William Weston) are included by Juan Santibañez in his gallery of distinguished members of the Andalusian province, *Varones ilustres de la Provincia de Andalucía*. Copies of the first three of his 'Centurias' (groups of one hundred short eulogies) are kept at the Jesuit archives in Granada and Alcalá.

Rectors of St Gregory's
Francisco de Peralta 1592-1607
Alonso Díaz 1607-12.
Francisco de Peralta 1613-21 (d.7 January 1622)
Francisco de los Cámeros 1621-27
Luis Ramírez 1627-28
Martin de Vega 1628-31
Diego de Ribera 1631-36
Juan de Armenta 1636-37
Fernando de Valencia 1637-40
Ximenes de Bertendona 1640-44
Pablo Federíqui 1644-48
Francisco Sotelo 1648-49
Pablo Federíqui 1649-51

ARTHUR (Arturo), *alias* BELL, HOARE, Gregory
Temporal coadjutor. b.Hurley, Berks, c.1574. S.J. at Montilla, 1593. At ECS 1599, Trigueros 1603, ECS 1604 (Baet.3/2/707)—1606. St Omer 1609-17. Watten 1618-39. d.Watten 1639. (Baet.8/88,136,181,216v; Belg.43-4).

BECKET (Vecheto), *alias* COVET, Joseph
Temporal coadjutor. b.Hants 1590. SO 1611-16 (CRS 69/30). ECV 1616-17 (CRS 30/128), 1618-20. Sacristan at ECM 1620 (AAW A16/77). S.J. at Seville March 1623 (Baet.9/1/20v). At ECS 1625-39 as eleemosynarius. In 1637 and 1639 he is listed as 'socius procuratoris Sancti Omer' (Baet.9/1/14). See Fo 7/44-5, 1418-9.

BEDINGFIELD, *alias* DE MENDOZA, Thomas. See p.53.

BELL, Gregory. See ARTHUR.

BELL, Henry

b.Notts 1563. From Rheims to ECR 1586. Priest 1586. To England 1591. S.J. at Villagarcía, Prov. Toledo, March 1596 (Tol. 21/1/177). Minister at ECS c.1598. To Cadiz, where he died c.1601 after returning from the Azores. See pp.153, 160; Ans. 1/29.

BENTLEY (Bencleus), Henry

b.Derbys 1585. ECR 1598-1603. In England from 1604. Priest at ECR 1609. S.J. 1611. Minister Operarius at Granada by April 1615 (Baet.8/272). At Cadiz in May 1618 when he was sent to Flanders (Baet.4/2/118v). d.in England before 1628. See Ans.2/22-3; Fo 7/51-2.

BILLINGTON (Verincton, Bilinton), John

Temporal coadjutor. b.'Cuelso' (?Kelsall), Cheshire, 1583. S.J. Liège 1617. At ECS 1619-49 as eleemosynarius (Belg.24; Baet.9/1, 9/2, 14).

CHAPMAN, Stephen

b.London, 1578. Joined S.J. in Flanders, 1606, as temporal coadjutor. According to his eulogy (*Varones* 2.78) 'he pleaded to be left in the rank of temporal coadjutor, in order that his rare talent for the mechanical arts might be put to use. Learning of this, the General instructed him to learn the art of printing, so as to serve in this capacity in the East Indies'. Instead he was promoted to orders. At SO from 1609. Priest c.1611. ECV 1614. ECS 1615-22. In Seville he heard confessions in Flemish and French, and served for eight years 'without ever taking money or gifts from his penitents'. d.Seville 15 November 1622, aet.44.

COLLINS (Colin), John

Temporal coadjutor. b. London 1573. S.J. Jan. 1593. Novice at Montilla by April 1593 (Baet.8/88; CRS 14/11).

CRATHORNE (Craton), John

b.Yorks 1592. S.J. 1611. At Salamanca 1614 (Cast.15/1/254v). Minister at ECS 1619 (Baet.8). Spiritual Director at ECS 1628 (Baet.9/1). On both occasions he was soon replaced on health grounds. d.1656. See Fo 7/180; CRS 30/96-8.

CRESWELL, Joseph.

b.London 1556. To ECR 1580. S.J. Rome 1583. Priest 1586. Rector ECR 1588-92. At ECS 1592-6. Madrid 1596-Nov.1613. d.1623. (Loomie, *The Spanish Elizabethans*, pp.182-229).

FECK, Thomas

b.dioc.London, 1573. ECR 1597-1601. S.J., Rome, Oct.1601. Minister at ECS 1606 (Baet.8). d.Liège 1647. See Ans.1/113; Fo 7/247-8.

FELTON, Francis. See p.66.

FORCER, Francis. See p.67.

GAGE, *alias* HOWARD (Hoardus), William

b.1599, son of John Gage and Margaret Copley, of Haling, Surrey. Brother of Col. Sir Henry Gage, Fr George Gage, and the renegade Dominican Thomas Gage. S.J. 1619. Priest c.1624. Minister at ECS 1628-9 (Baet.9/1; 14). To Flanders in ill-health 1629 (Baet.5/2/144). See Fo 7/283-4.

GARNET, *alias* GILFORD (Guifordo, Quarfrord), George

Temporal coadjutor. b.1597 at 'Chilbalbos,' Yorks (Baet.9/1/20v). Nephew of Henry Garnet, S.J. SO 1608-13 (CRS 69/110-11). S.J. Liège 1616. Eleemosynarius at ECS c.1619-30, 1648-49 (Baet. 8,9,14). Procurator at ECM 1630-48. See Fo 7/287.

GERARD, Thomas.

b.1608. Joined S.J. at Seville as temporal coadjutor, Jan.1628, aged 20 (Baet.9/66/104v).

HANMER, Francis

b.Leics c.1590. S.J. 1608. Student of theology at Cordoba in 1611, aet.20 (Baet.8/251). Priest at Marchena 1615. d.1666. See Fo 4/394.

HARGRAVE (Argrabro), Charles or James

b.Whalley, Lancs, 1586. Priest at ECV 1609. S.J. Louvain 1612. Operarius at ECS by 1615 (Baet.8/288v). Ordered to Flanders May 1618 (Baet.4/2/117). Later dismissed from S.J. See Ans.2/145; Fo 7/1432.

HIGGINS (Higinio), Michael, *vere* Adam

b.London 1559, brother of Isaac Higgins (Ans. 1/166-7). ECD 1571-82. S.J. 1582 at Rome, where he was a fellow-novice of St Luis Gonzaga and studied philosophy under Bellarmine. Taught at Dillingen for nine years and at Ingolstadt for fifteen (c.1587-1611). At Lisbon 1613-14 (Lus.). At ECS c.1615-21 as confessor, spiritual director and professor of 'cases' and controversy. At Malaga from 1622 to his death in June 1638 (*Varones* 3.99). See Fo 7/1433-4.

HOARE. See ARTHUR.

HOSKINS (Osquins), Anthony.

b.Herefords 1570. ECV 1591-4. S.J. 1594. Priest by 1597, when he was at ECS in charge of the philosophers (Baet.8/122v). At Madrid, 1599, as assistant to J.Creswell (Tolet.12/219v). To England 1601. Returned to

Madrid 1613 as Vice-Prefect of the English Mission. d.Madrid, Sept.1615. See Fo 7/373; CRS 30/14.

IGNATIUS, Thomas

Temporal coadjutor. b.1613. S.J. 1639. First vows, July 1641 (Baet.9/2/289v). At ECS 1641–4 (Baet.9/2/260). Dismissed Dec.1644 (ibid.302v).

IPSLEY, *alias* BLOFIELD, Thomas. See p.75.

JAMES (Jaime) Francis

b.London 1583. S.J. 1611. First year theologian at Salamanca 1614, aet.30 (Cast.15/1/254v). Priest at ECS 1615 (Baet.8/288).

JENISON, Thomas. See p.76.

JENKIN, *alias* DUARTE, John

Temporal coadjutor. b.Penzance 1596. Sent by his father to Malaga c.1608 to learn Spanish. S.J. 1612. At Guadix 1615, Baeza 1617–22, Jerez 1622–3, Trigueros 1625. Applied unsuccessfully to be sent to Japan, Dec.1617 (Baet.4/1/254v). ECV 1627–33. In November 1633 he was apprehended at Plymouth and stated that he had been given leave of absence by his Superior 'to see his friends'. He had acquired the name Duarte because his first employer at Malaga had been unable to pronounce the name Jenkin. With him he had a letter to his brother Thomas Jenkin of Penzance, written for him by John Wray of ECS, a copy of a letter addressed by Marina de Escobar to the Catholics of England, given him by Thomas Land S.J. at Valladolid, and a letter from P.Vitelleschi, the Father General. He refused the oath of allegiance. (SP 16/250/19; Fo 4/666–8, 7/403; Baet.8, 9/1, 14; Cast.15).

JOHNSON (Ayanson, Janson), Bernard

b.1629. According to his obituary (AHN Jesuitas leg.56) he was of noble family, sent by his father to Spain 'to save his soul'. S.J. at Seville 1645 (Baet.14/1/127). Student of 'dialectics' at Malaga 1648 (Baet.9/2/357v). d.Malaga 1649, aet.20.

JOHNSON, Thomas. See p.77.

JOHNSON, William I

b.1566, in dioc.Chester. Rheims 1585–90. ECV 1591–6. Priest. S.J. at Villagarcía 1596 (Tol.21/1/177). Minister at ECS 1599–1600. At Malaga 1603–14. d.Malaga 1614. See Ans.1/192; Fo 7/1436.

JOHNSON (Janson, Consonio), William II. See p.77.

JUSTIN, Richard

Temporal coadjutor. b.1596. S.J. at Seville March 1615, aet.19
(Baet.8/258). At Cadiz in Nov.1617, when he petitioned either to be
allowed to become a priest or to be released for family reasons
(Baet.4/1/253v).

KENDALL, Thomas

b.Devon 1612. SO 1631-5 (CRS 69/152). S.J. Watten 1635. At Sanlúcar
(not St George's, but the Jesuit residence) 1648-51 (Baet.9/2, 14).
Minister at Malaga 1655 (Baet.14/2/340v). Procurator at Madrid for
English Province S.J. from 1662 until his death in 1672. (CRS 29/157,
362; Fo 7/413).

KINSMAN (Guismans), Bernard

b.Middlesex 1611. S.J. Watten 1626. At Liege 1642-5. Minister at ECS
1648-1660, or later (Baet.9/2,10,14/2). Military chaplain in Belgium
1665. To England 1666. d.Suffolk district 1668 (Fo 7/421)

LAND, Thomas, *alias* COLLINS, John

b.Orford, Suffolk, 1586. Converted in 1603. SO 1606-8 (CRS 69/68-9).
To ECV 1608. S.J. in Castile, 1612. Priest c.1616. Prefect of Studies at
ECS 1619 (Baet.8/302). To England. d.Valladolid 1632. (RH 2/96-7; Fo
7/431, 1438; BS 2/96-7).

LEA, Thomas. See p.79.

LEWIS (Luis, Ludovici), George

b.London 1611. S.J. at Seville 1632 (Baet.9/1/122). At novitiate house,
Seville, 1633 (ibid.).

MARIN (= Mearing?), James (Didacus, Diego, Jacobus)

Temporal coadjutor. b.'Baiopte' (= Bridport?), Dorset, 1602. Travelled
to Malaga as a youth with his father and was taken in at the Jesuit college
where he became a Catholic. S.J. at Malaga 1622. At ECS as
eleemosynarius, etc, 1623-41. d.Seville August 1641. (Baet.9/1, 14; obit.
in Baet.26/58). Mearing is a name found in Dorset and seems the most
likely original.

MARSH, William

b.Lancs 1637. SO 1656-8. S.J. Watten 1658. Priest 1666. Signed accounts
as Minister at ECS 1669-70. To Worcs district 1671. d.Lincs district
1681. See Fo 7/488; CRS 69/172; 70/159.

de MENDOZA, *alias* LOVE, Christopher. See p.81.

METHAM, Francis

b.Yorks 1617. S.J. 1644. In Yorks 1658. At ECS by 1662 (CRS 29/307) and Minister there in 1665, aet.48 (Baet.10/167). In Oxon 1674. d.1681. See Fo 7/503.

MORGAN, Walter. See p.85.

NEWPORT, *alias* JENNINGS, Richard. See p.76.

PERSONS, George

Temporal coadjutor. 'Of Taunton in the diocese of Wells', b.1574. Kinsman of Robert Persons. S.J. 1595 in Castille. At ECV 1597–9 (Cast.14/2/308, 409). At St Hermenegild's , Seville, 1603, employed in 'house duties' (Baet.8). d.Granada, May 1607 (ALSJ 1607, pp.135–6).

PICKFORD (Picfort), *alias* DANIELL, Thomas . See p.89.

POLE (Polo), John

b.Derbys 1574. S.J. 1598. From Alcalá to teach at ECV, 1603 (see p.159). Prefect of Studies at ECS when he died there in 1605 (ALSJ 1605).

POULTON, *alias* POLLARD, Henry. See p.90.

PRICE (Pricio), John. See p.90.

ST GEORGE (San Jorge) William

Temporal coadjutor. b.Bristol (Perestol) c.1582. S.J. in Andalusia 1602. At Cordoba 1603–23 (Baet.8, 9/1). d.Sept.1623.

SALKELD, John. See p.93.

SANKEY (Sanchez, Sans), Francis

b.Lancs 1603. S.J. 1628. At ECS 1639 as spiritual director (Baet.9/1).

SNOW (Nieves), Thomas

Temporal coadjutor. b.Dorset c.1590. S.J. Liège, 1616. 'Hortulanus' at ECS 1619–21. Baker at St Hermenegild's 1622 (Baet.14). At SO by 1629 (Ang.10). d.Liège 1650.

SWINBURNE (Sumbuorno), Simon

b.Hunts 1561. To ECR 1561. Priest and S.J., 1586. From France to Andalusian province c.1590 (Baet.8/56) and was Minister at ECS (see p.160). At ECV 1593 (Cast. 14/224). At Tournai from 1598 (Belg. 43). d.1638. (Ans. 1/344).

TANCARD, Charles

b.Yorks 1563. S.J. at Naples 1584. Priest. At Cadiz, 1592, 'employed in assisting his fellow-countrymen' (Baet.3/1/28). Minister at ECS 1593 (Baet.8). Chaplain to the Spanish fleet (see p.153.). Minister at ECV 1595-6 (Cast.27/3v,20v). d.Valladolid 1599.

THOMPSON (Tonson), John

b.in dioc.Canterbury, c.1573. ECV 1590-8. S.J. at Montilla, Dec.1598. To Cadiz Dec.1600. Confessor (in five languages) at ECS by 1603 (Baet.8). At Granada 1606. Still in Andalusia in Jan.1611, when he was posted to ECV (Baet.4/1/93). d.Valladolid 1616. See p.155 and Ans.1/351; Fo 7/1456.

TICHBORNE, William, *vere* Henry

b.in dioc.Salisbury, 1571, S.J. Rome 1587. At ECS 1600-05 as Minister and professor of 'cases' and controversy (Baet.8). d.ECS 1605 (AL). See Fo 7/778-9.

WALPOLE (Vualpolo) Christopher

b.Norfolk 1570. S.J. in Andalusia 1597. Theologian at St Hermenegild's 1599-1600 (Baet.8/134v,159). Dismissed Dec.1600, in third year of theology. Not the C.W. of Ans.2/334 and Fo 7/186. See p.160.

WALPOLE, Richard *alias* BECKHAM (Beccam), Thomas

b.Docking, Norfolk, 1564. To Peterhouse, Cambridge, 1579. To ECR 1585. Priest 1589. To Valladolid 1591. To ECS, Feb.1592 (CRS 14/17). S.J. at Montilla Feb.1593 as Thomas Beckham (Baet.8/87). Prefect of Studies at ECS, 1597-c.1603 (Baet.8). At ECV by 1606 (Cast.15). d.Valladolid Sept.1607. See Ans.1/369-70; Fo 2/235; 7/809.

WALPOLE, Thomas

According to a 19th c.necrology (Baet.8), someone of this name died at Seville on 11 Nov.1625.

WARFORD, William

b.Bristol 1559. Trin.Coll.Oxon, 1574-82. Priest, Rome 1584. S.J. at Rome 1594. At ECS 1603-5 as confessor (in six languages) and working among English prisoners (Baet.8; 3/2/799). At Cadiz, 1606, when the General wrote to him approving his translation of the *Flos Sanctorum* (Baet.3/2/943). There is no record of its publication. d. ECV Nov. 1608. See Ans.1/370; Fo 7/815. For his catechism, see p.116.

WENSONIUS, Christopher

Minister at Malaga 1615, aet.33, in 10th year S.J. (Baet.8/276v). Identity uncertain.

WESTON, William

b.Maidstone c.1550. Ch.Ch.Oxon, 1564–69. S.J. Rome, Nov.1575.
Priest, Seville 1579. At Montilla, Cordoba, Cadiz, Sanlúcar and Seville,
1576–84. In England 1584–1603. At ECS 1605–14, as confessor and
lecturer in 'cases'. Rector ECV June 1614. d.Valladolid 9 April 1615. See
pp. 160–61 and P.Caraman, *William Weston* (1955), pp.252–3.

WHICHCOTT, *alias* SAVILLE (Sabel)., William

b.Lincs c.1580. S.J. Oct.1606. At ECS by 1611 and until 1615, as Prefect
of Studies (Baet.8). To England late in 1615 (see p.170). Worked in
London and Hants districts. d.Flanders 1654.

WHITE, Andrew. See p.102

WORTHINGTON, Laurence. See p.104

7. ANDALUSIAN IMPRESOS RELATING TO ENGLISH CATHOLIC AFFAIRS, 1590–1670

[c.1590] *Traslado de una carta de cierta monja inglesa llamada Isabel Sandera hermana del Doctor Nicolas Sandero escrita en Roan ciudad de Francia a Francisco Englefild cavallero ingles residente en Madrid: en que le da cuenta de sus persecuciones y trabajos que ha passado por nuestra santa fe en Inglaterra.* Sevilla: Clemente Hidalgo. (ARCR 965. Reprinted in Yepes, pp.724–37).

1599. *Nuevos avisos de Inglaterra de diez y seis del mes de enero de este año de mil y quinientos y noventa y nueve en los quales se da quêta de muchas particularidades de cosas de guerra y de sucesos y persecuciones de los catolicos que ay presos.* Sevilla: Rodrigo de Cabrera. (ARCR 1063). Fol.bifol. Based on reports sent to ECS on the transfer of William Weston from Wisbech to the Tower; the escape of two fathers from the house of Sr Abinton [Thomas Habington, of Hindlip House, Worcs]; the execution of a soldier [Edward Squyer] recently returned from Spain.

1600. *Relacion del martirio de los dos sacerdotes el P.Tomas Benested que fue del Colegio Ingles de Sevilla y de N.Sprat del Seminario de Duay en Flandes que padecieron en Linconia de Inglaterra primero de Iulio del año del Señor 1600.* Fol.bifol. (ARCR 91). The martyrdom of Blessed Thomas Benstead, *alias* Hunt, the protomartyr of ECS, and Blessed Thomas Sprott.

1601. *La prision del conde de Essex y otros condes y cavalleros de Inglaterra: y vando que echo la Reyna contra los dichos copiada de una de Londres de 22 de febrero de 1601 años.* Sevilla: Clemente Hidalgo. Fol.bifol. (RAH PJ 89/151).

1601. *Avisos de Londres de XIX de marzo de mil y seiscientos y uno de la muerte del conde de Essex.* Sevilla: Clemente Hidalgo. Fol.bifol. (RAH PJ 102/11). Also reports the death of Blessed John Pibush.

1603. *La declaracion que hizo el Consejo de Estado de la Reyna Isabela de Inglaterra difunta. En favor de Iacobo quinto [sic] Rey de Escocia por heredero y sucesor de aquella corona. A tres dias de abril 1603.* Sevilla: Juan de Leon. Fol.bifol. (ARCR 1064). A translation of the Privy Council's proclamation on the day of the Queen's death. Also reports the execution of 'Laurence Anderton' of ECS, i.e.Blessed William Richardson, *alias* Anderson whom the writer has confused with Laurence Anderton, *alias* Rigby, also of ECS (See RH 16, 1983, pp.316–18).

1603. Ditto. Granada: Fernando Diaz de la Montoya. (ARCR 1064.1).

1603. *Relacion muy verdadera del recibimiento y fiestas que se le hizieron en Inglaterra a Don Iuan de Tassis Conde de Villamediana Embaxador extraordinario de su Magestad del Rey Don*

Felipe Tercero nuestro señor por el nuevo Rey Jacobo de Inglaterra. Sevilla: Bartolomé Gomez. (SU 109-85). An account of the progress of the Spanish Ambassador from Dover to Greenwich, Windsor, Henley and Oxford. This *relación,* and the following, in BL at G 6256(1).

1604.   *La segunda parte de la embaxada de Don Iuan de Tassis.* Sevilla: Bartolomé Gomez. (SU 109-85). On the unprecedented honours paid to the ambassador at Winchester, the release of Catholics in November and the subsequent unrest among 'puritans'.

1604.   [Joseph Creswell], *Informacion a la ciudad de Sevilla por parte del Colegio Ingles de la misma ciudad.* Sevilla: Clemente Hidalgo. (ARCR 279). A petition to the city fathers not to discontinue the grant begun in 1592.

1604.   *Copia de una relacion hecha en el cabildo de la ciudad de Sevilla que mando imprimir el Assistente della don Bernardino Gonçalez Delgadillo de Avellaneda sobre un caso si la ciudad tratando de su desempeño y aviendo quitado para el mismo fin otras mercedes y limosnas podia continuar la que hazia al Seminario de los Ingleses.* Con pareceres de theologos sobre el mismo caso. Sevilla: Clemente Hidalgo. Fol. (ARCR 1072). Some had proposed that the grant of 600 ducats to ECS should be transferred to the redemption of captives, but expert opinion recommended its continuation.

1604.   George Doulye [*vere* William Warford], *A briefe instruction by way of dialogue concerning the principall poyntes of Christian religiõ.* Lovaine: Laurence Kellam [*vere* Sevilla: ?Clemente Hidalgo]. (A&R 877). See p.21.

[c.1604].   *Algunos motivos y razones que ay para favorecer los seminarios ingleses.* n.p.d. (ARCR 1062).

1606.   *Relacion verdadera que trato como el catolico don Iacob rey de Inglaterra trae a sus vassallos al conocimiento de la santa fe. Compuesta por Iuan de Godoy.* Sevilla: Clemente Hidalgo. (SP 14/24/56). Not a *relación,* but two highly imaginative verse *romances* celebrating the 'restoration' of the Catholic religion by the newly crowned James I, following his visions of Queen Elizabeth (in hell) and Santiago. See p.9.

[1614].   *Copia de una carta que el P.Francisco de Peralta de la Compañia de Jesus, Rector del Colegio de los Ingleses de Sevilla, escrivio al P.Rodrigo de Cabredo Provincial de la Nueva España en que se da quenta de la dichosa muerte que tuvo en Londres doña Luisa de Carvajal . . . y de las honras que se le hizieron en la yglesia de San Gregorio Magno Apostol de Inglaterra en el Collegio Ingles de Sevilla en 11 de mayo de 1614.* n.p.d. 4o. (ARCR 1065). An account of the solemnities at St Gregory's in honour of the lately deceased Luisa de Carvajal, including the panegyric delivered by Juan de Pineda, S.J. This is followed by the text of letters to the writer from Flanders and England giving details of Luisa de Carvajal's last days. The writer ends (pp.55-7) with a report on the current state of St Gregory's and thanks Fr de Cabredo (a former Rector of St Alban's, Valladolid) for his efforts in raising funds for St Gregory's in Mexico.

1615. *Algunos avisos de Inglaterra y de la persecucion grande que aora de nuevo ay en aquel reyno contra los catolicos.* Sevilla: Alonso Rodriguez Gamarra. Fol.bifol. (ARCR 1067).
Information based on a letter from London of a priest alumnus of ECS, dated 18 January 1615, reporting the death in Newgate of George Fairburn, another alumnus. Another letter, dated 9 April 1615, from an English priest in Brussels, reports a debate between John Ainsworth and George Muscote, *vere* Fisher, both alumni of ECS, and the Archbishop of Canterbury, the Bishop of London, Sir Ralph Winwood and others. (See Ans.2/2-3).

1615. *Relacion del martirio de Tomas Haso* [Hackshott] *inclito martir de Jesu Cristo y de Nicolas Sisburno* [Tichborne] *ingleses y de una muger varonil. Con otros avisos importantes embiados por un sacerdote del seminario de Sevilla testigo de vista que fue del todo.* Granada: Antonio René. Fol.bifol. (ARCR 624).
A belated narrative based on an eyewitness account by an alumnus of ECS, of the arrest and execution fourteen years earlier (1604) of Nicholas Tichborne and Thomas Hackshott (see RH 19, 1989, pp.411-25). Also reports the conversion of more than forty-six 'Lutherans' at Seville, following discussions held at St Gregory's.

1615. *Relacion verdadera embiado al seminario de Sevilla por un padre de la Compañia de Jesus que esta preso en Inglaterra entre otros muchos sacerdotes. Dase quenta de la prision de deziseys mil cristianos y de los crueles martyrios que algunos han padecido por nuestra santa fe catolica.* Granada: Bartolomé de Lorençana. (ARCR 1069).
Duplicates the report in *Algunos avisos*, 1615, with additional details. A verse *romance* based on this *relación*, by Martin de Luna, S.J., was published at Cuenca the same year (ARCR 1068).

1616. *Relacion que el P.Francisco de Peralta . . . escrivio a D.Antonio Vigil de Quiñones y Pimentel, Conde de Luna y Mayorga. En que se da quenta del estado que oy tienen las cosas de la religion catolica de Ynglaterra y la persecucion que padecen los catolicos. Y del martirio que el mes de Março passado padecieron dos sacerdotes y un lego.* Sevilla: Alonso Rodriguez Gamarra. (ARCR 1070).
The martyrdom of Thomas Atkinson, John Thules and Roger Wrenno.

1618. *Admirable y breve relacion sacada sumariamente de algunas*
       clausulas de una carta que escrivio el padre Rector de los Ingleses
       de Sevilla a el padre Provincial de la Compañia de Jesus de
       Mexico. Sevilla: Diego Perez. Fol.bifol. (ARCR 1066.1).
       A reprint of *Copia de una carta*, 1614, on the exequies at Seville in
       honour of Luisa de Carvajal.

1619. [Patrick Comerford], *Breve relacion de la presente persecucion de*
       Irlanda. Sevilla: Gabriel Ramos Vejarano. (ARCR 1074).
       See HMC, Franciscan MSS, p.73.

1623. *Copia de una carta de una señora inglesa catolica, ausente de*
       Londres, escrita a su marido: exortandole, que aun pierda su
       hazienda e hijos, no dexe de confessar ser catolico. Impressa a su
       instancia de Doña Catalina de Zuñiga y Sandoval, Marquesa de
       Villena, Duquesa de Escalona. Madrid: Diego de Flamenco;
       Sevilla: Francisco de Lyra. Fol.bifol. (ARCR 2). The writer signs
       herself 'A.A.'

1623. *Relacion de la venida en secreto y por la posta desde Londres a*
       Madrid del Principe Don Carlos de Inglaterra. Refierense los
       sucesos de su viaje, entrada en Madrid, salida en publico de la
       señora Infanta, visitas del Rey N.S. con el Principe, y otras cosas
       curiosas. Embiada de Madrid al P.Rector del Colegio de los
       Ingleses de Sevilla. Sevilla: Juan Serrano de Vargas y Urrena.
       Fol.bif. (ARCR 1071).
       The first of many news-sheets on the visit of the Prince of Wales to
       Madrid, based on information from ECM.

1623. *Relacion de la entrada del principe don Carlos de Inglaterra en la*
       Corte de Madrid, 17 de marzo 1623. Sevilla: Francisco de Lyra.
       (In RAH index of PJ, but missing).

1623. *Segunda relacion de la suntuada entrada con palio en Madrid del*
       Principe de Inglaterra . . . Va a la letra el pregon de la suspension
       de las prematicas en la corte. Sevilla: Juan Serrano de Vargas.
       Fol.bifol. (SU 109–85) Describes the amnesty granted by the
       Spanish crown to prisoners, to mark the occasion of Prince
       Charles' visit.

1623. *Relacion del torneo que dispuso en Madrid el almirante de Castilla*
       para festejar la venida del Principe de Gales, 16 de abril. Sevilla:
       Francisco de Lyra. Fol.bifol. (RAH PJ 129/11).

1623. *Relacion de las fiestas del Corpus a que asistieron el rey Felipe 4o,*
       los infantes y el Principe de Gales. Sevilla: Francisco de Lyra. (In
       RAH index of PJ, but missing).

1623. *Relacion de las fiestas reales de toros y cañas que la Magestad*
       Catolica de el Rey nuestro señor jugo en la villa de Madrid en 21 de
       agosto por festejar los felicissimos y dichosos despôsorios del
       serenissimo Principe de Gales y la señora Infante Dña Maria.
       Sevilla: Gabriel Ramos Vejarano. (SU 109–85).

1623.   *Respuesta que el Principe de Gales embio a su Magestad Filipo 4 nuestro señor sobre la junta que uvo en que la Infanta no saliesse de España dentro de el tiempo propuesto.* Sevilla: Gabriel Ramos Vejarano. (ARCR 1604). The Prince of Wales' reply to letters from Philip IV and the Count Duke of Olivares, renewing an earlier pledge of limited toleration for English Catholics.

[1623].   *Memorial que el serenissimo Principe de Gales dio en razon de que se concluya el casamiento con la señora Infante.* Sevilla: Francisco de Lyra. Fol.bifol. (ARCR 1603).
Another edition of the above.

1623.   *Gregorio Papa XV al venerable hermano Obispo de Cuenca Inquisidor General de las Españas.* Sevilla: Gabriel Ramos Vejarano. Fol.bif. (ARCR 1592–3).
The Spanish and Latin texts of a letter in which the Pope urges Bishop Enrique Pimentel to use his influence with Philip IV, on the occasion of the royal betrothal, to obtain better terms for English Catholics.

1623.   *Memorial en el qual suplican los catolicos de Inglaterra al serenissimo Principe de Gales . . . y otro que dieron los escoceses a su Magestad.* Sevilla: Matias Clavijo. Fol.bifol. (ARCR 355).
The English petition is for a Catholic university to be set up in England after the royal marriage. The Scots, in the name of Hugh Sempill, ask for a Scots seminary to be set up in a Spanish university.

1623.   *Fiesta eclesiastica que en el seminario ingles de Madrid mando hazer el dia de nuestra señora de agosto este año de 1623 su alteza de la serenissima Infanta Maria de Austria. Dase cuenta de la nueva congregaciõ de Ingleses Catolicos que en Madrid hizo el Padre Forcex* [Forcer] *de la Compañia de Jesus, y asimismo de las colgaduras de Iglesia, calles, puertas y ventanas, y de las grandi- osas invenciones de fuegos que se hizieron la vispera desta fiesta.* Sevilla: Francisco de Lyra. Fol.bifol. (ARCR 754).
The celebrations at ECM to mark the impending royal betrothal. An additional report from 'P.Planifan' [Blackfan] in England on the measures taken by the king to conciliate the Catholics.

1623.   *Relacion de la partida del Principe de Gales para Inglaterra.* Sevilla: Francisco de Lyra. Fol.bifol. (BCC 63–7–10; RAH PJ 117/92).

1623.   *Relacion en que se da cuenta del dichoso parto de la Reyna . . . Dase tambien cuenta de la llegada del Principe Don Carlos a Londres y el gran recebimiento que se le hizo y como mando dar libertad a los catolicos que estavan presos.* Sevilla: Gabriel Ramos Vejarano. (SU 109–85).
Fancifully describes how Aeolus and Neptune, envious of Spain's glory in having had the Prince of Wales as a guest for over six

months, detained him on his homeward journey with their winds and waves.

1623. *Entrada de Don Juan de Mendoza Marques de Inoiosa embaxador extraordinario en Inglaterra.* Sevilla: Francisco de Lyra. (SU 109–85; BL 593. h.17-2).

'After the arrival of the Marquess in England, more than twenty thousand professed themselves to be Catholics, to the great confusion of the heretics, the more so when they saw that the king was confirming the settlement and that a chapel was being prepared for the Infanta in the royal palace'. Includes an account of the solemn oath taken by the king to abide by the marriage treaty.

1624. *Verissima relacion de la partida de Londres que hizo Don Diego Hurtado de Mendoza embaxador extraordinario de su Magestad y los singulares favores que le hizo el Rey de la Gran Bretaña sentandole a comer a su mesa con el y con el Principe de Gales.* Sevilla: Juan de Cabrera. (SU 109–85).

1625. *Verdadera relacion de la armada aprestada en Inglaterra . . . y de la grande peste que ay en la ciudad de Londres.* Sevilla: Juan de Cabrera. (RAH PJ 93/86).
Includes an account of the discovery of the incorrupt body of Francis Tregian in the Jesuit church at Lisbon.

1625. *Relacion embiado a un personage de esta ciudad avisandole de algunos ordinarios que de Italia y otras partes an venido a la Corte de su Magestad y de la muerte de Jacobo Rey de Inglaterra y coronacion de su hijo.* Sevilla: Juan de Cabrera. (RAH PJ 93/84).

1625. *Avisos de Italia, Flandes . . . y otras partes desde 28 de julio hasta 3 de agosto deste año de 1625. Dase cuenta como en el palacio de Londres dixo Missa de pontifical el obispo que acompaño a la Reyna hermana del Rey de Francia a cuyo acto asistieron y comulgaron mas de 600 catolicos.* Sevilla: Francisco de Lyra. (RAH PJ 93/99).

1626. *Noticias de Inglaterra y sobre el estado de los catolicos.* Sevilla: Juan de Cabrera. (ARCR 387. Probably identical with the following).

1626. *Verissima relacion en que se da cuenta en el estado en que estan los catolicos de Inglaterra.* Sevilla: Juan de Cabrera. (ARCR 386). Fol.bifol. Describes the growing anti-Catholic mood. More than 600 Catholics arrested in London alone. The efforts of Queen Henrietta Maria on their behalf.

1627. *Vitoria que el Marques de Espinola a tenido en Inglaterra, entrando y saqueando la Isla de Lycuria y cogido en ella gran cantidad de ganado y otras cosas.* Sevilla: Juan de Cabrera. (SU 109–85).

Reports a Spanish landing in the Shetlands [Lycuria = Lerwick], described as exporting rough woollen cloth to Spain (cf.SP 16/75/98). Also reports the treaty between England and France, specifying the restoration to the Queen of her confessor and household, and permission for English Catholic exiles to return to their estates.

[1630]. *Relacion del grandioso recibimiento y hospedaje que por orden del Excmo Conde Duque se hizo en la ciudad de Sevilla a su Exca el Sr D.Francisco Continton* [Cottington] *embaxador del Srmo Rey de la Gran Bretaña.* n.p.d. (RAH PJ 109). Fol.bifol.
Describes the lavish reception given at Seville to Sir Francis Cottington and his retinue of eighty, whose tour of the city included a visit to St Gregory's. The gifts heaped upon the visitors included two paintings, by Tintoretto and Bassano, and marble busts of Brutus and Cassius from Cartagena.

1642. *Relacion verdadera de la insigne victoria* [at Knockfergus] *que los catolicos del reyno de Irlanda obtuvieron contra los ingleses que no son catolicos romanos. Dase cuenta del estado de la religion catolica en la Gran Bretaña.* Sevilla: Juan Gomez de Blas. (RAH PJ 90/42).
Mentions the martyrdoms in 1641 of an old priest [Blessed Richard Reynolds, *vere* Green, an alumnus of ECS] and a Benedictine [St Ambrose Barlow].

1642. *Manifiesto de los catolicos confederados de Irlanda a su legitimo senõr el rey Carlos en orden a dar algun medio para la pacificacion. Impresso en lengua inglesa en Dublin año de 1642 y en Latin en Lorayna el mismo año, y del original Latino traducido en Romance.* Sevilla: Juan Gomez de Blas. Fol.bifol. (RAH PJ 90/46).

[c.1644]. *Breve proposicion de algunos de los motivos que ay para favorecer los seminarios ingleses y en particular este de San Gregorio de Sevilla.* n.p.d. (ARCR 1071.1).
The date can be reckoned by the fact that the number of students at ECS is stated to have been reduced to twelve.

1647. *Relacion verdadera de las felizes victorias que han obtenido los catholicos confederados de el Reyno de Irlanda contra los Ingleses y Escoseses. Dase quenta del presente estado de Inglaterra. Impresa en Irlanda en la ciudad de Kilkeni en lengua inglesa.* Sevilla: Juan Gomez de Blas. Fol.bifol. (Cordoba, Bibl.Mun.).

1648. *Memorial por parte del colegio ingles sobre la pretension que tiene de que la ciudad de Sevilla le continue la limosna que desde su fundacion le ha señalado.* n.p. (BCC 63-9-87, f.25; RAH PJ 91/44;GU A 31-127).

1657. *Relacion de los nuevos decretos que el tiranisimo Cromvel ha hecho en Irlanda . . . con copia de una carta escrita al Reverendissimo Padre General del Orden de San Francisco por los Padres que han sido Provinciales de Irlanda.* Granada: Francisco Sanchez. (GU A 31–135).

1670. *Relacion de los trabajos que padecieron los catolicos en Inglaterra en 1670.* (In SU catalogue, but missing).

8. EXTRACTS FROM THE ANNUAL LETTERS

News about St Gregory's is to be found in the section relating to the Andalusian province in the published *Annuae Litterae Societatis Iesu* for the years 1593 (pp.318-20), 1594-5 (p.570-73), 1596 (pp.474-77), 1597 (pp.401-6), 1598 (pp.499-502), 1600 (pp.241-42), 1601 (pp.273-75), 1602 (pp.194-5), 1603 (pp.173-4), 1604 (p.204), 1605 (pp.297-300), 1606 (p.165), 1607 (pp.131-33), 1608 (pp.849-51), 1611 (pp.724-5), 1612 (p.49), 1613-14 (pp.645-46). However, these are extracted from the manuscript *Litterae Annuae*, which extend over a longer period and contain additional information. The selection of the latter that follows is taken from ARSI Baet.19/1 (Litterae Annuae Provinciae Baeticae, 1592-1617), 19/2 (1624-1639), 20/1 (1640-89) and 20/2. After about 1650 the information about St Gregory's in the Annual Letters is minimal, and I have taken information on the number of students during this period from the catalogues of the province (see p.106). The extracts are translated, but I have given the original Latin where it is of interest or relevance. The number of students is given in brackets after each year.

1592 (40).

1593 (almost 50). 3 Englishmen entered S.J., one a priest [Richard Walpole].

1594 (45). Death of a priest who accompanied six boys from England [William Ball]. Impression made by the students in Seville: 'When they have to go out in public they walk two by two, in column and keeping time, with downcast eyes and with such modesty and impression of piety that passers-by stop to admire the spectacle and call down blessings upon them'.

1595 Death of 3 students: Robert Waller, Thomas Egerton, George Johnson. Abundance of alms from well-wishers. To celebrate the feast of St Hyacinth, a tragicomedy was performed in the presence of Cardinal de Castro, the Inquisitors, the Regent and the Asistente: *Anglia Lapsa Resurgens*, 'a history of the principal events in England during the reign of Queen Elizabeth'. The play was written in Latin by a student, based on an outline prepared by Fr Persons.

1596 (60). Four priests departed to England, two to Rome, and two with the Spanish fleet. Ten arrivals from England, including a 15-year old boy who escaped disguised as a merchant's servant. Six ordained priest. Christmas celebrations at the college attended by the *flos civitatis*: the Duke of Alcalá, the Marqués de Tarifa, the Conde de Priego, the Bishop of Cuzco and the Regente of Seville. The visitors admired the crib and after being entertained with music, speeches and poems toured the college and noted the simplicity of the accommodation.

1597 (70). 3 priests to England, 22 admissions. Death of Fr Richard Thorne at Sanlúcar, where the crowds at his funeral (paid for by the Duke of

Medina Sidonia) testified to the esteem in which he was held. His command of seven languages meant that he was in much demand among foreign visitors in the port.

Deaths of the Briant brothers and John Cooper, and of Henry Clifton, aged 16, whose father had been a 'praetor' in Lancashire and the lord of four towns.

Visits to the college by the Dukes of Medinaceli, Medina Sidonia and Alcalá, the Marqués de Villafranca, Don Pedro de Toledo (Admiral of the Neapolitan fleet) and the Conde de Puñonrostro.

1598 (58). Dedication of the college chapel on the feast of St Andrew (30 November), attended by the Inquisitors. Speech delivered by a student in praise of the Inquisition. Death of a student, Richard Levison. Three performances of a play attended by Cardinal de Castro, the Marqués de Tarifa, the Duke of Alcalá, etc [Tragicomedia de Cicilii calliditate qua tam altum dignitatis gradum ex obscura familia in Anglia sibi comparavit, cui titulus *Cicilius ἄθεος non Anglicanus* quoniam Cicilii varios casus et astus temporisque vicissitudines continebat—*Deleted*].

1600 (36). 4 priests to England. One alumnus died for the faith [Thomas Benstead].

1601 (61). A deacon died of the plague. The custom of taking the discipline adopted by the college, following the practice at the English College, Rome. 20 admissions, some of whom arrived on foot *via* France.

1602 Fathers called on by the Inquisition to examine and instruct foreign prisoners.

1603 Increased numbers. 22 arrivals from St Omer. 5 priests to England. William Richardson died for the faith in England.

1604 (40). Six priests to England.

1605 (40). Death of two fathers [Henry Tichborne and John Pole] and a Jesuit novice, Thomas Johnson. 15 arrivals from St Omer. 4 to England. Death of a priest alumnus in England shortly after his public defence of the faith.

1606 (35). Fathers frequently called to attend the tribunals of the Inquisition or employed 'in cleansing the poisonous books of heretics with the sponge of correction'.

1607 A priest on his way to England [John Ainsworth] captured in Spanish waters by an English 'archpirate'[1] who took him to Alarache but there treated him kindly and freed him. He then fell into the hands of 'Mahometans and Jews' who promised to deliver him safely to the nearby Spanish garrison while secretly intending to sell him to an African chief. With the help of the English pirate (from whom he extracted a promise to amend his life) he escaped to Seville and resumed his journey to England.

1608 (39). Fathers summoned by the Inquisition daily and sometimes for weeks at a time.

1609 (26). 4 priests to England, one [William Newman] to Lisbon to take charge of the residence there. 9 arrivals from St Omer. A painting of St Gregory [by Juan de Roelas] bought for 1000 aurei.

1610 (21). 4 students joined the Dominicans.

1611 (34).

1614 2 students joined the Benedictines [one was Anthony Bury].

1615 (25).

1616 (32). 14 arrivals from St Omer. 6 priests to England. 1 student priest [Edward Smith] joined O.S.B.

1617 (32). Foreigners flock to St Gregory's, where the fathers are much in demand to hear confessions in German, Flemish and French, as well as English, since there are over 4000 foreigners of these nationalities in Seville. The chapel is crowded on feast-days. Of 12 students completing the philosophy course, 5 joined the Society, one in the Toledo province, one in Andalusia and three in Flanders.

1618 (29).

1619 (20). 2 students joined the Society, 5 joined other religious orders.

1620 5 students joined religious orders.

1624 (31). 12 came from St Omer, of whom one died on the way and one in sight of Sanlúcar. Apostolic work continues among the English at Seville, but 'the harvest is not abundant': one convert, and four under instruction. Account of the sufferings of two alumni who sailed to England on a heretical ship. Their ordeal included being roasted and subjected to tobacco fumes ('fumo hyosquyami, *vulgo* tabaco').

1625 (31). Deaths of a student and of a priest about to go to England.

1626 (27). 8 arrived from St Omer to begin philosophy.

1630 Twenty youths from the island of St Kitts (San Cristobal) put in at Seville, 'where under our guidance they boarded the safer bark of the Roman faith'. 'Books of controversy distributed among the homes of English Catholics in order to be exhibited at places where the heretics gather, have brought a significant increase of Christian faith'.

1631 (27).

1632 (25). A painting of St Thomas of Canterbury [by Francisco de Herrera] bought for 300 aurei.

1634 2 priests to England. One alumnus joined S.J. in Spain, one in Flanders.

1636 (17).

1637 11 arrivals from St Omer. Participation by students in literary contests.

1638 (15). 4 priests to England.

1640 (20 students, including 6 priests). One student died, one [James Barton] went to Rome to join S.J.

1641 (20, including 7 priests). Death of Brother Diego Marin. 8 arrived from St Omer, and also a young man who after admission to a Cambridge college ('in sodalitium Collegii Cantabrigiensis . . . cooptatus'), 'which is there a high honour, growing weary of the errors of unquiet England, undertook a journey to our Spain out of curiosity, not knowing that he was being drawn thither by divine providence; for when he put in at the port of Sanlúcar he realised that he had been brought to knowledge of the truth, and therefore, on a change of heart and having forsworn heretical perfidy, he enlisted in the Catholic faith and in our college'.[2]

1643 (15)

1644 Deaths of Fr Henry Pollard and Br Richard Newport.

1645 (10). 2 priests to England.

1646 (17). 4 priests to England. Severe shortages in Seville, and heavy taxes.

1647 (12). 14 Jesuits on the staff.

1648 (9). 2 priests to England.

1652 (11).

1655 (6).

1660 (11).

1662 (5).

1665 (3).

1669 (6).

1671 14 students from St Omer.

1675 (10).

1680 (5).

1681 (6).

1685 (5).

1686 4 priests to England.

1688 (4).

1689 (1).

1728 (6, all priests).

1729 (7, all priests).

1741-2 (8, of whom 3 were priests).

Notes

1. This was probably one of the English pirates operating at this time from Mamorra, on the Atlantic coast of Morocco. Captain Henry Manwaring, a native of Cheshire, made this the base of a pirate fleet of some forty sail, in two squadrons, under Sir John Fearne and Captain Peter Croston. See G. N. Clark, 'Barbary Corsairs in the 17th century', *Cambridge Historical Journal* 8 (1945–6), p.28. The archpirate is less likely to have been the notorious Captain John Ward (see DNB), who operated from Tunis.

2. The Cambridge man is difficult to identify but may be John Travers (q.v.), whose father Samuel Travers was a Cambridge man. John entered St Gregory's as a convictor in June 1639 (S 19). He is not recorded by Venn as a Cambridge graduate, but two of his brothers, Thomas and Henry, were at Magdalene College. See S. Smith Travers, *A Pedigree, with Biographical Sketches, of the Devonshire Family of Travers* (Dublin, 1898). It is likely, therefore, that John intended to go to Magdalene, even if he never actually matriculated.

DOCUMENTS

Document 1. The Mission Oath [edited by Mgr Henson]

Two different forms of the mission oath survive. Oath A is that prescribed by the constitutions of the College, 1 April 1600, the original of which, signed and sealed by Cardinals Borghese and Farnese, is preserved in the College archives (S 1). The Seville oath and constitutions are identical with those of Valladolid (cf.CRS 30/252). This oath was amended under Urban VIII, by a decree of the S.C. de Propaganda Fide dated 19 September 1625, to include a new clause stipulating renunciation of the right to enter a religious order (cf.CRS 10/242,409). This amended oath was later reimposed with some variations under Alexander VII, by a decree of Propaganda dated 20 July 1660 (cf.Knox, *Douay Diaries*, p.47). However there is no evidence that the amended oaths of Urban VIII or of Alexander VII were ever used either at Seville or Valladolid.

Oath B was used at Seville indiscriminately with the constitution oath. It was introduced before 1613, no doubt as the result of some internal unrest at the college. An analysis of the oaths preserved in the college archives (S XVII, B/67/1–37) is given below. The dates marked with an asterisk are those when Oath B was used. The constitution Oath A was used in the other years.

1660 (5)	*c.1686 (1)
c.1662 (1)	*c.1687 (2)
c.1663 (1)	*c.1712 (1)
*1667 (1)	1713 (1)
1672 (9)	1720 (2)
*c.1673 (1)	*1721 (1)
*c.1681 (1)	1725 (3)
*c.1683 (1)	1766 (4)
	undated (1)

Oath A: (S XVII, B/67/13)

Ego Joannes Langleus Collegii Anglorum Hispalensis alumnus considerans divina erga me beneficia, et illud in primis quo me ex patria heresi laboranti duxit, et Ecclesiae suae Catholicae membrum effecit, cupiensque tantae Dei misericordiae non penitus me ingratum praebere, statui me totum divino ejus famulatui, in quantum possum, pro fine hujus Collegii exequendo offerre, et promitto juroque Omnipotenti Deo me paratum esse animo, ac futurum semper, quantum divina ejus gratia me adiuverit, ut suo tempore sacros ordines suscipiam, et in Angliam ad proximorum animas lucrandas revertar, quandocumque Superiori hujus Collegii pro sui instituti ratione mihi praecipere visum fuerit in Domino. Interim vero dum hic vivo, promitto me quiete et pacifice victurum, et Collegii institutiones regulasque pro meo virili observaturum.

Januarii 4o, 1660   Joannes Langleus

Translation

I, John Langley, an alumnus of the English College, Seville, considering the benefits I have received from God, and particularly that he has brought me out of my country, oppressed by heresy, and made me a member of his Catholic Church; and wishing to show myself not altogether ungrateful for so many of God's mercies, have resolved to offer myself completely, in so far as in me lies, to his divine service in fulfilment of the purpose intended for this College; and I promise and swear to almighty God that I am, and always will be, ready with the help of his divine grace to receive Holy Orders in due time and to return to England to win my neighbours' souls whensoever the Superior of this College, in accordance with his office, shall see fit to order me to do so. Meanwhile so long as I live here, I promise to conduct myself in peace and quiet and to observe the customs and rules of the College to my utmost ability.

Oath B (S XVII, B/67/27)

Ego Paulus Savagius coram beatissima Virgine Maria cujus in dote Anglia est, et coram gloriosissimo martyre Sancto Thoma Cantuariensi Archiepiscopo Angliae Primate, et coram tota curia caelesti: promitto juroque Omnipotenti Deo me hujus Hispalensis Divi Gregorii Collegii Rectori sic obediturum, ut suo tempore sacros ordines suscipiam: et in Angliam ad proximorum animas lucrandas revertar. Interim vero dum hic vivo promitto me quiete ac pacifice victurum et Collegii constitutiones regulasque pro meo virili observaturum. Item promitto ac juro quod quamdiu in Collegio hoc vel alio seminario victurus sum, nihil agam aut moliar sponte ac de industria neque aliis persuadere nitar quod ad pacem Collegii vel disciplinae domesticae observantiam perturbandam pertineat. A cujus immensa bonitate et clementia peto suppliciter ut hanc meam oblationem admittere dignetur: et ut largitus est ad hoc desiderandum et offerendum, sic etiam ad explendum gratiam uberem largiatur. Amen.

Die 20 Aprilis anno Domini 1687   Paulus Savagius

Translation:

I, Paul Savage, in the presence of the most blessed Virgin Mary, who has England for her dowry, and the most glorious martyr St Thomas, Archbishop of Canterbury and Primate of England, and all the court of heaven, promise and swear to almighty God so to obey the Rector of this, the College of St Gregory, that in his time I will receive holy orders and return to England to win my neighbours' souls. Meanwhile, so long as I live here I promise to do so peacefully and quietly and to observe the customs and rules of the College to the utmost of my ability. I also promise and swear that as long as I live in the College I will not voluntarily or of set purpose do or devise, or endeavour to persuade others to do or devise anything that might tend to disturb the peace of the College or the observance of the discipline of the house.

I humbly beseech his immense goodness and mercy that he condescend to accept this my offering: and as he has granted me the desire, so may he grant me abundant grace of fulfilment.

20 April 1687   Paul Savage

Document 2. A Scotsman before the Inquisition, 1594

The Jesuit Pedro de León ministered to the inmates of the Seville prison for nearly forty years (1578–1616), and at the request of his superiors wrote, at the end of his life, an account of his experiences there. In his record of the year 1594, de León records his tireless efforts to reconcile a Scotsman, Jaime Bolen (?James Bullen) from burning by the Inquisition. A priest from the English College, Father John Sparchford, acted as his assistant and interpreter. While not questioning the principles and methods of the Inquisition, de León reveals something of the tensions between the Jesuits and the older religious orders—Augustinians, Franciscans, Dominicans—who normally attended those tried before the tribunal.

What follows is a translation of the relevant passage from a modern edition of selections from de León's unpublished memoirs: *Grandeza y miseria en Andalucía*, by Pedro Herrera Puga, S.J. (Granada, 1981), pp.490–95.

For this auto they brought out Jaime Bolen, a Scot and a most pertinacious heretic. It was impossible to reason with him, for he was obtuse, coarse and brutish, as well as obstinately attached to his accursed sect, to which he had belonged since childhood. His Lutheranism was unshakeable. My lords the Inquisitors requested that one of the priests from the English seminary should accompany me to the prison to act as interpreter, and this was Father John Sponsfors [Sparchford], now a martyr in England. In fact the prisoner had a reasonable knowledge of Spanish, having spent five years in the castle[1] in the company of Spaniards, for the prisoners there are not held in solitary confinement but are put with others who are held for different offences.

So the two of us went and . . . they released the prisoner to us. We were accompanied by many officers of the Holy Inquisition and their assistants and by the chief Constable of the Inquisition, Don Juan de Saavedra. They were there partly out of curiosity to see the man, who was said to be like a savage, and partly because they knew he was extremely violent and so ordered all these people to accompany us in order to manacle him for our safety. Though he was restricted by a brace and loaded with chains, the Inquisitors were extremely concerned lest any harm should befall us, for all his chains had not prevented him from doing great violence to those who brought him his food. So to make doubly sure of our safety, they ordered that some of their lay officials should keep special watch over us, in addition to the normal watch which is kept inside the castle every night of the *auto*.

So the two of us were left alone with him. When the secretary told him officially that he was due to die the following day, he flew into a rage and in spite of all his chains gave such a leap that his head hit the ceiling of the cell. It was terrifying to see him in such a passion, for throughout the five years of his imprisonment he had refused to have his hair or beard cut. He was like a savage, and let out a stream of blasphemies. 'Five years they keep me in castle', he shouted, 'then I get confessed and burned in one night!' There was no way we could talk to him or make him listen to reason. It was like being with a lion in his cage. We tried to pacify and comfort him, I in Spanish and Father Sparchford in English, but he would have none of it. We gave him something to eat with our own hands, for his were manacled, but he never stopped raving. Thus we passed the whole night. He did not sleep, nor did we. Several times we begged him to get some rest, but it was useless.

Day dawned, and my lords the Inquisitors asked us how it had gone, although they had already been told by our bodyguard. They commiserated with us for the bad night we had spent—and all the more as the man had not been reconciled. We said our masses, and one of us stayed with him in the interval. They provided a meal for all the penitents and ourselves. Thereupon they began to form the procession, consisting of ourselves and the penitents, with our man bringing up the rear as being the most stubborn heretic, bearing his insignia of devils.[2]

We emerged from the castle, and if he had not been constricted by a brace he would surely have laid hold of someone and seized his sword and caused havoc or even bloodshed. Even so he elbowed and shoved those of us who were around him, pushing us from one side to the other. When the crowd surged around him at the Puerta de la Mar, he frightened them and us into keeping our distance and standing well clear.

We reached the scaffold with great difficulty, not so much because of the enormous crush of people which gathers on such occasions as on account of this man's devilish violence. We stood by while the sentences of the condemned were read out, and from time to time either I or my companion would say something to try to win him over. Among the many arguments which God gave us, the one which first opened his eyes was when I said: 'Look, Jaime, all of us in this square and in this city and kingdom are on one road, whereas you alone are set on this other way followed only by yourself and some others of your country—and that only within the last sixty or seventy years. Is it possible that all those people in past centuries who did not take this road of yours—which had not yet been discovered by your apostate and his like—were lost? What about all the thousands of saints who have taken our road since the Church began? Were they in error? Or is it only this rabble of innkeepers, tapsters and low, unlettered folk who are in the right? My son, see how that fellow-countryman of yours whom they arrested for the same reason as yourself has been converted and has abandoned his wicked way, and how we and the holy Roman church, our Mother, have given him instruction, and how my lords the Inquisitors have taken pity on him and received and reconciled him with our Mother the holy Roman Catholic Church, bringing him out in the garb of a penitent and taking away the placard that hung around his neck and the other trappings of a condemned man'.

Our Lord be praised, though I had been talking to him the whole night and the whole day until three in the afternoon without making the slightest impression, this reasoning at last had its effect, and Our Lord opened his eyes and ears which until then he had kept sealed. He asked us to teach him this way of the holy Catholic faith, saying that no-one in all his life had ever taught him anything of what I had said, and that as he had been brought up from childhood in those teachings he knew nothing of these others of the holy Faith, and that he was ready to be instructed. And when I questioned him on all the points which he had stubbornly refused to concede, one by one, and catechised him on each, he admitted his error, and when asked if he wished to confess he said he did, in awareness that this was a sacrament. He and I went down to a small balcony below the penitents' seats, and there I began to hear his confession, intending to finish it after my lords the Inquisitors had reconciled him and absolved him from excommunication.

We returned to our seats, and there we found one of the Inquisitors who was taking statements from some Portuguese women who had declined to confess.[3] It was evident that God had brought him there more for our Jaime's sake than for theirs. After he had taken the man's statement and mine about his conversion, confirmed by my companion, the lord Inquisitor returned to his tribunal. Thereupon his colleagues and their censors and advisers were put in a great dilemma, mainly because this man had said that he had never been instructed in our faith and had known no other than that which his parents had taught him, and that he wanted to be instructed in the true faith. For that reason the *auto* was adjourned and the sentences were not passed. They retired within the council chamber to debate the matter, and after about an hour emerged with their decision. After they had filed out they proceeded to read the sentences, but Jaime Bolen's sentence was not included. The *auto* was then concluded with the customary solemn absolution, to a note given by the organ, and with the handing over of those condemned to the secular arm. They ordered Jaime Bolen to return to the castle along with the others who had been reconciled, so that his case might be reviewed. With that, our task was finished: we went back to our house, and they to the castle.

After ten or twelve days my lords the Inquisitors summoned my companion and myself to testify as to what had occurred while we were with this man, with particular reference to the crucial issue of his conversion. This each of us did individually, saying that his conversion had seemed to us genuine and not prompted merely by fear of death, if for no other reason that while he was pertinacious he was wild and violent, whereas on being converted his expression became calm, joyful, mild, humble, and as soft as silk. This had struck all the bystanders, who remarked on it to each other: 'See how his appearance has changed from when he was incorrigible!' There were enough witnesses to suggest that the conversion had been genuine. The other point was that the man never thought that his conversion would save him from death, for it was noticeable that when he realised he was not going to have to die that day, he looked no more joyful after hearing the news than before.

I only wish that had been the end of the story, and that the poor man had met his final end in as good a state as on that day when he showed unquestionable signs of salvation. But however many times a man may be put in a state of grace, he does not, like the angels, remain fixed and confirmed in that state, as we know, but is liable to change from one moment to the next, being endowed with free will. So it was with this wretched man. A few days later he tried to kill the governor of the castle and bit and maimed him, causing I know not how many other injuries in the prison. To conclude his lamentable and tragic story, as a final result of all his crimes he was brought out for a subsequent *auto*, far more defiant and savage than on the previous occasion, and in this state he was burned alive.

This time the Inquisitors did not call us, saying that they had to meet their obligations to the older religious orders and that there were already enough condemned persons for us to look after. But it was common talk throughout Seville at the time that if the man had been put in the charge of the same fathers as before he would have been converted by their good efforts as he had been on the previous occasion. God alone knows, and his judgments are known only to him, to whom be glory in all things. They burned him alive. Some Augustinian fathers were with him.[4]

Notes

1. The Castillo de Triana, where the Inquisition had its offices and prison.
2. Those sentenced to be 'relaxed' (i.e. handed over to the secular authorities for execution) wore a black penitential garment (*sambenito*) on which were painted devils, flames and similar insignia. The *auto* itself was probably held in the Plaza de San Francisco, the city's main square.
3. *Negativas*, i.e. those who refused to confess or to testify against themselves.
4. Jaime Bolen was burned at the *auto* of 1597. The historian of the Andalusian Province, Juan Santibañez, writing for the benefit of his fellow-Jesuits some years later, remembered the deep impression the event made on the Seville public, such was the raging defiance with which the Scotsman met his end. Evidence of the existence of a heterodox underground is implicit in his interesting observation that 'those of his sort regarded and still regard him as a glorious martyr', and that 'there were some heretics of his sect in Seville who came to the place of burning early the following morning looking for relics of their martyr. But they paid for their devotion by being arrested and punished by the officials of the Inquisition' (*Historia de la Provincia de Andalucía de la Compañía de Jesús*, Parte 2a, Libro 3o, chapter 59).

Document 3. Henry Piers: An Anglo-Irishman at Seville, 1597-8

Henry Piers (1568–1623), of Tristernagh, Co.Meath, was the son of William Piers, Constable of Carrickfergus. He was married to Jane, the daughter of Thomas Jones, Archbishop of Dublin and Chancellor of Ireland, a prelate noted for his severe treatment of recusants in Ireland. Though his parents and his wife were Protestants, his sister Mary was married to a Catholic alderman of Dublin. By the time Henry left Ireland in 1595 his Catholic sympathies had, he wrote, 'bred dislike in my greatest friends of me'. His destination was Rome, where he made a prolonged stay at the English College and recorded his visits to the city's churches and shrines. He returned via Spain, where he spent six months (1597–8) at St Gregory's, studying metaphysics. He returned to Ireland in 1598, and seven years later (1605) wrote *A Discourse of His Travels*, now preserved among the Rawlinson MSS in the Bodleian Library (Rawlinson D83). The work is dedicated to Richard Haydock, sometime Dean of Dublin (Ans.1/159–60). 'One reason moving me thereunto', the author wrote, 'was to show my thankful mind towards you, for that as an immediate instrument under God of my happiness, you did place me in the English College in Rome, where I gained great store of spiritual treasure'.

The account of Piers in the *Dictionary of National Biography*, written by Sir John Gilbert, is largely based on memoirs of the Piers family collected by Henry Ware, the grandson of Sir James Ware (National Library of Ireland MS 2563). Henry Piers' son James (fl.1635) was a priest and doctor of divinity, who taught philosophy at the Irish College, Bordeaux.

The section of Piers' *Discourse* which relates to his stay in Seville is reproduced below by kind permission of the Bodleian Library. I have had the advantage of being able to use the transcript made by the late Mr Thomas Frank, who edited the MS for a B.Litt.thesis in 1954. As well as providing a valuable first-hand account of St Gregory's in its earliest years, the *Discourse* illustrates the dangers to which English and Irishmen were liable at Seville at this time.

[p.205] The xviijth day to the Ritche Cittie of Civill, there I was intertainede verie kindly by Father walpoule, a graue and learned Jesuit, and was admitted as Convictor in the Englishe Colledge there. where I studied methaphisicke for the space of half a yeere, and went in priestes aparrell. at my Comminge thether there was a merchant of Galwaye named Richard Skernett whose godds were seased vpon to the Kinges vse, for the same Cause that those merchaunts of Dublin and waterfford (as before I named) were trobled, but vpon my intreatie Father walpoole soe vsed the matter with the Regent of Civill, as he was Restored to his owne and about the same tyme one valentine blake a merchant of the same towne had his Shipp and

goods confiscated to the Kings vse and himself Committed to prison, where he endured a longe tyme to his great chardge and hinderance these and many other the licke percedents (which might be named) beinge Considered doe prove evidentlie that the merchants of Irelande which trafficke for Spaine were then in a verie
[p.206] harde Case, for there, they weare, for / the moste parte suspected of heresie, and reputed for spies. heere in Ireland vexed and ill thought of for beinge papistes, and mistrusted as intelligencers for the Spaniardes.

Civill is the welthieste Cittie of all Spaine there the Kinge hathe a mente house wherein is coyned Dailie when they Doe worcke one hundred thousande Duckettes at leaste, This Coyninge house is not far from the Kinges Pallace, which is verie faire and lardge, nighe vnto which is in buildinge an exchange house of Stone verie spatious and Costlye, and adioyninge almoste vnto the same is the Cathedrall Churche which in greatnes Dothe everie way excell that of Tolledo, in itt as is Constantly affirmed, is a picture of oure blessed lady which was made by Angells and in the Chappell where this picture is placed lie three Kinges of Spaine interred. in the Chappell of our lady Called Antiqua is an antient picture of the blessed virgin, before which are Continvally burninge fiftie Silver lampes of Divers greatnes, there is another Chappell wherein there Relickes are kepte with wonderfull Reverence, amongst which is the heade of Saint Leander and an arme of St.Bartholomewe ye apostle Ritchly sett in
[p.207] Silver and golde as the Reste are, this Churche is exceedingly well / served, as well in Respecte of there musicke as alsoe in Regarde of stately Ceremonies and sumptuous Churche stuffe, The archbusshopp of Civill is Comonly a Cardinall, his revenues Doethe amounte at least to one hundred and fiftie 1000 Duckettes yeerely, the Dignities and Cannonries are verie good and great some of them amountinge to eight thowsande Ducketts by the yeere, there are noe lesse then five hundred masses Daily saide in it. In Civill is a Churche of Saint Fraunces which hathe a Cloister wherein is Curiously painted his liffe, with the pictures and names of soe many Kinges and noble men as haue been of that order, there is also in Civill a picture of our blissed lady Called Devalia which hathe Done great myracles besides many other Churches monestaries and Colleadges. The river which Runethe by itt sometymes Dothe soe ouer flowe his banckes as it Drownethe muche land and a great part of the Cittie, in this Common wealthe as also in all Spaine, the Kinge hathe paied vnto his Cofers the tenthe peny of all suche Comodities as are bought or sold, which amountethe to an infinitt som of mony by the yeere. the government of Civill for cheefeste matters of warre or busines of state is managed by an assistant soe named who is of
[p.208] great worth & reputation. for the Kinges / excheates and hearinge of many other Causes is a Regent and a Courte of avdentia, for the Kinges revenues and matters of treason against his majestie the

house of Contractation, for enquire of heresie and punishinge of heretickes, the holy house of inquisition, For Desydinge matters of lesse importance are fowre and twenty in maner of Aldermen Called the vintie quators.

The xijth Day of September I went to a fayre which was [in] a towne Called Entrero[1] five leages from Civill where is a picture of our lady, which Dothe great myracles, and iorniead backe againe thether on the 14 of the same, in the Almeda of that cittie stande two pillers which are certainly affirmed to be those which in olde tyme were Called Hercules pillers vpon which are written *non plus ultra*. In the suburb therof is an hospitall *Desangre* soe Called only for women, verie fayere and lardge, the Revenues thereof Come to 1400 Ducketts by the yeere, at my beinge in Civill there was in makinge a hearse for the Kinge lately Deseaced of wonderfull Coste and worckmanshipp, beinge builded with three heights Reachinge to the topp of ye Cathedrall Church in the higheste height was sett forthe the orders of Spaine, in the Seconde the Kinges proper heirs, and in the theerde his fowre wives statues with many other pictures and Rare imagerie of Divers sortes it was thought that it woulde Coste eare it were finished aboue 24000 Duckettes and ye artificers wadges [p.209] would Come to no less then 1500, / the wax Candles and tapers which sett it out Coulde be noe fewer then three thowsande,[2] when the Kinge Died all those which weare able Did mourne in black as well strangers as others, vpon my Departure from the College I changed my self vnto lay apparell, and one the verie same Daye one Capten Hawkins an Englishe gent. which had bene longe prisoner in Civill Did finde meanes to escape, and for that I did vse in my other attyre to visitte Mr.Blake which laie in the same prison I was suspected to be accessorie vnto his Departure and for as muche as I was then vpon my Cominge for Irelande I bought som wyne fruite and bankettinge stuffe, with entent therewith to paie my waye vnto the Fathers and Scollers of the Colleadge, which at that Daye weare Recreatinge themselves in ther venyarde nighe adioyninge vnto the Cittie, and soe passinge with this provision throwe the streates accompanied with Certaine gent. of this Contrie, it was thought that I wente to releave Hawkins, and therevpon I was apprehended by an officer and Carried to the house of Contractation, where I was imprisoned and examyned, vpon the which examynation, notwith-standinge my inocency, I was sent to the Rackinge house and had bene Racked the next day in the morning, had not Capten Hawkins that night beene founde, whom they which persued him overtook in a venyard som two leages from Civill,[3] This Hawkins had before [p.210] that tyme / bene taken by the Spaniardes at sea and was Converted and Reconsiled in the prison wherin he laye (by Father Richard Wallpoll) whoe in his nede lente him som two hundred Crownes the which he himself Confessed when he was examyned Concerninge me. wherevpon the iudges Did mistruste that he Did sett Downe the plotte for Hawkins his escape to the ende that thereby the Englishe Jesuits might get the greater favor in Englande [*supposinge that I was his instrument for effecting that busines*] but after theie had fully examyned Capten hawkins vpon his Returne, and with exacte Diligence loked into the matter vnderstanding as well by Father Wallpoll as by Divers others of the maner of my behaviour and the places of my Residence sithence my Dep*a*rture from Ireland, theie at lenght founde me Cleere of the Cryme w*h*ich was laid to my chardge and Delivered me out of prison But I muste Confesse that these presumptions being soe many and pregnant Did give them great occation to Condemne me.

wee maye by this accidente and suche others of that nature consider howe Carefull and sircumspecte iudges ought to be in ther p*r*oceedinges espetiallie when theye sitt for matter of life and Deathe, for somtymes the inocent man is putt awaye by means of suspitious licklyhoods and often it fallethe oute, that moste wicked offenders are served by Craftie sleights and Deceetfull practises.

Aboute the same tyme I hearde from Irelande of the Deathe of [p.211] Divers of my frend*e*s and of / the burninge wastinge and prayinge of my land, these casuall mischaunces concurringe together were great Crosses vnto me, yet did I as patiently as I coulde endure them, knowinge that my sins had Deserued greater punishments then these were. In Civill the Jesuits haue a good Colledge where they doe vse to Reade Divinitie and Philosophie theie haue also there a profeste house w*h*ich is verie faire and Ritchlie adornede, but the greateste Coste is bestowed vpon the Churche, the w*h*ich is Curiously made and furnished exceedinge Costlye nighe vnto the Colledge of the Jesuits is a fayere Pallace belonginge vnto the Duke of medena, Scidonia, adioyninge vnto the w*h*ich standethe the Englishe Colledge, the w*h*ich was builded as I p*a*rtely touched befor, by the meanes of Father parsons whoe procured Divers as well noblemen as others to Contribute to the settinge vp of the same, but the greateste benefactor to the Englishe there was a widdowe in Civill, which gave vnto Father parsons for makinge vp [of] a Churche for the Colledge (wherein Shee himself shoulde be buried and Daily praied for), the som of forteene thowsand Crownes, and after the Churche was builded w*h*ich was finished at my beinge there, she bestowed three thowsande Crownes for makings of Churche stuffe [p.212] for the same, Right before the highe altar is hir buriall / place, vnder the w*h*ich is a vaute w*h*ich is Couered w*i*th a verie fayre tombe stone, wherein is ingraven hir name and armes,[4] the Colledge hathe in it som twentye Chambers, a verie fayre hale and Divers howses of office requisite for suche a building, I haue harde Father parsons saye that the Daye before that this great som of 14 thowsande Crownes was bestowed (as before is Resited) there came to enquire for him (he beinge then at the Duke of medena Sidonia his house) a poore widdowe, w*h*ich had earnestly sought for him w*i*th whom

when he had talked shee protested vnto him that the Cause whye
shee Came to speake to him [was] for that shee harde the prieste of
ye parishe wherein shee Dwelled, exortinge of his parishoners to
extende there beste helpe towardes the settinge vp of a Colledge for
the Englishe nation, affirminge howe meritorious a thinge it weare
to gyve meanes of maintenance vnto suche laborers as shoulde
worcke in Englande, for ye purginge and Rootinge out of suche
weedes of heresie as weare growen in it, by Reason of the innyquite
of these later tymes, and therefor imitatinge the poore widdowe
spoken of in the Scriptur shee presented him with a shillinge the
which Father parsons verie thanckfully Receaved not Doubtinge but
that god which Did move that poore woman to yelde hir benevol-
ence accordinge hir smale abbillitie, woulde also moue greater
persons to bestowe franckly accordinge to there welthe and sub-
stance the which answerably vnto his expectation was the next Day
[p.213] after performed by the Ritche / widdowe, which before I made
mention of, this Colleadge maye finde three score Schollers besides
there teachears and servants,

From the tyme of my Departure out of the Colledge vntill that I
was Ready to take my Jorney for Ireland I laie at a Frenche mans
house nighe vnto the great Churche of the Cittie and Did happen
then to be exercised with more trouble, for I was suddenly areasted
in my hoste is house by two officers which Carried me to the Regent
of Civill, whoe was informed that I Determyned to Carrye awaye an
Englishe youthe which was his page into Ireland. And therevpon
sente me to prison, Commandinge that I shoulde be well loaden with
Irons. at the which tyme I Deliuered vnto him my pasports which I
brought from Rome, the which after he had perused he sente backe
againe for me and toulde [me] that he perceaved by those writtinges
that I was a good Christian and therefor perswaded himself that I
was wrongfully accused, but before he had vewed those certificattes
of my behavior he did mistruste that I was a Lutheran or [of] som
other newe secte and that my intente of the supposed takinge awaye
of his Servante was to perverte him in Religion, and soe beinge fully
satisfied of me, he gaue me verie good wordes and Cryed me mercy
for that he [had] vsed me soe hardly, assuringe me that from that
tyme fourthe he woulde stande my good frende to the utermoste of
his power and therewithall he verie Corteously Dismissed me.

I departed from Civill [on] the xxvijth of October by barke
[p.214] passinge harde by Careo,[5] where there / is searche made of all which
passe for prohibited ware, and landed at Saint Lucars the xxixth of
the same, this towne belongethe to the Duke of medena Sidonia it is
in the mouthe of the Riuer of Civill. the Duke his Revenue amounts
as I was informed to three hundred 1000 Duckettes yeerly, there is a
Residence for Englishe pristes whose Churche there is Dedicated to
Saint George.

The xxxth Daye to herrishe,[6] vpon the land of this Cittie the beste wynes in Spaine are made, there I mett with Sabastine Fleming a merchant of Drogheda which lente me mony for Dischardginge of my Debts in the Colleadge and furnished me for my passadge into Irelande I was by him verie frendlye and kindely vsed, The second Daye of Nouember I went backe againe to Saint Lucas.

The fourthe I tooke horse for Civill in my trauell I was benighted and was fayne to lye in a fearm house, of one of the Ritche merchants of Civill I did obserue the allowance of meate gyven vnto his plowmen, which was only breade oyle and garlicke, and there Drincke water, they Did Cooke there meate in this sorte followinge, firste they boyled som water then they brake there breade into small peeces, and putt it into great boules and scalled it, there breade beinge soaken they Caste oute the Remainder of the water and sprinckled oyle vpon it minglinge the same, with good stoore of garlicke, and eate the same, with spownes,[7] there wadges as they tolde me was ix d str. a day, The Bailiffe of that place gaue me parte [p.215] of his meate, and his bedd for that / night which was verie homely,

The vjth Daye I wente to Civill where I paied my Debtes and tooke my leaue of my frendes there,

The xth I Departed from thence and tooke horse for hereeshe and laie at one Mr.Flather, his house an Englishman which had longe tyme Dwelled there,

The xvth Daye we Did Ride from thence to St.*maria* Porte,[8] there I mett with Capten Cripes an Englishe gent. which vsed me verie kindely, and gaue me a faire bloodstone,

The xxiijth we wente by boate to Cales,[9] which Cittie som yeere and a half before that tyme had bene sacked by the Earle of Essex, the inhabitantes of Cales Did Cale him an honnorable enemye, for at his beinge there he suffred all the ladyes gentlwomen Nunnes and Religious men to goe out of the Cittie, vntouched with as much welthe as they Coulde Carrye about them,

The xxviijth of nouember wee tooke Shippinge for Ireland in a Frenche vessell Called the litle Delphine of St.maloes the which Sabastin Fleminge had fraighted, and ladded hir with wynes, after we weare a shipboard, it was my happ not to Departe without more trouble, for an officer of Cales borded vs and woulde haue areasted me affirminge that I was an Englishman and a spie, and althoughe I had there a sufficient testimonye of my behaviour and Contrey yet was I fayne to Recompence his paines, and to speake fayere while my head was in ye lyons mouthe./

Notes

1. Utrera, 9 miles from Seville. There was an annual *fiesta* there on 8 September in honour of Our Lady of Consolation whose image was venerated in the Convento de los Minimos.

2. Philip II had died on 13 September 1598. What Piers saw being erected in the Cathedral was the colossal and hubristic 'monument' designed by the city's leading architect Juan de Oviedo and decorated with sculptures by Martínez Montañés. When the funeral ceremonies finally began on 24 November there was a public scandal when the representatives of the Inquisition and members of the local judiciary quarrelled over precedence. The mass was interrupted and the exequies were not resumed until the end of the following month. Cervantes voiced the popular derision in a sonnet which mocked the vaingloriousness of the 'famous structure'.

3. Richard Hawkins, the son of Sir John, had been captured off Peru in 1594 and held at Lima. In 1597 he was transferred to prison in Seville. After his escape and recapture in September 1598, related here by Piers, he was moved to Madrid in 1599 but released three years later. For Hawkins' own account of these events, see his letter to the Earl of Essex in HMC Salisbury 8, pp.289–91.

4. Doña Ana de Espinosa, widow of Don Alonso Flores Quiñones, Captain-General of the Fleet of the Indies. Her tombstone does not survive. See Appendix, p.199.

5. Coria.

6. Jerez.

7. Gazpacho, once the staple diet of Spanish 'ploughmen', now an international delicacy.

8. Puerto de Santa María.

9. Cádiz.

Document 4. [Francisco de Peralta]. Some reasons why the English seminary at Seville is no burden to the Province, but rather to its advantage, honour and good repute [1604].

The MS reproduced and translated below is in Book XVII in the Seville archive at ECV. It may be dated by internal evidence to c.1604[1] and can be attributed with some certainty to Francisco de Peralta, then Rector of the College and deeply committed to its cause. It was written to counter criticisms from some Jesuits at Seville (see p.7) that the College was a foreign body which was diverting benefactions away from the Professed House. Peralta's aim was to vindicate the College and to show how the Andalusian Province derived kudos and advantage from it. The document also shows the extent to which the English fathers at St Gregory's were involved in pastoral work among foreigners of many nationalities at Seville. The Spanish text is given first, followed by a translation on p.152.

Summa de algunas razones que pruevan que el Seminario Ingles de Sevilla no es cargoso a la provincia sino provechoso y de honra y reputacion.

1. Ayuda a los ministerios muy proprios de la Compañia dentro de Sevilla y en los puertos del Andalucia como se vera, a que no pudieran acudir los padres naturales de la provincia por falta de la lengua, por que los tres padres ingleses que hoy ay aqui pueden confessar y predicar en 6 o 7 y de ordinario acuden al seminario a confessar gran numero (y mucho mayor en la quaresma) de Franceses, Valones, Ingleses, Escoceses, Irlandeses, Flamencos, Italianos, y muy a menudo acuden los padres (y a vezes ayudan los alumnos) a las carceles, galeras y hospitales, a catechizarles, hazerles platicas, confessarles, y ayudarles a bien morir, con gran edificacion de los que lo ven, y mayor provecho de sus almas, y a menudo se reducen algunos herejes, y algun año han pasado de 150 y mucho de ellos de buena capacidad y entendimientos y hecho confessiones generales de toda su vida, de los quales algunos han muerto con gran dolor de sus peccados y vida pasada, y otros han perseverado en nuestra santa religion y los que de cerca tocan esto ven el fruto que se haze, y los que se han ganado que al parecer se hallavan sin otro recurso ni remedio; y lo que esta provincia gana de reputacion en tener quien acuda a cosa tan propria de su instituto, y a que mas en particular fue llamada de Dios nuestro Señor. Solo dire dos cosas de muchas que pudiera. La primera que en la carcel real de esta ciudad ay algunos capitanes y soldados Ingleses presos, los quales (y otros que han muerto Catholicos y recibido los sacramentos) quando entraron eran herejes, y todos se han reducido, y algunos ay tan aprovechados el dia de oy que cada dia tienen tres horas de oracion mental de rodillas y leccion espiritual, y el cura de la carcel dize que son el exemplo de todos los que alli ay. Y a ellos y a otros de la nacion se les han dado algunos libros espirituales que ha compuesto el

Padre Personio con que mucho se han aprovechado. Y para ellos y otros de la nacion ha traducido un Padre desta casa en su lengua un catechismo, y modo de confessar y otros tratados pios, y un methodo y direccion para tratar con los herejes quando vayan a su tierra, de modo que no sean de ellos pervertidos, antes ellos puedan ganar a otros. La segunda, que en dos o tres dias que he ydo escriviendo esto han pedido de la carcel real que vaya un padre para un Ingles, y de un hospital para dos Franceses y un Valon, y en casa se confesso un Frances y dos Francesas, y me han pedido sus amos que quieren embiar a catechizar dos Ingleses, un Frances, y un Holandes y otro Aleman. Y otros dos o tres Ingleses que han ido de paso en Romeria se han confessado y comulgado, y es casi desta manera lo ordinario. Y aunque los padres estan ocupados en sus lecciones y officios dentro de casa, y hazen todo lo que pueden no basta *quia messis quidem multa est, operarii autem pauci.* Y assi pido agora otro padre. Y si en la casa professa uviera [2] un par de padres que acudieran a los estrangeros, estuvieran muy bien ocupados y empleados; por que como acuden aqui tantos de las regiones septentrionales, que estan o del todo inficionados o tocados de la herejia, y no hallan quien sepa su lengua, ni trate de su bien espiritual, hasta agora se bolvian en sus mismos errores, y aca no hazian ningun provecho.

Y en San Lucar ay una residencia deste Seminario con un sacerdote grave y docto que es Superior de alli, con otro compañero y a vezes otros dos, los quales en lo que acude a acquel puerto y al de Santa Maria hazen los mismos effectos que aqui, de lo qual el Duque de Medina y los Generales de las galeras de España estan muy agradecidos y reconocidos de los buenos effectos que ven cada dia a los ojos, y a uno de la casa y nacion de los de alli le ha cometido el Santo Officio y el Duque el visitar los navios y mirar los que vienen; y los sacerdotes que de aqui parten a Inglaterra, los dias que se detienen en San Lucar ayudan a lo mismo.

2. Fuera de la ciudad estos tres años precedentes, han ydo tres Padres de la Compañia Ingleses a cinco missiones con los padres de la provincia. Y el año antes el Padre Henrique Belo ministro de este Collegio estuvo algunos meses ayudando a confessar en Cadiz gran numero de estrangeros y de la ciudad donde fue muy amado de todos; y fue embiado por el Padre Provincial con el Adelantado a la Jornada que hizo a las Terceras, y murio a la buelta. Y otro año antes el Padre Walpolo fue de aqui una o dos vezes a Cadiz adonde andavan mas de 200 Ingleses trabajando en la fortificacion, y les hizo varias exhortaciones y se reduxeron algunos y en lo temporal se les ayudo, que estavan en gran miseria. Y el general Don Pedro de Toledo dio licencia que algunos de menor edad, los sacasse de con los demas, y los accommodassemos donde los tratassen bien, y enseñassen la religion Catholica, como se hizo. Y antes desto el Padre Carlos Tancardo ministro deste Collegio anduvo dos o tres años con el Adelantado en sus galeras y en dos o tres jornadas que hizo. Y el Doctor Stillinton, Preposito de San Jorge (hombre muy grave y docto) y otros muy buenos sujetos de los Seminarios, yendo en la misma

demanda murieron en Ferrol y en la mar.

Y por estar aqui este Seminario y hallarse el Padre Personio en esta ciudad, aviendo el Adelantado tomado unos navios Ingleses, acudio al puerto de Santa Maria y les hizo varias platicas y tuvo muchas disputas y conferencias con ellos, oyendo y saltando sus dudas [3] hasta que el Señor fue servido se reduxessen todos, y dio traça con el buen Adelantado, para que su Magestad les diesse a todos su libertad. Y el dia que se reconciliaron a la fee los vistieron de nuevo, y fueron a la iglesia y comulgaron, y el Adelantado les hizo gran fiesta, sirviendo a la mesa el Marques de Montesclaros, que oy es Assistiente de Sevilla y Virrey de Mexico, y otros Señores, y creo el mismo Adelantado segun me han referido; de los quales unos se quedaron a vivir por aca, otros sirviendo al Rey en las galeras por marineros y soldados (y hasta oy quando vienen las galeras aqui acuden a confessar) y otros se fueron a Inglaterra agradecidissimos, y se les dio instruccion como avian de tratar con los herejes, y procurar ganarlos y conservarse a si. Y una docena de muchachos de poca edad no consintio el Padre Personio que bolviessen a su tierra, ni quedassen sirviendo a los cavalleros ni capitanes de las galeras, sino dio orden con el Padre Bartholome Perez (a quien Dios nuestro Señor dio gran luz de la importancia desta obra de los Seminarios y con ella les ha ayudado mucho en todas ocasiones, y ganadoles las mejores limosnas que han tenido, y dadoles a conocer a personas gravisimas) que se repartiessen por los Collegios de la Provincia, y dos con el santo obispo de Jaen, Don Francisco Sarmiento, para que sirviendo en ellos fuessen enseñados en la fee, como se hizo, dos de los quales estan oy en la Compañia, y esto fue cosa de gran edificacion para todos los que la vieron y supieron, y como tal la he leydo en un libro latino impresso en Flandes, y esta en otros Ingleses.

Y deste buen principio resulto que todas las vezes que el Adelantado, Don Pedro de Toledo, y el Principe Doria, y otros Generales han tomado navios, no dexan bolver los muchachos a Inglaterra, sino los embian aqui para que los enseñemos y acomodemos, y assi se ha hecho, y algunos han tomado estado en Sevilla y saben officios con que ganan de comer; y otros han muerto bien, y otro tercero ay en la Compañia Hermano Coadiutor como los demas. Y solo dire de uno de diez años de muy lindo exterior y gran abilidad que embio el Adelantado; el qual entro en casa con muchas lagrimas, y haziendo burla de todos y llamandolos Papistas y rebeldes a la Reyna y locos, y que le truxessen una biblia en Ingles y que el los convenceria a todos y a todos puso espanto ver quan inficionado estava en tan tierna edad, trayendo lugares y argumentos de la sagrada escritura para sus herejias y dezia que el sabia mas que todos los papistas juntos, los quales eran ciegos pues no querian recibir la nueva luz del evangelio. Y dentro [4] de pocos dias, oyendo sus dudas (que las ponia como si fuera de 30 años) y soltandoselas, y declarandole la falsedad de la herejia, le hallaron un dia llorando, sin admittir razon ni consuelo ni regalo, y preguntado la causa respondio muy turbado, que el veya claramente que la religion de la Reyna de Inglaterra y de los herejes era mala y falsa, y que el la queria dexar, y que la de los Papistas no avia de tener por lo mismo, y que assi se hallava sin religion ninguna como una bestia; mas dentro de pocos dias se reduxo, y era de gran consolacion ver lo que obro la gracia de nuestro Señor en el y la devocion y lagrimas con que reçava el rosario y oya missa y los ratos que estava en la iglesia de rodillas. Y pocos dias despues el Principe Doria que llego con sus galeras a Cadiz nos embio otros tres muchachos para ser catechizados y enseñados, y el niño les dixo de si proprio, que mirassen que estavan engañados y que se hiziessen Catholicos porque el antes era mayor hereje que ellos aunque ya por la misericordia de Dios era Catholico y estava en el verdadero camino para poder salvarse.

Otro menor nos embio el Adelantado muy gracioso, que quando tomaron su nao dezia que no amaynassen las velas por el Papa, ni por el Rey de España, ni por los Papistas. Estuvo sirviendo en este Seminario siete años, hasta que el de 600 murio de peste, y creo se salvo porque era muy bonito y muy bien entendido. Y llevando yo un dia a visitar los Señores Inquisidores unos aluños recien venidos, y que les dixessen unas oraciones breves latinas y griegas, quedose este niño a la puerta del tribunal con los sombreros y le mandaron entrar, y le hizieron dezir las oraciones, y la doctrina cristiana, y les respondio con tal gracia y tan bien, que dixo el mas antiguo y los demas, que aunque este Seminario y los de la Compañia que en el estavan no uviessen hecho aquel año mas que ganar y reducir aquel niño y criado, era bien empleado todo quanto trabajavan ayudando esta obra.

3. Con ser tan pocos los padres Ingleses ayudan lo que pueden en los Collegios a los ministerios. Oy es ministro y muy bien obrero en Malaga el Padre Jhonson, y el Padre Tomson leyo dos años de Mayores en Cadiz, y confessava muchos estrangeros y de la ciudad. Y otros dos Hermanos Coadiutores Ingleses ay en Cordova y Trigueros que hazen lo que pueden, y otros dos hermanos oyen en tercer año de Theologia en Cordova y Sevilla, que a su tiempo podran ayudar. Y el Collegio de Sevilla ha ganado mucho pues cada 2o año ay 22 o 28 estudiantes que entran a oyr el curso de artes que se comiença, y de ordinario ay buen numero de [5] Theologos que van saliendo cada 2o año, y en comun son todos buenos estudiantes, y algunos aventajados como se ve en las conclusiones generales, que desde que esta aqui el Seminario han defendido todos los años de Artes y Theologia. Y el Cardenal que estuvo en las ultimas que se dedicaron a el, fue admirado de ver lo bien que lo hizo el sustentante, y los buenos soldados que cria este Seminario para pelear contra los hereges, y los religiosos y personas graves que de ordinario acuden no acaban de alabar esto estimando a la Compañia que lo tiene a su cargo, y que saca y cria tal gente de reyno tan estragado. *Ex quo infero* que si algunos Padres de la Casa Professa o Collegio se occuparon en ayudar 50 o 60 mancebos que tienen este fin, y los fueran embiando a Inglaterra, fuera de gran estima y abono desta provincia, y gran servicio de nuestro Señor, y propriosissimo de nuestra vocacion.

Pues esso es lo que haze el Seminario y sin el trabajo goza la provincia del provecho, y de la estimacion. Y lo mismo pudiera dezir si se ocuparon otros en ayudar, enseñar, confessar y socorrer a gran numero de estrangeros de varias naciones, pobres que acuden a esta ciudad, y ultra de lo espiritual se les procuran amos, y ponenles a officios, y se les aiuda con limosnas conforme a la pobreza desta casa.

4. Por el gran servicio que haze a Dios esta provincia criando Apostoles y martyres para Inglaterra, es bien probable (y algunas personas graves y espirituales de la Compañia me lo han dicho) que nuestro Señor la ha augmentado en tantos Collegios y dos casas de probacion desde que se fundo esto Seminario. Y podria ser que en su triennio le dio Dios tantas y tan extraordinarias limosnas al Padre Elifonso de Castro (como se sabe y se ve por lo que labro siendo preposito en la casa professa) y los dos a tres mil ducados que repartio quando se fue a Mexico, por el amor con que abraço esta obra desde que vino a Sevilla, y por el cuidado con que le procuro muy gruesas limosnas, y la voluntad con que la acredito con personas muy graves, y con todos sus amigos. El qual me dixo con gran sentimiento varias veces que no tenia esta provincia cosa mas honrosa ni que mas la acreditasse con gente principal, ni mas propria de su vocacion que este Seminario, y que devria yr recibiendo todos los alumnos que pudiesse, para que a su tiempo fuessen en nombre della a Inglaterra, porque en sus ojos valia mas y estimava mas lo que uno de la Compañia hazia y padecia en un dia en aquel fuego de Inglaterra que quanto el y otros muchos hazian por aca en un año. *Haec ille.*

5. Por la educacion de estos alumnos la Compañia de esta Provincia y aun toda ella en comun esta muy acreditada de toda suerte de gente, y mas de la mas principal [6] y mas grave (con que quiza se sueldan otras murmuraciones y dichos) y por este medio se han ganado y afficionado muchos.

El Duque de Medina Sidonia una de las vezes que vino a esta casa, fue con el Cardenal pasado, y me dixo que ninguna cosa avia dado de mejor gana en su vida que la paja de agua que dio al Seminario, y que a no tener ocho hijos, ninguna obra pia en religion fundara con la voluntad que esta, porque la tenia por la mejor de España, y aun de la Christiandad, y que devian los obispos, Señores y ciudades ayudarla con gran cuydado y amor, y que ya que el no la podia fundar, que en todas las ocasiones la favoreceria, y que en qualquiera que se le offreciesse a esta casa acudiesse a el. El Adelantado Mayor de Castilla me dixo varias veces, lo que se devia a la Compañia por esta obra, y su gran importancia, y que viendo las armadas que se avian perdido con tiempos contrarios, entendia que Dios no queria conquistar acquel Reyno sino con armas espirituales y sangre de sus naturales que aqui se criava. Y una persona muy grave que se hallo con el Duque de Guisa el año de 1588 quando se perdio el armada que llevo el Duque de Medina me refirio que le dixo lo mismo; y assi el en su ciudad de Lugo [*vere* Eu] tenia un seminario de 12 alumnos, y los sustentava, y aqui ay oy algunos dellos. El Conde de Puñonrostro siendo Asistente aqui, no acabava de alabar esta obra y a la Compañia por tenerla a su cargo. Y me dixo varias veces que por lo que avia entendido siendo Maestro de Campo en las guerras de Flandes y Francia y otras partes, juzgava que en razon de estado y de religion le estava muy bien a España el llevarla adelante, ya que otros medios no havian y que de aqui a cien años que se leyessen las historias admiraria el mundo. Y pudiera referir el sentimiento y dichos notables de mas de 20 grandes y Señores de titulo, y de el Cardenal presente y passado de Sevilla y del de Toledo, y de mas de otros 10 Arçobispos y Obispos que a mi me han dicho. Solo dire lo que le oy al Arçobispo de Burgos siendo Obispo de Cadiz; que si la Compañia solo tuviera este assumpto devia ser amada y estimada de todos; porque le tenia por el mayor que ay en la Iglesia de Dios, y a los Catholicos de Inglaterra por los mejores y mas acrisolados del mundo, y que mediante esta obra, esta la religion Catholica victoriosa contra los herejes en Inglaterra, pues con tan largas y tan crueles persecuciones no han prevalecido, y que tenia por cierto que oy se salvavan mas en Inglaterra que en tiempo que era Catholica. Y esso mismo me han dicho confirma el Padre Thomas Darbigier, Ingles de nuestra Compañia, que es mas de 90 años [7] y alcanço los tiempos Catholicos y fue Dean de Londres en ellos, y salio desterrado al principio que commenço a reynar esta Reyna, y se entro en la Compañia. Y el santo Obispo de Jaen, Don Francisco Sarmiento, a quien Dios dio extraordinaria luz y ponderacion de la importancia desta obra, las vezes que me hablava de ella era no con pocas lagrimas, y me dixo una, que se le representavan los tiempos de la primitiva Iglesia los que agora corrian en Inglaterra. Y el Padre Roberto Personio un San Athanasio (lo mismo me dixo algunas vezes el Padre Juan de Cañas, persona tan grave y tan santa como todos los que le conocieron saben) y que no veya el obra en la Iglesia de Dios como ella, y assi con gran amor dava cada año mil ducados adelantados a este Seminario y al de Valladolid, y quando murio mando se continuassen por otros dos años, sin otras limosnas particulares que hizo a este. Y tuvo consigo algunos muchachos de los que el Padre Personio retuvo en el puerto, y los vistio y trato con gran amor y charidad, el tiempo que los tuvo en su casa.

Y las vezes que han ydo algunos que vienen de nuevo, y otros antes de partir a su mission por la bendicion a los Señores Inquisidores, ha dicho aquel Santo Tribunal la gran estima que tiene desta obra y la buena dicha de los que la ayudan, y en todas ocasiones le han mostrado y socorrido con algunas limosnas en comun y cada uno en particular. Y en una ocasion los convidamos y vino a una fiesta todo el tribunal en forma de tribunal con todos sus oficiales y ministros, que es cosa que nunca o rara vez se ha visto en Sevilla, y la ultima vez que fueron 4 sacerdotes a despidirse antes de partir se los recibieron con notable amor, y el mas antiguo (no sin lagrimas suyas y de los circumstantes) en nombre de todos lo agradecio mucho, y pidio quedassen los nombres escritos en aquel santo tribunal para consuelo suyo.

El Padre Fray Gaspar de Cordova que oy es Confessor del Rey nuestro Señor, sciendo Provincial desta Provincia, y el Maestro Calahorrano que le sucedio en el officio, hombre gravissimo, y que en esta ciudad predico mas de 50 años con gran satisfacion y concurso, los oy hablar con gran estima de la obra, y de la Compañia por tenerla a cargo, y que era la mayor de sus empressas. Lo qual dezia el Maestro Salucio era assi y que *ab initio nascentis ecclesiae* no avia leydo el que uviesse avido obra como esta, y en los pulpitos hablava en qualquiera ocasion que se le ofrecia con notable sentimiento, y el mismo tienen hombres gravissimos de su religion y de otras. Y [8] personas seglares y religiosas declaradas por enemigos della Compañia nos favorecen con sus limosnas, y hablan con gran estima de la obra, y dizen que no hay aqui de que murmurar, y de los seglares algunos que no tienen fama de que viven bien, dizen que es gran dicha de esta ciudad que se crie en ella gente dedicada y obligada con juramento a dar la vida, y derramar la sangre por Jesu Cristo y su fee y religion. Y muy pocos dias vinieron aqui dos cavalleros de Moron a esta ciudad a solo ver este Seminario, del qual tenian noticia por un libro que habian leydo, y con extraordinaria devocion y lagrimas querian besar las paredes del, y me rogaron fuesse alguno desta casa a su tierra, y que ellos pidirian limosna para esta casa de trigo &c. Y lo hizieron assi.

Y de la bondad de nuestro Señor y de la luz que ha dado desta obra ha resultado que todas las vezes que hemos pedido algunas cosas (que han sido no pocas) en el Cabildo de la ciudad, de la Iglesia y de los demas tribunales, nunca ha avido contradiccion, antes me ha dicho que ando corto en lo que pido. Y algunos de los veintiquatros y canonigos no contentos con lo que han hecho sus Cabildos se han movido a pedir limosnas a particulares, y lo mismo han hecho algunos grandes y Señores de titulo que sustentan algunos estudiantes, con otros Señores que hagan lo mismo por la gran estima que tienen de la obra, y de la Compañia que la tiene a su cargo. Y algunos ecclesiasticos graves y prebendados han pedido y deseado con affecto, por tener parte en esta obra sustentar y criar en su casa y darles estudio a algunos estudiantes pequeños, que alguna vez vienen no con la sufficiencia necessaria para oyr artes, como se reciben en el Collegio. Un doctor Theologo de este Arçobispado nos crio uno tres años, que es oy de los mejores Theologos que ay aqui. Y el Licenciado Francisco de Sepulveda, Vicario y Theologo de Baeça (hombre de gran piedad y exemplo, y de quien hizo gran confiança y se sirvio el santo Obispo Don Francisco Sarmiento, y lo mismo haze oy el que es obispo de Jaen) con gran amor y charidad y luz que Dios le ha dado de la importancia desta obra y gran deseo de la reducion de Inglaterra, el año de 600 nos embio un sobrino de un glorioso martyr sacerdote, aviendole criado dos o tres años, que es muy lindo latino y griego, y de los mejores philosophos que tenemos, y de gran virtud y no menos esperanças; y este año pasado nos embio otro que tuvo mas de otro año, que sera muy bien sujeto, y a ambos se les echa de ver la piedad, Christiandad y cuidado con que los crio tal padre. Y otras personas ecclesiasticas y seglares piden otros con el mismo deseo. Y otras

Provincias de la Compañia sin tener Seminarios por tener parte en esta obra han recibido [9] y criado algunos sujetos y dadolos luego a la mission y a los Seminarios, como la de Toledo que nos ha dado a este Padre Belo que murio en Cadiz y fue aqui Ministro y al Padre Jhonson que lo es oy en Malaga, y al Padre Antonio [Hoskins] que es compañero del que haze officio de Provincial en Inglaterra. Y este año pasado de 1602 dio al Padre Juan Polo, que acabo en Alcala, al Seminario de Valladolid, y lee alli Moral, y al cielo al Hermano Guillermo Worthington, que oya Theologia en Murcia, y los que se reciben en Inglaterra salen a hazer su noviciado a Flandes, Francia y Roma, y luego acuden a la mission, y de ordinario ay 4 o 6 novicios, que se reciben cada año en Roma, y otros tantos estudiantes en el Collegio Romano.

Y a N.P. General desde que entro en el govierno, se le ha conocido particular affecto y animo de ayudar a esta obra por todas las vias possibles, y he sabido que su Paternidad dixo a una persona grave de la Compañia hablando de esta obra, que no se hartava de favorecer y ayudar a esta mission, y que era la mas honrada y de mayor estima que la Compania tenia, y de gran servicio de nuestro Señor y de su Iglesia, pues en espacio de 22 años que avia que se començo, siempre avia crecido y prevalecido contra la furia y brava persecucion de los herejes y en este tiempo derramado la sangre mas de 150 sacerdotes y entre ellos 9 o 10 de la Compañia sin otro gran numero de Catholicos.

6. Ultra del bien espiritual y reputacion que se le ha seguido a la Compañia por este Seminario, hasta aqui por la bondad de nuestro Señor no ha dado ningun cuydado en lo temporal a la Provincia ni sido cargoso: pues hasta agora ni para el sustento de los nuestros, ni de los alumnos ha dado nada mas que dos o tres hermanos Españoles y un Padre antes que todos fuessen Ingleses. Ni la casa professa ha perdido algo de sus limosnas (como al principio algunos temieron) antes si bien se considera, parece que nuestro Señor ha acudido con mas liberalidad, y mas larga mano estos años que ha que vino aqui el Seminario como se ve por lo que ha edificado y labrado y la gente que sustenta que es la ordinaria y mas 25 novicios, y las gruesas mandas que ha tenido estos años. Lo qual varias vezes me dixo el Padre Cordesses, que en virtud de ayudar a esta obra, avia Dios de augmentar la casa professa y la Compañia en Sevilla, y que nadie pensasse que unas limosnas estorvarian a otras, y assi se ha cumplido lo que este santo Padre dixo. El qual ocho años o nueve que fue preposito y subdito ayudo con extraordinario amor a esta obra, y la favorecio con todos los conocidos, y le procuro varias limosnas, porque le dio Dios gran luz de su importancia, y lo que dexo Alonso de Paz de diez mill ducados para ambos Seminarios de la orden y en otro testamento dexaba uno 18 mill ducados. Y si dos padres que se criaron aqui que fue el Padre Richardo Walpolo y su hermano el Padre Christoval Walpolo fueron a los Seminarios de Roma y Valladolid, el primero despues de un año de noviciado trabajo ocho en este con edificacion, y el otro fue por su salud que estava quartanario [10] y por

ellos han venido 8 de otras provincias y seminarios a ayudar en este.
El Padre Henrique Walpolo, Martyr, vino al principio que se fundo el
Seminario, de Flandes.
El Padre Carlos Tancardo, que fue ministro, de Italia.
El Padre Simon Suimborno, que fue ministro, de Francia.
El Padre Henrique Belo, que fue ministro, de Toledo.
El Padre Guillermo Jhonson, que fue ministro, de Toledo.
El Padre Antonio Hoskins, de Toledo.
El Padre Henrique Tichborn, que oy es ministro, de Francia.
El Padre Guillermo Warfordo, que oy es confessor y lee, de Roma.
Y con estos Padres fuera de aliviar a la provincia de dar otros, es muy
ayudada en sus ministerios como se ha visto.

Y no parece carga yr recibiendo algunos novicios, que pueden yr
ayudando a la mission y a la provincia, como otros lo hazen; y lo que
otras provincias tienen por ganancia aun no teniendo seminarios a que
acudir, ni aviendose de quedar en ellas para trabajar.

7. Y parece que Dios nuestro Señor ha querido servirse mucho desta
provincia para la conversion de Inglaterra, aun muchos años antes que
uviera seminarios en España: pues el año de 1577 vino a ella novicio y
estudio, y se ordeno el padre Guillermo Weston (varon verdaderamente
santo como confiessan todos los que le conocieron) y fue obrero y leyo
griego en el Collegio de Sevilla y en el de Cadiz con grandissima
edificacion; que aun oy en dia le llaman los seglares que le conocieron el
santo Padre Guillermo. Y desde aquel tiempo movio Dios los coraçones
de algunos desta provincia a ayudar a los Seminarios y les dio gran estima
de la obra y deseo de emplearse en ella, y despues que ay Seminario en la
provincia otros muchos de los mas graves y doctos estan con vivos deseos
de lo mismo, y se han offrecido a pasar alla, y estan con gran embidia de
los naturales que trabajan, y se emplean en esta viña del Señor tan
necessitada de buenos obreros, y por solo tener parte en tal mies,
quisieran ser naturales de la nacion. Y porque muchos desta provincia me
preguntan de aquel verdadero siervo de Dios y fiel hijo de la Compañia el
Padre Guillermo, y yo he tenido particular cuidado de saber lo que ha
pasado, dire brevemente que el año de 82 por orden de N. Padre fue desta
provincia a Inglaterra (y tengo una carta suya de 4 planas que escrivio
desde Paris antes de entrar en el Reyno, lleno de zelo y espiritu de Dios) a
supplir por el Padre Campiano que el año antes de 81 gloriosamente avia
derramado la sangre y sido ahorcado y hecho quartos. Tres o quatro años
que el buen Padre estuvo libre, trabajo con gran fervor y espiritu y de
todos era muy estimado por su gran virtud [11] y modestia. Hizo muchas
y muy señaladas conversiones de personas principales y entre ellas de una
hija de un Señor de titulo, no obstante que la procuro estorvar, uno de los
mas famosos herejes y estimados predicadores que avia en Inglaterra.

Dieziseis años ha que esta preso en varias carceles adonde ha dado tales
muestras de sanctidad que los mismos herejes lo veneran y reverencian. Y
me dixo varias vezes el Padre Personio que era el hombre mas estimado

que avia en Inglaterra y que de todo el Reyno era consultado aun estando en la carcel, en la qual le conto al mismo Padre Personio un sacerdote, que estuvo junto con el un año, que en todo aquel tiempo nunca se acosto en cama, aunque la tenia, y que pasava casi todas las noches en oracion de rodillas, y que si algun rato descansava oprimido de sueño, se arrimava a un banquito que tenia, y en breve despertava y se bolvia a su oracion de rodillas, y que assi paso un año que estuvieron juntos. Y el año de 89 un sacerdote ingles que paso por Marchena me dixo que era publico entre herejes y Catholicos, que todo el tiempo que estuvo preso no se acostava en cama, y que de ordinario estava de rodillas, y que el sabia que con la señal de la cruz y el agua bendita avia sanado enfermos, y que era tal su penitencia, y rigor con que se tratava, que era comun dicho entre los Catholicos *si habuero eloquentiam P. Campiani, pennam velocem P. Personii et vitam austeram P. Guillermi, charitatem autem non habuero, nihil mihi prodest*. Y quando vivio en el Collegio de Sevilla me dixo el Hermano Toribio de Palacio que vivo un invierno en un aposento con el, que todas las noches a media noche se disciplinava con gran rigor, y que siempre que entro en el aposento le hallo de rodillas y otras cosas de notable edificacion, y que casi toda la noche tenia oracion.

Viendo los herejes el exemplo y vida suya, y los que se convertian por medio del lo llevaron a la carcel de Wisbich, adonde estavan presos 20 sacerdotes Catholicos los quales movidos con su exemplo y sanctidad quisieron ponerse debajo de su obediencia, y como el Padre por su humildad lo rehusasse, lo pidieron al Superior de la Compañia, y a N.P. General pidieron lo mismo. Y nuestro Padre le mando que sin titulo de Superior los governasse y ayudasse al modo que lo hazen los nuestros a las congregaciones de los clerigos en los Collegios y casas de la Compañia. Lo qual el buen Padre hizo con tanto cuydado y con tanta charidad y tal exemplo que parecia aquella carcel una religion reformada. Un alumno que ha estado aqui me conto (como testigo de vista, porque el se havia criado en aquella carcel, y servia misas y estudiava) que cada dia se dezian 18 missas y mas: y les leya el Padre dos liciones [12] [de casos, *in the earlier draft*] y resolvia muchos que le consultavan de fuera, y oya gran numero de confessiones, y reducia muchos herejes. Por lo qual avra tres o 4o años le mudaron de aquella carcel a la torre de Londres donde esta oy preso con tal rigor que nadie le puede hablar, y en una destas carceles hizo estos años pasados profesion. Y otras cosas muy particulares se pudieran referir de este santo varon que por abreviar se dexan.

Y de lo dicho consta como este Collegio es provechoso a la provincia en lo espiritual y temporal, y en nada cargoso ni costoso.

[Endorsed] Apologia pro Seminario.
n.4. occupationes y empleos de los Padres Ingleses.
Pot. dici de vida del P. Jhonson en Malaga 12 años hasta que murio el de 614.
Lo que el P.Forcer en 7 años limosnas y conversiones.
N.S.

Translation:

1. Both in Seville and in the Andalusian ports the seminary helps in ministries very appropriate to the Company which the native-born fathers of the province cannot perform because they lack the necessary knowledge of foreign languages. The three English fathers who are here now can hear confessions and preach in six or seven languages, and a considerable number of French, Walloons, English, Scots, Irish, Flemish and Italians regularly call at the seminary for confession, particularly in Lent. The fathers, sometimes accompanied by students, frequently visit prisons, galleys and hospitals to catechize, preach, hear confessions or assist the dying, to the great edification and spiritual profit of all who witness it. Heretics are frequently reconciled, and one year there were as many as 150 converts, many of them men of considerable parts and understanding. They all made general confessions and some of them died in great sorrow for their sins and past life, while others have persevered in our holy religion. People who witness all this at close quarters can see the harvest which is being reaped, and the converts see that otherwise they would have been left without any recourse or remedy. The province itself gains in reputation from having men ready and able to devote themselves to work which is so appropriate to their Institute and to which it was especially called by Our Lord.

I will only mention two specific examples out of many. The first is that in the royal prison in this city there are some captive English officers and soldiers who were heretics when they entered but who have all been converted. Some of them died as Catholics and received the sacraments, while others have made such progress at the time of writing that they spend three hours a day on their knees in mental prayer and spiritual reading. The chaplain of the prison[2] says that they are an example to everyone there. They and other Englishmen have been given some spiritual books written by Father Persons, from which they have derived much profit. For their benefit and that of others, one of the fathers of this house has translated into English a catechism[3] and form of confession and other pious tracts, and instructions on how to treat with the heretics when they return home, so that they may not be perverted but rather convert others.

To give a second example: within just the last two or three days we have received a call from the prison for a father to attend an Englishman there, and another call from a hospital for a priest to attend two Frenchmen and a Walloon. A Frenchman and two Frenchwomen have called at the house for confession and we have received requests from masters to instruct two Englishmen, a Frenchman, a Dutchman and a German. Two or three other Englishmen on pilgrimage have called on us for confession and communion. Such are the typical demands made on us. Though the fathers are busy with their teaching and other duties, they do what they can, but it is not enough, *quia messis quidem multa est, operarii autem pauci*. That is why I am now asking for another father. If there were two fathers in the Professed House assigned to look after foreigners they would have their hands full, so numerous are the visitors who come here from northern regions who are altogether or in part infected with heresy, but there is no-one who knows their language or who can attend to their spiritual welfare, so that hitherto they have been allowed to return to their errors and have derived no profit from their stay.

In Sanlúcar [de Barrameda] this seminary has a residence presided over by a reverend and learned superior, with one companion and sometimes two more. These perform the same functions in Sanlúcar and Puerto de Santa María as we do here, for which the Duke of Medina Sidonia and the commanders of the Spanish galleys are very grateful, seeing the good effects which are produced daily. One of the English priests of that house has been charged by the Holy Office and by the Duke with the task of inspecting the ships and examining arrivals. Priests who are on their way to England assist in this task for as long as they are detained at Sanlúcar awaiting passage.

2. During the last three years three English fathers of the Company have been on five missions outside Seville with fathers of the Andalusian province. The year before, Fr Henry Bell, Minister of this college, spent some months at Cadiz helping to hear the confessions of a large number of foreigners and citizens, by whom he was greatly beloved. He was then sent by the Father Provincial to accompany the Captain-General [Adelantado] on his expedition to the Azores, and he died after returning. On an earlier occasion Father Persons made one or two journeys to Cadiz when more than two hundred Englishmen were employed in building the fortifications there. He addressed them on various occasions, converting several and attending to their temporal needs, for they were in a wretched state[4]. Don Pedro de Toledo allowed him to remove some of those who were of tender years, and to have them lodged where they would be treated well and taught the Catholic religion. Earlier Father Charles Tancard, Minister of this college, accompanied the Captain-General on several voyages which he made with his galleys over a period of two or three years. Dr Stillington, the reverend and learned superior of St George [at Sanlúcar] along with other seminary priests died at El Ferrol or at sea while engaged on similar service.

When the Captain-General captured some English ships along with their crews of more than 200 hundred English sailors, Fr Persons who was then in Seville was able to go to Puerto de Santa María where he addressed them on several occasions and had many discussions and debates with them, listening to and answering their questions until— thanks be to God—they were all reconciled[4]. He prevailed upon the Captain-General to obtain his Majesty's pardon for them all, and the day they were reconciled to the faith they put on new clothes and went to church and communicated, after which the Captain-General gave them all a great feast at which they were waited on at table by the Marqués de Montes Claros, the present Asistente of Seville and Viceroy of Mexico, and by other gentlemen including the Captain-General himself, I believe.

Some of the men settled here, while others took service on the King's galleys as sailors or soldiers (to this day they always call here for confession whenever their ships come to Seville), while others returned gratefully to England after being instructed on how to deal with the heretics and how to convert them and defend themselves. In the case of a dozen young boys, Fr Persons would not consent to their returning home or remaining in their present service, but prevailed upon Fr Bartolomé Pérez (whom Our Lord enlightened with a clear understanding of the importance of the seminaries, and who has accordingly taken every opportunity to assist them, obtaining substantial donations for them and making them known to influential persons) to have them taken into service in some of the colleges of the Province. Two of them were taken into his household by the good Bishop of Jaen, Don Francisco de Sarmiento, to be instructed in the faith. Of this group of boys, two are now members of our Company. This caused great edification among all who witnessed or heard of it, and I have read an account of it in a book written in Latin and published in Flanders, and there is an account of it in other books written in English.

Following this good precedent, whenever the Captain-General, Don Pedro de Toledo, and Prince Doria and other generals capture English ships, instead of letting the boy prisoners return to England, they send them here to be taught and lodged. Some of these boys settled in Seville and learned a trade to support themselves, another is a lay-brother in the Company, while others died a good death. One of those sent us by the Captain-General was a ten-year old boy of winning appearance and much intelligence who on arrival shed many tears and made mock of everyone, calling them papists and rebels against the Queen, and fools. He bade them bring him a bible in English, saying he would refute them all, etc, and everyone was dismayed to see how infected he was at such a tender age, quoting passages from Sacred Scripture to prove his heresies and saying that he knew more than all the papists put together and that they were blind since they would not receive the new light of the gospel. But a few days later, after they had listened to his objections (which he put to them as if he were a man of thirty) and answered them and shown him the folly of his heresy, they found him one day in tears. He would not listen to reason or be consoled or comforted, and when they asked the cause he replied in great distress that he saw clearly that the religion of the Queen of England and of the heretics was false and wicked and that he wanted to renounce it, but that he could not accept the religion of the papists either, for the same reason, and thus he was left without any religion at all, like a brute beast. Within a few days, however, he recovered, and it was a great joy to see the grace of Our Lord at work in him and the devotion and tears with which he recited the rosary and heard mass and prayed in the chapel. A few days afterwards Prince Doria put in to Cadiz with his galleys and sent us another three boys to be catechized and cared for, and this boy told them, on his own initiative that they should realise they had been led astray and should become

Catholics. He told them that he had been an even greater heretic, but now by God's mercy he was a Catholic and on the true road to salvation.

Another of those sent us by the Captain-General was a boy of quick wit who told his ship's captors that they would not lower sail for any Pope, or King of Spain, or Papist. He became a servant in this seminary and was here for seven years until he died of the plague in 1600, and I believe he was saved, for he was a good boy and possessed of much understanding. One day, when I brought some newly arrived students to see the Lords Inquisitors, in order to deliver some brief speeches in Latin and Greek, this boy waited at the door of the Tribunal keeping our hats. When they bade him enter and asked him to recite his prayers and Christian doctrine, he answered so well and gracefully that the eldest of the Inquisitors and the rest said that if this seminary and the fathers in it had done no more that year than to win over that single servant boy, then all the assistance they had given to our work had been of good avail.

3. In spite of being so few in number, the English fathers give what assistance they can in various colleges of the Province. At the present moment, Fr Johnson is an active minister in Malaga, and Fr Thompson taught the senior class in the Cadiz college for two years as well as hearing the confessions of many people, both citizens and foreigners. Another two Englishmen are laybrothers at Cordova and Trigueros, and two more brothers are in their third year of theology at Cordova and Seville[5]. The Seville seminary has made great progress. Every other year 22 or 23 new students arrive to start the humanities course and a good number of theologians complete the theology course. In general they are good students, and some of them are outstanding, as is evident when they defend their General Conclusions which have been held in public every year since the seminary started. When the Cardinal attended the last Conclusions, which were held in his honour, he was amazed to see how well the defender of the thesis performed, and how well the seminary was training its soldiers to combat heresy. The learned men and religious who ordinarily attend these occasions never cease to praise the Company for undertaking this work and for rescuing and educating such fine young men from so corrupt a kingdom. *Ex quo infero* that if the Professed House or College [of San Hermenegildo] were employed in training fifty or sixty youths for this purpose, to be sent to England, it would be considered a great credit to the province and of great service to Our Lord and most fitting to our vocation. Yet this is exactly what the seminary is doing, while the province without any effort on its part enjoys the benefit and the credit. The same could be said if others were occupied in teaching, confessing and succouring the large number of poor foreigners who come to this city, attending to their spiritual needs and also helping them to find service or employment or giving them as much alms as the poverty of the house will allow.

4. It is probably as a reward for the great service which this province does

for God in training apostles and martyrs for England, as some reverend and spiritual fathers of the Company have said to me, that Our Lord has blessed it with so many colleges and with two novitiate houses in the period since this seminary was founded. The extraordinary scale of the donations raised by Fr Ildefonso de Castro during his three years in charge of the Professed House—which is reflected in the building programme he carried out there and in the sum of two or three thousand ducats which he distributed on his departure for Mexico—may well have been God's reward for the support he gave to our work from the time he arrived in Seville, for his efforts in obtaining generous donations for us and gaining the support of influential persons and of all his acquaintances. He remarked to me on several occasions with deep feeling that this province had no more praiseworthy undertaking, nor one more likely to gain it credit in high places, nor one more in keeping with its vocation than this seminary, and that it should continue to take as many students as it could so that in due course they could proceed to England in its name. What one single father of the Company did and suffered in that furnace of England in one single day was, he declared, of more worth and value than all that he and others did here in a whole year. That is what he said.

5. The education of these students has gained for the Company, not only in this province but at large, the good opinion of every class of society and in particular those of influence and importance (which may perhaps counteract certain other murmurings and gossip), so that by this means it has gained many supporters.

    On one of his visits to this house, the Duke of Medina Sidonia, who was accompanied by the late Cardinal, told me that nothing in his life had given him greater satisfaction than to be able to furnish the seminary with its water supply, and that were it not for the fact that he had eight children there was no pious work in religion which he would more willingly endow than this, for he considered it to be the greatest in Spain and indeed in Christendom. The bishops, nobility and civic authorities should assist it, he declared, with great care and devotion, and although he could not endow it he would use every opportunity to promote it, and the house should come to him whenever it was in any difficulty. The Captain-General of Castille also told me on several occasions how important our work was and how creditable to the Company. The loss of our armadas in contrary weathers had made him realise that God wanted to conquer the kingdom of England only by spiritual weapons and by the blood of its own countrymen, trained here. An important person who attended the Duke of Guise in 1588, the year the Duke of Medina Sidonia's fleet was lost, told me that he said the same thing. That is why in the city of Eu the Duke at his own expense maintained a seminary of twelve students, some of whom are now here with us. When the Conde de Puñonrostro was Asistente here he never tired of praising our work and congratulating the Company for undertaking it. He remarked to me on various occasions that his experience as Field Marshal in the French and Flemish wars had made him realise that Spain's support for this work was to its benefit for reasons both of state and religion, since no other means were now practicable, and he added that when history was read a hundred years from now this story would arouse the admiration of the world. I could go on to report the similar views of more than twenty grandees and titled gentlemen, and of the past and present Cardinals of Seville, the Cardinal of Toledo and more than ten other archbishops and bishops, but I will simply record the comment made to me by the present Archbishop of Burgos when he was Bishop of Cadiz—that were this the only work undertaken by the Company it would deserve the love and esteem of all, for he believed it to be the greatest in God's church and he considered the Catholics of England to be the best and the most tried and tested in the world, and that by means of this work the Catholic religion had proved victorious, for the heretics had not prevailed in spite of their long and cruel persecutions. He was convinced, he told me, that more souls were saved in England today than when it was a Catholic country. The same opinion was expressed to me by Fr Thomas Darbyshire, an English father of our Company who is now more than 90 years old and was Dean of London in Catholic times and went to England at the beginning of the present Queen's reign and entered our Company[6]. The good Bishop of Jaen, Don Francisco de Sarmiento, to whom God granted an exceptional appreciation of the importance of our work, spoke of it to me on several occasions with tears in his eyes and said that the present situation in England reminded him of the primitive Church. He regarded Fr Robert Persons as a modern Athanasius (a comparison which was made on several occasions to me by Fr Juan de Cañas, known to all his acquaintances as a holy and learned man) and said he could see no more important work in God's Church. This explains the yearly grant of a thousand ducats which he lovingly bestowed on the seminaries in Seville and Valladolid, and when he died he left instructions that this grant should be continued for another two years—not taking into account other gifts which he bestowed. He also took in several of the boys whom Fr Persons rescued in Puerto de Santa María, and clothed them and treated them with great charity and generosity for as long as they were in his household.

Whenever new students, or those departing for the mission, call upon the Lords Inquisitors to seek their blessing, the Holy Tribunal has expressed its great esteem for this work and its commendation of those who support it, and as a practical token of their support they have donated money both collectively and individually. On one occasion we invited them to a college celebration and the whole Tribunal came with all its ministers and officials—something almost unprecedented in Seville. The last time four priests went to take their leave before departure the Tribunal received them with marked affection and the eldest Inquisitor thanked them, not without tears, on behalf of all his colleagues and asked them to record their names in their register as a favour.

Fray Gaspar de Cordova formerly Provincial and now confessor to His Majesty the King, and Master Calahorrano, his successor as Provincial, a man of great influence and regarded as a great servant of God, and Master Spinola, another influential churchman who for more than 50 years preached to large congregations in this city to great effect, all expressed to me on various occasions their great esteem for this work and for the Company in supporting it, declaring that it was the most important of their undertakings. Master Salucio said the same: that from the earliest times of the Church he had never read of an undertaking to compare with this, and he spoke of it in the pulpit, whenever opportunity arose, with deep feeling, as did other learned members of his and other orders. Even seculars and religious known to be unfriendly to the Company contribute to this work of ours and find no cause in it for complaint. Some seculars who have no great reputation for virtue say what great good fortune it is for this city that it should foster men who are dedicated and sworn to give their lives and shed their blood for Jesus Christ and for their faith and religion. Only a few days ago two gentlemen from Morón came to this city just to see this seminary, which they had read about in a book, and with extraordinary devotion and tears begged to be allowed to kiss its walls and asked that someone from the house should visit their district and said they would raise contributions of corn etc on its behalf. Which they did.

As a result of Our Lord's goodness and the renown he has given to our work, every time we have asked help from the city council, the Church and other institutions here (and there have been many such occasions) we have never been refused—indeed I have been told that I am too modest in my requests. Some of the city councillors and canons, not content with what their chapters have contributed, have taken it upon themselves to raise funds from private individuals. Some of the grandees and titled gentlemen who support individual students have persuaded others to do the same, out of the great esteem they have for our work and for the Company in undertaking it. Some reverend ecclesiastics and prebendaries have volunteered, out of their eagerness to contribute to our work, to maintain and educate in their own households some of the young boys who often arrive without the grounding required to start the philosophy course in the college. A doctor of theology in this archbishopric educated at his expense for three years a student who is now one of our best theologians. And in 1600 the licentiate Francisco de Sepulveda, Vicar and Theologian of Baeça (an exemplary man of great piety, a trusted colleague of the good bishop Don Francisco Sarmiento and of his successor the present bishop of Jaen), out of the great love and charity and appreciation of the value of our work and his earnest desire for the conversion of England, sent us a nephew of a glorious priest martyr whom he had educated at his own cost for two or three years. This young man is an excellent Latin and Greek scholar, and one of our most gifted philosophers, and possessed of much virtue and promise. This year the same reverend gentleman sent us another student whom he had maintained for more than a year and who promises well. Both of them give evidence of the Christian piety and care which their good patron devoted to their education. Other ecclesiastics and laymen also have offered to support students. Furthermore, other provinces of the Company in Spain which do not maintain seminaries associated with this work have taken in and educated some of our subjects before sending them on to the mission or to the seminaries. The province of Toledo sent us Fr Bell who was Minister here and later died in Cadiz, and Fr Johnson who is now Minister in Malaga, and Fr Anthony [Hoskins] who is assistant to the present Fr Provincial in England. Last year it sent Fr John Pole, after he had finished at Alcalá, to the Valladolid seminary where he is now teaching theology, and it gave to heaven Brother William Worthington, who was studying theology at Murcia. Those who are accepted for the Company in England do their novitiate in Flanders, France or Rome before returning to the mission. Generally speaking, about 4 to 6 novices are accepted at Rome each year, and the same number of students enters the College there.

From the beginning of his term of office the Father General has shown a marked eagerness to promote this work in every possible way, and I understand that when he was speaking of it to a senior member of our Company he stressed his unremitting support for the English mission and said that it was the finest and most estimable of all the Company's activities and of great service to God and his Church: in the 22 years since it first began it had gathered strength and resisted the furious and savage persecution of the heretics, while more than 150 priests had shed their blood including 9 or 10 from our Company, as well as a great number of laymen.

6. Apart from the spiritual benefit and credit which this seminary has brought to our Company, it has never yet, by God's grace, been a burden to the Province or occasioned it any temporal concern. The Province has so far not had to contribute anything to the support of our fathers or students, except for one or two Spanish brothers and one Spanish father who were on the staff before it became entirely English. Nor has the Professed House suffered any decline in its income from private contributions (as some feared it would). On the contrary, it appears that Our Lord has blessed it more liberally and generously in these last years than in the period prior to the seminary's establishment, as can be seen from all the building extensions and improvements they have been able to undertake and the support they have received from the ordinary public—not to speak of their 25 novices and the substantial legacies they have been left this year. Fr Cordesses declared to me on several occasions that God would reward the Professed House and the Company in Seville for supporting this work, and that contributions to the one would in no way affect contributions to the other, and he has been proved right. In the eight or nine years he was here as superior or subject he supported our work with extraordinary zeal, promoting it among all his acquaintances

and securing for it a number of donations including the bequest by Alonso de Paz of 10,000 ducats to the two seminaries and another bequest of 16,000 ducats. He did so because God had given him a keen appreciation of the importance of this work.

Two fathers trained here, Fr Richard Walpole and his brother Fr Christopher Walpole, have gone to the seminaries at Rome and Valladolid. The former, after his year of novitiate, worked here for eight years to great effect. The latter had to leave for health reasons, as he had quartan fever. Eight fathers have come to work here from other seminaries and provinces:

Fr Henry Walpole, the martyr, one of the founder members of the seminary, from Flanders.
Fr Charles Tancard, Minister, from Italy.
Fr Simon Swinburne, Minister, from France.
Fr Henry Bell, Minister, from Toledo.
Fr William Johnson, Minister, from Toledo.
Fr Anthony Hoskins, Minister, from Toledo.
Fr Henry Tichborne, the present Minister, from France.
Fr William Warford, at present confessor and lecturer, from Rome.

As I have said, these Fathers save the Province labour because of the assistance they give in its ministries.

It would not be a burden to start taking in some novices who would help the mission and the province, as is done elsewhere. Other provinces consider this to be to their advantage even when they have no seminaries to support and when the novices are not obliged to remain there to work.

7. Our Lord was pleased to make much use of this province for the conversion of England even before there were any seminaries in Spain. In 1577 Fr William Weston, a man of true sanctity as all those who knew him will acknowledge, came here to this province for his novitiate and studies, and he was a missioner and teacher of Greek in the colleges at Seville and Cadiz, giving great edification. Even today the laymen who knew him remember him as 'holy Father William'. From that time on, God moved the hearts of several fathers of this province to support the seminaries and gave them a high esteem for this work and a desire to contribute to it, and now that there is a seminary in the province many others, including the most senior and learned, share this eagerness and have volunteered for the work. They envy those of their brethren who are working in this vineyard of the Lord and would willingly become Englishmen just to share in the harvest. Since many in this province often ask me about that true servant of God and faithful son of the Company Fr William, and since I have taken great pains to enquire about him, I can say briefly that in 1582, at the bidding of our Father [General] he left this province for England. I have a 4-page letter he wrote from Paris before crossing to England, full of zeal and the spirit of God. He was to take the place of Fr Campion who had shed his blood and been hanged and quartered the previous year. During the two or three years he was at

liberty the good father worked with great fervour and zeal and won universal esteem for his virtue and modesty. He made many distinguished converts, including the daughter of a titled gentleman, in spite of the obstacles put in his way by one of the most famous heretics and renowned preachers in England.

He has been a prisoner for 16 years now in various gaols where he has given such signs of sanctity that even the heretics love and venerate him. Fr Persons told me that he was the most highly regarded man in England, and that even in prison people came to consult him from all over the kingdom. Fr Persons also told a priest that he lived with Fr William for a year and that throughout that time the latter never slept in his bed but spent every night kneeling in prayer: if he was momentarily overcome by sleep he would lean on a stool for a short while until he revived and could return to his prayers. In 1589 an English priest who passed through Marchena told me that it was well known among Catholics and heretics alike that all the time Fr William was in prison he never slept in his bed and that he usually spent the night on his knees, and that to his knowledge he had healed the sick with the sign of the cross and holy water: such was his mortification and austerity that it was a common saying among Catholics: 'Si habuero eloquentiam P. Campiani, pennam velocem P. Personii et vitam austeram P. Guillermi, charitatem autem non habuero, nihil mihi prodest'. When Brother Toribio de Palacio lived in the Seville college, he told me that he once shared a room with Fr William for a whole winter and that every night the latter took the discipline with great severity: whenever he entered the room he would find him on his knees.

When the heretics saw the example he was setting and the number of conversions made by his means, they removed him to the prison at Wisbech where thirty Catholic priests were held. Moved by his example and sanctity, these priests wished to put themselves under obedience to him, and since the good father in his humility would not consent, they sent a petition to the Provincial of the Company and to the Father General. The latter instructed him to govern and assist them, though without using the title of superior, being in the same relation to them as our fathers are to the clerics in their colleges and houses. The good father carried out this task with such exemplary care and charity that the prison came to resemble a religious house of the reformed observance. One of our students here[7] was brought up in that prison and served mass and studied there, and from personal experience he told me that every day as many as 18 or more masses were said and Fr William gave two lectures of cases of conscience, besides counselling the many visitors who came to see him and hearing confessions and converting many heretics. As a result they moved him three or four years ago from Wisbech to the Tower of London, where he is now held in such strict confinement that no-one can talk to him. It was in one or other of these prisons that he made his profession recently. Many other remarkable things could be related of this holy man, but I must be brief.

So from what has been said it is evident that this college is advantageous to the Province both spiritually and temporally, and is in no way a liability or burden.

[Endorsed] A defence of the seminary.
no. 4. Occupations and assignments of the English fathers. It could be added that Fr Johnson spent 12 years in Malaga until his death in 1614. The fund-raising and conversions by Fr Forcer over 7 years. N.S.

Notes

1. The narrative was evidently written after the publication of William Warford's catechism in 1604 (see note 3), and before the arrival at ECS of Fr John Pole, who died there in 1605.
2. Pedro de León, S.J. See Document 2.
3. [William Warford] *A briefe instruction by way of dialogue concerning the principal poyntes of Christian religion . . . by the reverende M. George Doulye, priest*. Lovaine: Laurence Kellam, 1604. (A & R 877). In his Oxford D.Phil. thesis 'English Catholics and the Printing Press 1558–1640' Dr D. M. Rogers argues conclusively that this work was written by Warford and printed at Seville in 1604. One Giles Arkenstall, in a letter to the Earl of Salisbury dated 22 November 1605 (SP 14/16/99) reproted that in the course of visiting the colleges at Seville and Sanlúcar he had seen 'a book which as it seemeth is the work of one George Dowlies as appeareth, being printed in English purposely to be sent into England to do some great work'.
4. On this episode, see Robert Persons, *Newes from Spayne*, 1593 (facsimile reprint 1977), p.2.
5. In 1603 Laurence Worthington and Bro. William St George were at Cordoba, Bro. Gregory Arthur at Trigueros, and John Price at St Hermenegild's College Seville (Baet.8).
6. Thomas Darbyshire, b.1518, a nephew of Bishop Bonner of London. Studied at Broadgate Hall, Oxford. D.C.L. (Oxon), 1555. Successively Archdeacon of Essex, Canon of St Pauls, Chancellor of the diocese of London and Dean of St Pauls. S.J., Rome, 1563, aet.45. d. Pont à Mousson, 1604. Peralta overestimates his age, as he was 86 in the year of his death.
7. William Arton. See p.50.

Document 5. Joseph Creswell and his Spanish Jesuit opponents: The Evidence of Andrew White, S.J., October 1612.

The letter of Andrew White, now in the archives at Simancas[1], which is printed below, was probably written originally in English. Creswell translated it into Spanish and sent it with his comments in the margin to Claudio Acquaviva who is addressed as 'Your Paternity', the traditional title given by the Jesuits to their Father General. The letter is now in the Estado collection at Simancas because Creswell added it to the dossier of documents which he used to defend himself before the three councillors of state (the royal confessor, the Cardinal Primate and a nobleman) appointed by Philip III to investigate the charges against him and the English colleges. The letter is not in Creswell's own hand but in that of one of his secretaries, probably Francis Fowler I[2]. There is an endorsement in the same hand which reads: 'A letter from Seville, in which it is shown that the letter of Father General was not sent for his own purposes but because of the manoeuvres of interested persons here [i.e. in Spain]'. This is explained by the endorsement to the preceding folio, which reads: 'The reply of Fr Creswell to the letter of Father General of the Society of 9 October 1612'. That reply is an 8-page document in which Creswell reviewed the charges accumulating in Rome from the 'interested parties'[3].

The letter is included here because it throws some further light on the complex machinations which led up to Creswell's final departure from Madrid in November 1613. It has already been shown elsewhere[4] how some Spanish Jesuits, notably Hernando Lucero, the Provincial of Toledo, conspired with the Duke of Lerma's faction at the Spanish court to have Creswell removed. The new evidence reveals the role played in the affair by Francis Forcer, S.J.

Other documents at Simancas and Rome fill in a little of the background. On 22 May 1612 Creswell wrote to Rome asking to be allowed an assistant, with the wish that this should not be Francis Forcer (then at Cadiz)[5]. However, on 17 July 1612 the General wrote instructing Forcer that he was to proceed to Madrid without delay to assist Creswell in his duties as Prefect of the English mission[6]. Evidently this move was temporarily averted, for Forcer was still in Cadiz in October, as Andrew White's letter shows. On 9 October 1612 the General wrote to William Weston at Seville telling him that as Creswell had been summoned to Rome, he was to take his place at Madrid[7]. In fact, Creswell obtained permission to remain in Madrid and set about organising his defence. He had enemies not only at court and in the Toledo province, but in Andalusia. The Superior of the Casa Profesa at Seville, Iacobo Vaderfort, was alarmed by the threat which his fund-raising posed to the income of his house, and objected to his negotiations with a rich lay patron in Granada to found an English seminary there[8]. Evidently Creswell's enemies in Andalusia found a willing collaborator in Francis Forcer whom they saw as a more pliable and amenable replacement. In fact Forcer was to remain at Cadiz until 1617, and Creswell was replaced at the end of 1613 by Anthony Hoskins. Creswell's attempt to appeal over the head of Rome to his powerful friends at the Spanish court evidently provoked the General to final action. On 5 November 1613 Acquaviva wrote to Marcos del Castillo, the Andalusian Provincial, expressing his displeasure at Creswell's recruitment of the Duke of Medina Sidonia to plead his cause and telling him that he had written to the King and to the Duke of Lerma requesting their cooperation in his decision to recall Creswell. He reassured Castillo that 'all would be resolved' when the latter left Spain[9].

De Una del Pe Andres Vitus de Sevilla del 16 de octubre de 1612

a. Llama revolucion de planetas la secreta negociacion de los conspirados.

b. Fue traça de Dios que este moço con su poco secreto publicasse toda la conspiracion.

c. Oy decir a personas graves en Roma que este mismo solia con estas mismas mañas y negociaciones de cartas de terceros tirar a V.P. a traças suyas haciendole creer que nacian de las Provincias.

d. Bien veen que no es para este puesto. Pero buscan instrum^tos. para sus fines. La mission y nacion recibiran daño si V.P. no pusiere aqui persona de respecto *de quien tengan satisfacion los Catholicos de nrã nacion que dependen de España y pueden tener ocasion de correspondencia en qualqr tiempo con los Ministros de su Magd: y tal he procurado muchos años ha.*

e. Al P^e. Prov^al. del Andaluzia toca el remedio desto, y al V.P^d ya que lo sabe.

V. Ra dessea saver quien fue el primum mobile *que revolvio a estos planetas^a. El Pe* Forcer^b me dixo q̃ N.^c fue la persona que començo traço y compuso estos ingenios no tanto por amor que tenga al Pe *Forcer^d* (segun parece) como para sacar Demosthenes de Athenas, y apartar el mastin del ganado persona que con authoridad puede defender la mission prudente y constantem^te, para poner en su lugar a otro, cuya flaqueza por todos caminos se puede pisar facilm^te, y por el toda la mission y nacion rescebir agravios.

Y quanto al Pe Forcer se puede dudar, si conviene *que el resida en Cadez.^e* Porque el que ocupare aquel puesto ubiera de ayudar a los Ingleses, y combidarlos a ser Catholicos, con buenos documentos y obras de charidad como an hecho otros sus

f. El Obispo electo de Cadez advertio que pretende acreditarse por esta via, y no le pareçio bein.

g. *Como viene esto con lo que an informado al P. que* estoy desacreditado con los Ministros? *Querrian desacreditarme con ellos si pudieran.* Pero aqui se va de espacio en creer invenciones y los Ministros nos conocen a todos.

h. No parece sueño sino professia. Pero *de aca salio.*

j. *Que diran quando supieren* que V.P. *les a dado credito.* Por lo menos con esto les acabara deconoçer.

k. Pesa me que se vayan descubriendo estas cosas porque *la Compañia pierde* con ellas.

l. No erro en el tiempo: de manera que de aca fue la resolucion para que volviesse en Noveᵉ de V.P.

m. Le an hechado a perder y a otro compañero suyo.

antecessores, y no espantarlos y ponerles miedo y horror: pues se quexan del los Ingleses que es *el mayor enemigo* que tiene en España nr̃a nacion.ᶠ

Tenia casi olvidado de dezir a V.R. que me dixo el P. Forcer que esos Padres *temen lo que puede V.R.* con el Rey:ᵍ y por esso que prevendran a su Magᵈ y al Consejo que quando el Pᵉ General aya de llamar a V.R. a Roma (que ellos *sueñan*ʰ sera en viendo las cartas que an escrito los conspirados contra V.R.) no tenga arrimo, ni en su Magᵈ ni en su consejo. Pero no pienso que el Padre General *dara credito a nr̃os enemigos*ʲ antes de aver oydo a nr̃os amigos.

Tengo ya avisado a los nr̃os *en Flandes*ᵏ de los daños que an de seguir si estos otros saliessen con sus intentos, y ellos mismos seran los primeros que se arrepentiran.

Pero no dudo sino que el Pᵉ General estara sobre aviso: aunque el Padre Forcer tiene el seno lleno de buenas esperanças, *que al principio*ˡ de decembre a de volver a Madrid: y ya ha dicho algunos de los designios en que le an puesto *al pobre moço*ᵐ o el mismo se ha puesto. Porque le han echado a perder, y el vendra a ser el mejor testigo de sus miserias.

Translation:

From a letter of Fr Andrew White from Seville, 16 October 1612

a. By 'revolution of the planets' he means the secret plot of the conspirators.

b. It was God's plan that this young man[10] should with typical indiscretion have made known the whole conspiracy.

c. I have heard it said to senior persons in Rome that this same one used to try to draw your Paternity over to his side by relying on these same artifices and letters supposed to be by third parties, leading one to believe that they originated in the Provinces.

d. They can see quite well that he is not suitable for this post. But they are looking for tools to serve their own ends. The mission and the English nation will be damaged if your Paternity does not put here a respected person who will be acceptable to the Catholics of our nation who are dependent on Spain and may need to negotiate on occasion with His Majesty's ministers. Many years ago I managed to secure such a person.

e. The remedy for this lies with the Father Provincial of Andalusia and with your Paternity now that you are aware.

f. The Bishop elect of Cadiz[11] noticed his efforts to win esteem in this fashion and did not approve of it.

g. How does this accord with what they have told your Paternity about my being in low regard

Your Reverence wishes to know who was the primum mobile who set these planets in revolution.[a] Fr Forcer[b] told me that N.[c] was the person who laid the plan and assembled these talents, not so much out of love for Fr Forcer[d], it would seem, as to remove Demosthenes from Athens and to separate the guard-dog from the flock (one with the authority to defend the mission prudently and steadfastly) and to replace him with another whose weakness can in every way be easily exploited, to the disadvantage of the whole mission and English nation.

As for Fr Forcer, it is doubtful whether he is suitable to reside in Cadiz.[e] The person who occupies this post should assist the English and attract them to become Catholics by his good credentials and charitable works, as his predecessors have done, not put them off and cause them alarm and fear. The English complain that he is the worst enemy our Nation has in Spain.[f]

I almost forgot to tell your Reverence that Fr Forcer told me that these fathers are afraid of your Reverence's influence with the King[g], and so they will try to predispose His Majesty and the Council so that when the Father General has to summon your Reverence to Rome (which they fondly dream[h] will be when he sees the letters the conspirators have written against your Reverence) there will be no support forthcoming from His Majesty or among the officials? They would like to discredit me if they could, but people here are slow to believe stories and the officials know us all well.

h. It is no fond dream but a prophecy. But it originated here.

j. What will they be saying when they find out that your Paternity has taken them in earnest? At least after this one will cease to ignore them.

k. It pains me to see that they keep making these things public, because the Society is damaged by them.

l. He is not wrong about the time, since the decision that he should return from here in November came from your Paternity.

m. They have made him ready to be the loser, and his other companion too.

the Council. But I do not think that the Father General will give credence to our enemies[j] before he has listened to our friends.

I have already warned our fathers in Flanders[k] of the harm that must ensue if these others succeed in their plans, and that they will be the first to regret it.

But I have no doubt that the Father General will be on the alert, even if Fr Forcer has a dream full of high expectations and has to return to Madrid at the beginning of December.[l] He has already talked about some of the schemes in which they have involved the poor young man[m], or in which he has involved himself. They have made him ready to be the loser, and he will turn out to be the chief witness of their misfortunes.

Notes

1. Estado 2858, f.42. For Andrew White, see p.102.
2. See A. J. Loomie in RH 12 (1973), pp. 75–77.
3. Simancas E 2858, f.41.
4. A. F. Allison, in RH 15 (1979), p. 80–81. See also A. J. Loomie, *The Spanish Elizabethans*, 1963, pp. 182–229, on Creswell's career in Spain.
5. Simancas, E 2858.
6. Baet.4/1/120.
7. Baet.4/1/132.
8. See the letters of Vaderfort and Francisco de Porres, Rector of Madrid, in Simancas E 2858. The latter supported Creswell.
9. Baet.4/2/45r.
10. i.e. Forcer. It is not clear who 'N' was
11. Juan Cuenca, Bishop of Cadiz 1612–23 (C. Eubel, *Hierarchia Catholica*, Münster, 1935, 4, p. 192).

Document 6. A Petition for an English Rector, 1613

(Source: Simancas, leg. E 1771)

The petition is contained in a folder, or *pliego*. The endorsement reads:
'En 24 de mayo 1613 el Sr Duque de Lerma con un memorial y carta de los sacerdotes y colegiales de los seminarios de ingleses de Sevilla y Vall^{id}. Su Magd escrivio al general de la Compañia que permitiese a estos seminarios que tubiesen y les diese superior de su propia nacion como le tienen otros. No se ha cumplido esto, y vuelben a suplicar los dhos seminarios mande su Magd que tenga efeto'. (*In the margin*: El provincial de la Provincia informe de lo que le parece en esto').

Translation: The Duke of Lerma, 24 May 1613, with a petition and letter from the priests and students of the English seminaries of Seville and Valladolid. His Majesty wrote to the General of the Society of Jesus for permission for these seminaries to have and be given a superior of their own nationality, as others do. This was not done, and the aforesaid seminaries are again petitioning Your Majesty for it to be put into effect'. (*In the margin:* 'Obtain the opinion of the Provincial on the matter'.)

The text of the petition reads:

Señor

Los Sacerdotes y Colegiales yngleses del Seminario de Sevilla supp^{can} humilmente a V.Mag^d mande que tenga efeto la Mrd que les hizo y a toda su Nacion con la carta cuya copia va inclusa con perpetua obligacion y agradecimiento como agora quedan rogando por su salud y larga Vida y la Prosperidad de sus Reynos.

25 de Março

Sacerdotes	*Colegiales*
Guilielmus Astonus	Philippus Mayler
Edoard Hoptonus	Marcus Drurius
Rogerus Stonus	Ricard^s Cortesius
Joannes Noricius	Joan: Monaxius
Antonius Berius	Joanes Tylnicus
Guilielmus Symsonus	Joanes Martin[u]s
Henricus Pollardus	Thomas Blacklow
Odoardus Roffus	Petrus Alanus
Nicolaus Harington[u]s	Johannes Sidneus
Andreas Varnesius	Edmundus Campianus
Gulielmus Tyndallus	Joannes Polus
Robertus Personius	Carolus Florus
Joannes Molens	Joannes Gallicanus
Thomas Chetelt^s	Edoardus Leus
Robertus Bartonus	Gulielmus Talbottus
	Joannes Hattonus
	Georgius Olcornius

(**Translation:** 'The English priests and students of the Seville Seminary humbly beg Your Majesty that he should give orders for the putting into effect of the favour granted to them and all their nation in the enclosed letter. They remain his eternally grateful debtors, praying for his health and long life, and for the prosperity of his Kingdoms').

Also enclosed in the folder is a copy of the letter sent by Philip III to Acquaviva from Aranjuez on 11 May 1612, asking that the English seminaries in Spain might be granted English superiors.

A similar petition from the college at Valladolid was also attached. A note on the front of the folder indicates that the whole file was passed to the Council of State on 29 May for further discussion.

Document 7. William Whichcott's Letters from England, 1616

The letters below are translated from a rare *impreso* of which one copy survives in the Biblioteca Nacional, Madrid (Varios 58–98): *Relacion que el Padre Francisco de Peralta de la Compañia de Jesus, Rector del Colegio de San Gregorio de los Ingleses de Sevilla escrivio a Don Antonio Vigil de Quiñones y Pimentel, Conde de Luna y Mayorga, en que se da quenta del estado que oy tienen las cosas de la Religion Catolica de Inglaterra, y la persecucion que padecen los Catolicos* (Sevilla: Alonso Rodriguez Gamarra, 1616). The main part of the book consists of three letters to Fr de Peralta, written from St Omer and London by an English Jesuit priest who had been a member of the Jesuit community at St Gregory's and left for Flanders via Sanlúcar in January 1616. The letters are signed simply G.S.

An examination of the Jesuit catalogues suggests that the writer was most probably William Whichcott, *alias* Saville, S.J., who according to the records of the Andalusian province was on the staff of St Gregory's from about 1611 to 1615. He was of the diocese of Lincoln, was born in 1580 and joined the Society in October 1604. In 1615 he was Prefect of Studies at St Gregory's. He then disappears from the Andalusian lists, but the catalogues of the English province reveal that he was working in the London district from 1621, was in Wales in 1628 and in the Hampshire district by 1633 and until about 1645. He was back in Flanders in 1649 and died in 1654.[1]

The initials G.S. (Gulielmus Sabellus) and the dates point to William Whichcott as the writer. He may be identical with William, the son of Thomas Whichcott of South Kyme and Anwick, Lincs, who was a legatee in 1575 and of his wife Mary Saville of Newton. If so, his *alias* corresponds, as might be expected, to his mother's maiden name. There is a difficulty, however. In the letter he writes from London in March 1616, Whichcott declares his intention of travelling to his native parts in the hope of converting his parents (*mis padres*), but the family pedigree shows that Mary Whichcott died in 1591/2. The Anwick register records the christening there on 17 December 1581 of John and Matthew, (twin?) sons of Thomas Whichcott and so perhaps William's younger brothers.[2]

The tone and content of the letters suggest that they were intended for publication by Peralta, for the purpose of promoting the work of the college and raising funds. The person to whom the book is dedicated, the Conde de Luna, had held high office in Seville, and while there had been an influential patron and benefactor of the English College. In his dedication, Fr Peralta recalls the benefaction of the Count and his late wife in sponsoring two students a year at the college, and alludes to the Count's interest in English Catholic history which inspired him to commission a series of portraits of English royal saints, kings and queens, copies of which were made and sent 'to various parts of the world'.

f.1. From a letter by an English father of the Society, written a few months after he left this seminary, dated from St Omer, 6 February 1616.

I wrote to your Reverence the day I left Sanlúcar; this sequel will give a brief account of what befell me on the journey. After crossing the harbour bar we had very good weather for eight or nine days, then many storms, and at one time we were in extreme danger of perishing; but after twenty-two days, by Our Lord's favour we all arrived safe in Flanders. By God's grace I had good health all the way, and in all the colleges of this province—which are numerous and very large—I was most hospitably received; but I was particularly heartened by the sight of our college at Louvain which, though recent, is well established. I saw also the monastery of the Carthusians at Malines, and that of the Benedictines at Douai, both English foundations, and the convents at Brussels [defect in the original, with loss of ? two words] Gravelines and in this city. The nuns in all three are English, and of such virtue and perfection that I have great hopes that by the prayers of these holy souls Our Lord may take pity on our unhappy country. But what has given me special satisfaction is the seminary of St Omer, which I find it difficult to describe in words. It has a hundred and seventy boys between twelve and eighteen years old, all so well instructed in letters and virtue that one might go many leagues to see them. They celebrated the Vespers and Mass of the Purification of Our Lady with a solemnity that can hardly be surpassed in the Papal Chapel. The music was excellent, all performed by students of the house, and the same thing happens on all the solemn feasts of the year. Many of them appeared in surplices and copes, like canons, and their composure and modesty belied their years. Many gentlemen, prelates and persons of quality who attend these feasts are amazed to see with what dignity and grace the students celebrate them. I saw one boy among them, twelve years of age, the son of a prominent English gentleman, who on arrival at a port on his way to this country was asked by the guards if he would take the oath. The boy replied that in his parents' house he had been taught never to swear. When after further exchanges he persisted in refusing to take the oath, they took him back to London under arrest and put him in prison, from which he later emerged and came to this college.[3]

The difficulty of getting out of England is very great, as is clear from this case and many others, but entry to the kingdom is far more difficult, by reason of the spies who are posted by the heretics at all the ports, the vigilance of the guards in imposing the oath and rigorously examining all who enter, and the punishments meted out to any ship masters who smuggle Catholics in, so that none dares to bring in a person who is not a known heretic for fear of putting himself in evident danger of prison and confiscation of his ship and property. Yet in spite of all this, by Our Lord's grace, fathers and priests still manage to get through, such is their desire to help their country.

Your Reverence will already have heard about the five priests imprisoned in England who were released and deported at the petition of the Archduke's ambassador, on condition that they never returned to the kingdom. Among them was Father F., an alumnus of this seminary whom Your Reverence sent to the mission more than twelve years ago, but *multum mutatus ab illo*. I spoke to him in Brussels, and found him in good health and of stout heart. He is a great worker in that vineyard of the Lord, and will shortly return to England notwithstanding the perpetual exile they imposed on him when they released him from prison.[4]

Letters from England report how they have recently confiscated the estates and property of sixty gentlemen in the province of York, and committed their persons to perpetual imprisonment for refusing to take the oath, which is the normal punishment for recusancy. This matter of the oath, as your Reverence knows, is a new method that the heretics have devised to discover, catch and harass the Catholics and seize their property, because it is additional to the old penalties of 80 ducats a month for those who do not attend their churches, 250 ducats for hearing Mass, and death and confiscation of goods for harbouring a seminary priest in their house or possessing an Agnus Dei, medal or indulgences. The justices, who are very numerous, can impose this oath on anyone they like. Although it has some fair clauses at the beginning which it binds all subjects to keep and observe, it contains other things which are directly contrary to the authority, jurisdiction and power of the Pope and to other principles of the Catholic religion, such as that neither the Pope nor anyone else can absolve them from the said oath. If anyone refuses to take this oath, they arrest him without further evidence or charge, and maltreat him and condemn him to perpetual imprisonment, confiscating his goods, as they have done with the aforementioned gentlemen and many others. The wickedness of this oath has been written about at length by Cardinal Bellarmine, Father Francisco Suarez and other learned gentlemen, as your Reverence has seen.

The Archduke and Duchess show consideration and favour to our seminaries at every opportunity, but the King of England's ministers who reside at this court do all they can to harass the Catholics who live in these parts, both those who are in the seminaries and the other gentlemen and persons of quality who have fled to these states from the vexations they suffered from the heretics, fulfilling the words of the Apostle: *Persecutionem patimur, sed non angustiamur, dejicimur, sed non perimus. Quia Dominus supponit manum suam.* Many fathers of the Society and priests known to your reverence here in Flanders send you their greetings, in particular the Father Rector of St Omer[5], Father Flack[6], Dr Norton[7], Father Henry Mailer (who is shortly to receive his doctorate)[8], and Mr William Evans, a good friend to your Reverence and to this seminary, who came to Flanders with his wife and family to escape the harassments and vexations which as Catholics they had daily to endure from the pursuivants. He enquired much of me concerning your Reverence's health, as many others have done. They were very pleased to hear that Brother Fabricio[9] is in good health after having worked for our countrymen for twenty-five years. May Our Lord reward him and all of them.

This is the news I have concerning Flanders, being on the point of departing for England. If God is pleased to allow me to arrive there safely, I will write to your Reverence about the situation there. Give my greetings to all the Fathers, friends and acquaintances of the house and college, and likewise to my friends outside, and I humbly beg them all to commend me to Our Lord, that he may help me on this journey and in the dangers that await me. May he preserve your Reverence for us for many years. Date as above.

G.S.

f.3v. Copy of the letter from the Bishop of St Omer to His Majesty (3 February 1616)

[A progress report on St Omers College written at the suggestion of Joseph Creswell]

f.4v. From another letter of the same Father, dated London 12 March 1616.

Since I last wrote to your Reverence from St Omer I have entered this country safely, thanks be to God, though not without great danger of being arrested. After entry, which is always the most perilous part, thinking myself safe, my companion and I fell into the hands of justice. We were in an inn on the way to London when the innkeeper, happening to notice that we were somewhat modest and that we did not curse or swear as the heretics do, began to entertain some suspicion of us and then went to summon the ministers of justice to examine us to see if we were Catholics. When the justices arrived they found us sitting at table, and after they had questioned us as to who we were and where we came from, and we had answered the first thing that came to mind, we invited them to eat with us. We entertained and treated them with such courtesy that they departed without making further search, saying that we were honourable people who gave no grounds for suspicion. Thus God delivered us out of their hands, for if they had been thorough we would have been finished, since I had my breviary in one pocket and my rosary in another, together with some little pictures of Our Lady of Sichem.[10]

Now I am in this city of London, whence I shall depart in two or three days, for my chief business, which is the conversion of my parents, makes me eager to go to my own part of the country. Here I am evidently in danger of falling into the hands of the justices, for they have so many spies in the prisons and in the houses of all known Catholics and of the ambassadors that it is impossible to go in or out of them by day or night without being caught. They follow anyone they see coming out of one of these until he enters some other house, and then they fetch the justice and ransack the house from top to bottom and take the people they are looking for to gaol unless they give them the money they demand. On other occasions they lay hands on them in the street and search them for letters, books, rosaries or similar things, and even if they find nothing they take them to be examined by the bishops or the justices and cause them so many vexations and injustices that I marvel at the patience of the poor Catholics.

It is true that they do not make so many martyrs as they did, neither is the treatment in the prisons as bad as it has been (though there are large numbers of people imprisoned for the Faith in different parts of the kingdom, and in this city there are many men and women in six or seven different prisons), but for all that the persecution is more vexatious than ever, as I have been told by experienced and well-informed persons who have been here for more than twenty years and can compare present with past. The present policy of the heretics is to avoid doing anything which might make a noise outside the kingdom, and within it to do as little as possible, so that everyone may think there is no persecution and so cease to have compassion for the Catholics. On the other hand they give such ample commissions to the pursuivants to harass them and plunder their possessions that there is no Catholic in the kingdom who can be sure of holding on to a single sovereign.

Someone who knows as much about the affairs of the Catholics as anyone in the kingdom told me that in fact there is hardly a Catholic in the whole kingdom who is not in debt, and the majority are more than half ruined, so that although there is great charity among them and they are very generous with what they have, they can scarcely maintain themselves and their families, the priests, and other poor Catholics inside and outside prison. No great faith is needed to believe this, for although I have been here no more than a fortnight I have seen so much of these conditions that I am moved to the utmost pity and compassion, even though it comforts me to see the patience with which they bear it all. The only human consolation they have is to share their troubles with such as myself who are bound to take pity on them. Some heretics laugh at them and take them for madmen because they are willing to forfeit their possessions, honour and reputation for the sake of their faith. Others take pleasure in seeing them afflicted and ruined out of the hatred they feel for them in professing our holy faith. The mob, stirred up by wicked preachers who in their sermons do nothing but speak evil and lies of the Catholics, heaps a thousand curses on them, attributing to them every evil that occurs. In recent months a Count who is a great favourite of the King, was discovered along with his wife and others to have had a hand in the murder of a gentleman, and although it is quite certain that they were no more Catholics than Luther or Calvin, and those of them who were condemned made public profession of heresy at their execution, nevertheless the people, by the cunning of the ministers, are firmly convinced that they were all Catholics. I myself have heard it asserted as if it were Gospel truth, and am amazed at the scale of the slanders heaped on Catholics as a result.[11]

Consideration of such things often leads me to wonder how long the Catholic faith can last in this country, seeing that the heretics are gradually depriving the Catholics of all that they possess within the kingdom; that they will not let them leave the kingdom with what few possessions they have left, as many wish to do; that they go to amazing lengths to stop students going to the seminaries. There is so much wickedness in the heretics, and so little fervour and commitment in some who could and should help, that from a human point of view it does not seem possible that the faith can long survive. Yet in spite of all this I hope in the Lord that *nunc propior est nostra salus, quam cum credidimus* (Rom.13). The constancy of the Catholics in professing their faith; the patience with which they bear their dishonours, the loss of their possessions and the insults of their persecutors; the zeal with which they deprive themselves of their children and send them to the seminaries to be brought up in learning and virtue and to prepare themselves to be instruments in the salvation of their country; above all, the courage with which these children face dangers on sea and land, and the hardships of exile, and take such pains to elude the vigilance of those who wish to hinder them—all these are manifest signs *quod digitus Dei est hic* (Exod.8). These reasons give me hope that Our Lord will further his work, *attingens ad finem fortiter* (Sap.8), giving us the consolation and the victory we hope for, to his greater glory, even though meanwhile, *disponens omnia suaviter*, he permits all this so that the Catholics may gain greater merit and that all may see that the work is His, as is the cause.

I have seen Father N. and another Father of the Society imprisoned with him, and ten other priests as well as laymen. I have also visited Father Maxey,[12] who is in another prison. His own father had him arrested when he returned home after an absence of sixteen years. I shall omit the long and extraordinary story of his capture, because he told me he would write to your Reverence about it himself.

Father Baldwin[13] is in the Tower of London, where he is not allowed to speak or write or see anyone save only the guard who brings him his food. I chanced to meet Father W. and Father Thomas in this city, and they particularly asked me about your Reverence's health. I beg your Reverence to do me the kindness of giving my many and humble greetings to all my friends and acquaintances inside and outside the house. I keep them all in my memory and heart, and ask them to remember me in their holy prayers and to ask Our Lord to help me with his holy grace to be of service to him in this desert. I intend to return to this city for Whitsun, and then I shall advise your Reverence of what befell concerning the conversion of my parents. Meanwhile grant me your holy blessing and commend me to God at your holy mass and in your prayers. May he preserve your Reverence. London, date as above.

G.S.

f.7v. From another of the same. London, the 6th of April.

When I wrote to your Reverence on the 12th of last month, I intended to go straight to my native parts to discharge the main business for which I came, but afterwards my Superior thought fit to detain me until after Easter, seeing that if I had made such a long journey during Lent I would have run the risk of arousing suspicion in the inns on the way. If you do not eat meat like the other guests they begin to suspect you. Since I last wrote, therefore, I have been in this city and some other places five or six leagues distant, helping the Catholics as far as in me lies, deriving great consolation of soul from finding such good people and such pure souls in the midst of the great wickedness that surrounds us. I assure your Reverence that I am very humbled at seeing the devotion and fervour and great virtue of these Catholics who, although they are layfolk, are superior to me in every respect, even though as a priest and religious I have the greater obligation to set them an example and take the lead.

The same day, or the day before I wrote last to your Reverence, a priest was martyred at York, and later another priest along with a layman at Lancaster.[14] I shall not give your Reverence the details as I understand that others have already done so in full.

A little later the pursuivants took forty people who were coming away from hearing a sermon preached to them by a priest imprisoned in the Gatehouse. They took them to the Bishop of London who assigned them to various prisons where they are now with little prospect of liberty. Some noble ladies who were among the rest he delivered to the captain of the pursuivants who detains them in his house, each one paying him forty reals a day for board and lodging.

Although Father John Maxey related the story of his capture to me the first time I saw him and told me he would send you a full account of it by letter, I have since heard that he cannot easily do so in prison and so I shall relate his story to your Reverence just as he told it to me. This last winter, in fulfilment of the vow he had taken in the College to return to England, he entered the kingdom secretly and in disguise, as all priests are accustomed to do, and when after three days he arrived in London, hearing that one of his sisters was married and living in the city he went to find the house and asked for her, only to be told she was not at home. When her husband asked what he wanted, he said he brought her greetings from one of her brothers who was in Flanders. The husband asked him to wait a little, as she would soon be back. While he was waiting his father suddenly came in, but the two did not recognise one another, since it was more than sixteen years since they had last met. Shortly, having learned from his son-in-law that the visitor (his son, in fact, though unrecognised) brought news of his son John, he went up to him and asked how his son was and when he would return to England. He answered that he was well and was thinking of returning in three or four months if he gave permission, for he would not return without his father's consent and had delayed several months in Flanders so as not to arouse his displeasure by his return, being the man he was. 'I love him', said the good old man, 'as much as any of my other sons, and long to see him, and though he be a priest I will receive him with as much joy as the others who are ministers'. The conversation between the two continued a long time, and the old man was much affected and appeared most anxious for his son's return. He invited Father Maxey to sup with him so that he might hear more details about the son whom, without knowing, he had beside him, and he never tired of asking about him and his affairs. Seeing such great affection in his father, Father Maxey thought that he could safely reveal himself, not without hope of being able to do him the favour of preparing him for conversion to the Catholic faith, which was what he desired above all else. And so taking him apart he told him that he was his son, and going down upon his knees he besought his blessing in accordance with the custom of the country. The good old man was overjoyed and embraced him with great tenderness, and not being able to contain his pleasure went to a brother of his who was a lawyer, a great heretic and a man of much sagacity and cunning, and told him with great joy how his son John had come home safe and sound. 'Then he is not a priest?', said his brother, on hearing this. 'Yes he is', replied the other, 'but what matter?' At that the lawyer took his brother's hand and told him of the great danger he ran in harbouring a priest: by merely talking to him he had incurred the charge of treason, and he had no choice but to go in person and take him and deliver him to the Bishop of London. The good old man, alarmed by what his brother had said, resolved to take his son to the Bishop. So the following day he took him out of the house, saying that he must bring him to see some friends in town. Suspecting nothing, Father Maxey accompanied him, and when they entered the Bishop's palace asked his father whose house this was. He said it was the Lord Bishop's. 'The Bishop's?', answered his son: 'Then what are we doing here?' 'I want to take you to his Lordship', said his father. 'I have no business with him, nor he with me', replied Father Maxey, 'and so you will excuse me for I will not see him or listen to him'. But his father said that he would raise the alarm if he refused, and that he must go perforce, whether he liked it or not. Seeing this, Father Maxey tried reasoning with his father, telling him plainly how bad it would look for him to hand over his own son to his enemies, who were thirsting for his blood, the more so as he had come from such a distance to see him, out of love alone, and had been promised complete safety. However (he continued), lest he should think he was afraid of the Bishop, or of any Bishop in England, he would willingly go with him, since he wished it thus, trusting in Our Lord that none of them, however much they tried, could cause him to waver in his faith and religion. Arriving at the Bishop's hall the old man declared the cause of their coming, at which the Bishop greatly commended him. Turning to Father Maxey he began to call him traitor and a thousand bad names. Father Maxey told him it was wrong to insult him thus, in that he was as good and loyal a subject and vassal of the King as he, and that the Catholics were as good and loyal as they were—and more so. At this the Bishop grew exceeding angry and ordered him to be taken to a prison where Fr N. and many other priests were confined. Soon afterwards his father obtained leave of the Archbishop of Canterbury to have him taken to another prison, so that he should not have anyone to help him in the disputes he has daily with the heretics, for he has two brothers who are ministers, one being preacher to the King, and a cousin who is a Dean.[15] His father brings other ministers besides to talk to him. Now that they have seen that they can do nothing with him, they promise that if only he will take the oath they will procure him his liberty, but by the grace of God he remains steadfast and refuses to accept any of the favours they offer him, however licit, so as not to put himself under any obligation to them. I went to see him one day, and we comforted each other greatly, and I have sent various people to see him. All speak highly of him, and with reason.

While I was writing this, there came into the house where I am lodging one of our Fathers of the Society, to whom I related the story of Father Maxey and his father. He told me his own, similar, story which I think will interest your Reverence and so I shall recount it briefly, although it happened some time ago. This priest[16] was the only son of parents who are of good station and wealth. God brought him to the knowledge of the Catholic faith and gave him the desire to serve him in a state of perfection. So, being already Master of Arts of the University of Oxford, he left his native country and went to the seminary of Valladolid where he completed his studies and was made priest. Having news that he was in Flanders, his parents wrote and invited him most insistently to return to England. He, hoping to be able to bring them to the Catholic faith, came and arranged to meet them in the house of a certain Catholic friend. At their second meeting, they secretly informed on him to the justice who suddenly entered the house when he was on the point of leaving, took him prisoner and carried him off to gaol. His parents obtained permission from the Council to keep him in their own house, as a prisoner, and there, though they gave him every possible comfort, they tormented him by bringing in all the ministers of the neighbourhood to dispute with him, and all his kinsmen to persuade him, bombarding him day and night, now with threats, now with blandishments, and not knowing their son was a priest and so bound to chastity they offered him the hand of beautiful women and said they would give him all their estate; and thinking he would prefer to marry a Catholic they offered one lady a dowry of three or four thousand ducats if she would consent to marry him, but she would not agree. About this time the King issued a proclamation in which he ordered all Jesuits and priests to leave the realm, and the good father, having little hope of gaining his parents and being weary of the life he was enduring in prison, seized the opportunity and declared he would leave the kingdom in accordance with the proclamation. When they learned of his resolve, his parents caused all their friends, kinsmen and acquaintances to come to their house, and there they all joined in entreating him clamorously, with tears in their eyes, not to distress them so, nor cause his parents to pass their old age in sorrow. But he, seeing that his remaining there would be of little profit to their souls, and could be injurious to his, seeing that they neglected no opportunity to draw him to their will and make him fall, persisted in his determination to leave the kingdom and go into exile, even though his parents had obtained leave of the Council that he might stay if he wished. As a result he was taken to the prison where the other priests were in whose company he was to go into exile. He now thought he was free of his parents, but this was not so, for they obtained leave to be with him in prison in a place apart from the other inmates, and there they never left him alone, importuning him now one, now both, his father taking him by one arm and his mother by the other. They besought him on their knees, with tears in their eyes, to take pity on their grey hairs, and this they did on several occasions, alone and in the presence of others. Those who witnessed it waxed indignant at his hardness of heart and unwillingness to give way. They kept him under such close watch that they would not allow him converse with any Catholic or permission to read any papers he was sent. Again they brought in learned ministers to dispute with him and try to persuade him to abandon the Catholic faith and embrace their sect. But by Our Lord's grace he emerged victorious in everything. When the time came for him to leave prison for exile, his father flung himself on the ground at the foot of the staircase which led down from the prison, so that he could not pass without stepping over him—a cruel predicament! But Our Lord gave him the strength to overcome all obstacles and so he made his departure, not without shedding bitter tears at seeing the great distress of his parents and grieving even more at seeing how little his coming had profited their souls. After three or four years in exile in Flanders, he returned here this last year in order to help others even if he could not help his parents. Having heard of his coming, they were very eager to see him, but he would not trust them again or allow himself to see them.

All this I have written that your Reverence may know the different kinds of combat we have to engage in here, sometimes with declared enemies and sometimes even within our own household, and that you may obtain for me the grace of Our Lord that I may fight valiantly against them all. In two or three days I must go to my own region to see if, with his help, I can have any effect with my own parents, though from what I have been able to learn from some who know them I have as yet little hope. But with God's help anything is possible. I beseech your Reverence to commend myself and them to God in your masses and prayers, and to have others do likewise, for the greater the danger [gap of ? 4 words] the greater the need of heaven's assistance. This will add further to the countless obligations by which I am bound to your Reverence, whom may Our Lord preserve for many years with health and life. London, the 6th of April 1616.

G.S.

f.11. Extract from a letter from the Father Rector of the English College of Louvain,[17] 16 May 1616, in which he refers to the martyrdom of two priests and a layman.

[*Summary:* Three martyrs were executed in March, one a priest more than seventy years old who had laboured more than thirty years in York and was arrested in the house of a Catholic nobleman.[18] To protect his hosts, he neither denied nor admitted his priesthood, and was condemned solely on the evidence of a rosary and other religious objects found on him. A Catholic servant was arrested after purchasing the martyr's remains from the executioner, and was imprisoned.

One week later a priest, 'N.Tules',[19] and a layman were executed at Lancaster. On the scaffold a knight, pitying the priest, offered him an annuity of eighty ducats in perpetuity if he would take the oath, but the offer was refused. The priest was quartered, the layman hung. But the rope broke with the man's weight. He was again offered a reprieve but again he refused to take the oath and was hung.]

ff.12v—14v. Postscript [by F. de Peralta]

[*Summary:* Eight priests have been sent to England from ECS in the last year: two Jesuits and six seculars. The last four left in April, having had an audience of the Cardinal Archbishop, asking for his blessing and thanking him for his support of four students at the college. They also took leave of the Inquisitors, 'in appreciation of the great benefits which that Holy Tribunal had bestowed on this house since its foundation, and in order to be able to tell the Catholics and the heretics what fatherly protection they had given to the good English Catholics, and that if on occasion they were severe with miscreants, it was only in extreme cases and for their good. One of the students delivered a brief but affecting address in Latin, appropriate to the occasion, asking for their blessing, telling them of the dangers awaiting them and asking for prayers. He ended by expressing their wish to see the Holy Tribunal established in England and other provinces which were plagued by heresy, in order that by its means religion should be kept pure and undefiled, as it was in Spain and other parts where it was established'.

Two students have recently arrived at the college, and another twelve are expected. The college owes much to the support of the city, which last year [1615] extended its annual grant of 200,000 maravedis for another ten-year period. Their benefactors can be assured of the prayers in heaven of the martyrs from the college—now eight in number—whom they helped on earth.]

9 August 1616   Francisco de Peralta

Notes

1. Fo 7/832.
2. A.R.Maddison (ed.), *Lincolnshire Pedigrees*, Harleian Society Vol.52 (1904), p.1071. If my identification is correct, then Fr William Whichcott's paternal grandparents were Sir Hamon Whichcott, of Harpswell, Kent, and his wife Alice Redish. The Anwick christenings are taken from IGI.
3. With this description of St Omer's, compare the account by the papal nuncio Guido Bentivoglio written in October 1609 (translated extracts in Fo 7/1152-55).
4. The five priests were Francis Kemp, Gervase Pole, Edward Smith, Thomas Blunt and Thomas Browne (SP 14/83/25). Francis Kemp is probably to be identified with Francis Boniface Kemp (SO 1598-1602, ECV 1602-3, OSB Montserrat 1603), who was released from the New Prison by the agency of Gondomar on 29 June 1618 (SP 14/97/129; CRS 10/127). He appears in several London prison lists between 1614 and 1618. However, if he is 'Father F.', it is difficult to see how he can be described as an alumnus of ECS.
5. Gilles Schondonck, S.J. (H.Chadwick, *St Omers to Stonyhurst*, 1962, p.404). Though the English Jesuit novitiate had been transferred to Liège in

1614, the scholasticate remained at Louvain until 1623 (RH Oct.1979, pp.84–5).

6. William Flack, S.J. (1561–1637) studied at Cambridge and was later a fellow-novice of St Aloysius Gonzaga in Rome. After a short period at ECV (1590–92), he spent the remainder of his life at St Omer (Fo 7/261–2).

7. *vere* John Knatchbull, an alumnus of ECS who later became Vice-President of ECD (see p.78)

8. Another alumnus of ECS. See p.82.

9. Fabricio Como, a Milanese laybrother at ECS for 35 years (1593–1627). Obituary letter in AHN, Jesuitas leg. 56.

10. Sichem is a small town in Belgium near Montaigu (*anglice* Montacute), where there was a miraculous statue of Our Lady much venerated at this time. On his visit to St Omer in 1609 the papal nuncio in Flanders 'carried in the procession a statue of Our Lady carved out of the wood of a tree that grew in the forest of Sichem, where the apparition occurred' (Fo 7/1153; cf.A&R 578).

11. The Earl and Countess of Somerset were brought to trial in May 1616 for the murder of Sir Thomas Overbury.

12. John Maxey, an alumnus of ECS.

13. William Baldwin S.J. (1563–1632). Vice-President of the English Mission at Brussels c.1599–c.1610, he was captured by the Elector Palatine, handed over to the English government and imprisoned in the Tower. Released in 1618, he was Rector of St Omer 1622–32 (Fo 3/501–20).

14. Blessed Thomas Atkinson was martyred at York on 11 March 1616, aged 75. Blessed John Thulis and Blessed Roger Wrenno were martyred at Lancaster on 18 March 1616.

15. Probably Anthony Maxey, Dean of Windsor (DNB).

16. James Sharp, *alias* Pollard S.J. (1578–1630), of Bradford, Yorks. At Oriel College, Oxon, 1593–1600, ECV 1602–4, ECD 1604–7, S.J. 1607. In England as a priest, 1607–11, 1615–30 (Fo 2/617).

17. Henry Bedingfeld, *alias* Silesdon, S.J..

18. Blessed Thomas Atkinson (see n.14 above) was arrested at the house of Mr Vavasour at Willitoft, East Riding.

19. A printed note in the margin reads: 'This priest appears to be from the Seville seminary, which he left more than twenty years ago'. Peralta is confusing the martyr Blessed John Thules, educated at Rheims and Rome, with Robert Thules, who was at ECS 1593–4 and died in 1602.

Document 8. Henry Gerard's Stir, 1693.

By 1690 the supply of English students to St Gregory's had almost completely dried up. Only one Englishman was left at the college, Paul Savage, a brother of John Swinburn S.J., the Vice-Rector of St Omers.[1] Juan Bernal, the Rector of St Gregory's, wrote to the English Jesuits asking for more students, but military operations by the English and Dutch in Flanders prevented their departure. In any case, the authorities at St Omers may well have lost confidence in the ability of the Andalusian province to provide a training suitable for the English mission.

Relations between the Spanish Jesuits and their charges at St Gregory's sister-institution, the Irish College in Seville, had long been strained. There had been troubles there in 1637, and again in 1647, in the course of which some students had appealed over the heads of their superiors to the city authorities.[2] In 1692 the only three students at the Irish College, Roger O'Casey, Terence Kiernan and Walter Flood, were expelled. They obtained the support of the local Irish community in their campaign against the Jesuits, for in July 1692 thirty-eight Irish merchants resident at Cadiz and Puerto de Santa María signed a letter to Cardinal Howard asking for both the English and Irish colleges at Seville to be removed from the Society and placed under his jurisdiction and that of the Archbishop of Seville. The colleges, they complained, were simply being used by the Andalusian province for its own convenience. There were eight Spanish Jesuits at St Gregory's and only one English student, while at the Irish college there were no students at all, the three remaining ones having been driven out.[3]

The situation was now exacerbated by the arrival at the English college of Henry Gerard, one of those artful dodgers who from time to time bedevil seminaries. He was able to impose himself on St Gregory's only because the Rector there was anxious to obtain English students in order to perpetuate the college's claim to be 'English'. Gerard was a Lancastrian who had been admitted to the English College at Rome in 1688 but was dismissed about four years later as being 'unsuited for the mission'.[4] He made his way to Cadiz where he threw himself on the charity of a local English Catholic merchant, Francis Malbrank, and wrote to the Rector of St Gregory's to ask for admission to the college. Fr Bernal was encouraging, but wanted assurance that Gerard had left Rome only for health reasons, as he stated, and not for any misdemeanour. Gerard's ecstatic and flowery reply should have put the Rector on his guard. Among other things he claimed to have influence at St Omers and promised that within a year students would again be flocking from there to Seville in his wake.

Gerard's anxiety lest his bluff be called is evident from a letter he wrote a few days afterwards to a contemporary from his Venerabile days, Thomas Fitzjames, now a chaplain in the service of Cardinal Howard at Rome. Signing himself 'poor old Gerard' he asked Fitzjames to make sure that the Rector of the Venerabile, Fr Antonio Luca, did not report unfavourably about him to Seville. Besides revealing Gerard's character, the letter to Fitzjames casts some interesting sidelights on other matters. There is a reference to a contemporary of theirs at the Venerabile, Henry Rawlins, having been captured by the 'Salleymen', that is the Barbary pirates. Gerard saw much of the Irish community at Cadiz, and reported that they 'hate and speak against James [II] more than anybody'.[5]

One of the Irish whom Gerard met at Cadiz was Walter Flood, recently expelled from the Irish College in Seville, so he was already well informed about the Jesuit colleges when he arrived at St Gregory's in December 1692. It did not take him long to put into action a plot which evidently he and Flood had planned earlier. 'God send we prosper and cast away the Phylistian yoke', Flood wrote to him from Cadiz in January. That month Gerard wrote a letter, from St Gregory's to the Jesuit General in Rome, above his and the forged signatures of Savage and two Irish students, listing all the shortcomings of the college, and he sent a similar letter to Cardinal Howard in Rome, purporting to come from Savage. This letter was assumed by Fr Anstruther to be by Savage, but an examination of the original handwriting (AAW 36/27) confirms that it was the work of Gerard. In the letter Gerard refers to complaints already sent to the Cardinal by a certain 'Roger'. Anstruther took this as to be the English priest John Rogers, but it is much more likely to be Gerard's accomplice, the Irish student Roger O'Casey who was then in Rome pursuing his case against the Seville Jesuits.[6]

When the Father General wrote back to Seville enclosing the letter he had received from Gerard, the latter's game was up. Interrogated by the Rector of St Gregory's, Paul Savage swore 'on the oath of a priest' that the letter and signature were not his and that he was not privy to the plot. On searching Gerard's room, the Rector found a dossier of other conspiratorial and forged documents. There were drafts of letters to the Archbishop of Seville, the Pope, the Congregation *de Propaganda Fide* and the Congregation for Religious, petitioning for the suppression of the college or its transference to the archdiocese. Gerard was ejected from the college forthwith. He sought asylum with some of the English or Irish merchants in the town but was turned away. Eventually, the Rector reported, he was taken in by 'heretics'. The *Liber Ruber* of the English College, Rome, says briefly of his later career: 'Postea apostatavit factus ministellus, sed deinde resipuit'.[7]

St Gregory's might be assumed to have learned, from the lesson of Henry Gerard, to beware of English *vagantes*, but when after an interval of nearly twenty years the college again opened its doors to students it made much the same mistake with an equally disreputable character, John Mottram (see p.86). However the college was henceforward to function as an annexe to the Irish college, and was to be 'English' in name only.

One of Henry Gerard's many 'memorials' is printed below.

Memorial of Henry Gerard. (ARSI FG 1606/6/III no.20). c.1693.

Ego Henricus Gerard, Collegii Anglicani Hispalensis Alumnus, pro nunc existens motu proprio, certa scientia, et experientia tum propria tum aliena in conscientia et veritate testor statum collegii hujus per multos retro annos sic habuisse et pro *hic* et *nunc* sic se habere; et nisi res adeo publice notoria esset ut vel omnes quotidie vident et sciunt, iamiam plurimorum Anglorum Hibernorum, Hispanorum sigilla, manus proprias, syngraphas in rei fidem et testimonium habere possum, sed ridiculum est velle probare testibus, solem luce meridiana lucere:

1. Contra Bullam Clementis 8, quo proxime et immediate uni Sanctae Sedi Apostolicae hoc Collegium subiecit, Jesuitae per suam impudentiam mendacissime asserunt, hoc idem collegium sui iuris et potestatis esse; immo arroganter praetendunt dominium absolutum, regimen despoticum et potestatem independentem.

2. Fundatio Collegii est pro 35 alumnis; immo per 50 et amplius annos sustinebat 40,50,60,70 vel etiam 80 alumnos: a triginta vero annis nunc 3, 4, 5 plus minus, pro praesente unum tantum, ac ne illum quidem prout deberent.

3. Summa redituum annuorum ex ore et confessione ipsius Doctoris est 1200 ducati, 600 ex Capitulo seculari, 100 ex ecclesiastico, 100 Gadibus, et 400 ab Illustrissimo D.Didaco de Corduba; praeter vineam Collegii, quae reddit ad minimum 200 ducatos; tota vero haec summa non sufficit alere unum alumnum; ratio est, quia consumitur ab ipsis Jesuitis.

4. Loco alumnorum introducunt suos nonagenarios ad comedendum, bibendum et dormiendum; ita ut non sit Collegium Missionis Anglicanae, sed potius Jesuitarum, immo vero Asylum et baculum senectutis Patrum et Coadjutorum moribundorum.

5. Pessime tractando alumnos, cogunt eos necessario fugere ex Collegio ad redimendam vitam; ita nuper multae Missiones periere.

6. Jesuitae neque observant regulas Societatis neque regulas Collegii, sed vivunt ut volunt, nulla habita cura vel ratione alumnorum, an studeant vel non.

7. Non dant victum, vestitum, vel ulla instrumenta ad studia, unde alumni coguntur instar menduabulorum ostiatim ab Anglis et Hibernis catholicis mercatoribus necessaria omnia ex charitate et eleemosyna petere.

8. Intendunt mittere falsas informationes contra Rogerium; ad hunc finem noster Doctor P.Joh:Bernardo petiit a Anglis et Hibernis catholicis et haereticis ut vellent subscribere manibus propriis eius informationes.

Translation:
I Henry Gerard, alumnus of the English College, Seville, of my own accord, acting on certain knowledge and on the experience of myself and others do testify in conscience and truth that the state of this college is now and has for many years past been as follows; and were not the facts so far a matter of public notoriety that they are seen and known to all, I could cite as evidence the signed and sealed statements of numerous English, Irish and

Spanish witnesses, but it is as foolish as seeking to prove by witnesses that the sun shines at mid-day.

1. Contrary to the Bull of Clement VIII, whereby he placed this College directly under the jurisdiction of the Apostolic See, the Jesuits brazenly and most falsely claim that this college is subject to their jurisdiction. They go even further in pretending to an absolute, despotic and unlimited control over it.

2. The College was founded for 35 students. For over 50 years it maintained 40, 50, 60, 70 or even 80 students, but for the last thirty years there have been only about 3, 4 or 5, and at present only one, and even he is not maintained as he should be.

3. On the Doctor's own admission the annual total income is 1200 ducats: 600 from the city, 100 from the cathedral chapter, 100 from Cadiz and 400 from His Grace Don Didaco, Archbishop of Cordoba—not to speak of the proceeds from the college's vineyard, which yields at least 200 ducats. Yet all this does not suffice to maintain one student, the reason being that it all goes to the Jesuits themselves.

4. Instead of students they bring in their nonagenarians to eat, drink and sleep, with the result that it is not a college for the English Mission but rather an asylum and rest house for moribund fathers and laybrothers of the Society.

5. Students have been forced by their ill-treatment to flee the College in order to survive, and thus the missions have suffered.

6. The Jesuits observe neither the rules of the Society nor the rules of the College, but live as they please, showing no concern for the students or their studies.

7. They provide no food, no clothes, no means for study, so that the students are compelled like beggars to seek charity at the door of English and Irish merchants.

8. They intend to lodge false charges against Roger, and to this end Fr Juan Bernal has asked some English and Irish catholics and heretics to subscribe to his allegations.

Notes

1. Fo 7/752 and CRS 70/239-40.

2. For the troubles at ICS in 1637, see IER IX (1872), p.215. See also the Spanish *folleto* in Bodleian Arch.Seld.A subt.4(11). For an earlier attempt by students to remove the Rector in 1630, see *Wadding Papers 1614-38*, ed.B.Jennings, Irish MSS Commission 1953, pp.352-3.

The 1647 stirs are discussed in the article by Francis Finegan, 'Irish Rectors at Seville, 1619-1687', IER 5th series, CVI (1966), pp.53-5. Further light is thrown on them by the documents from the Fondo Gesuitico cited in the following note.

3. Spanish translation of a letter to Cardinal Howard of 30 July 1692. This and all the other relevant papers cited here are in FG 1606/6/III, 1–29 (copies at Farm Street). I am grateful to Fr Francis Edwards, S.J., for making them available. Of the Irish students named, Kiernan is listed by Silke (143) as having been ordained in 1691, but the other two do not appear in Silke's list of ICS students.

4. CRS 40/106–7.

5. Letter of 25 November 1692, in FG loc.cit. For Fitzjames, see Ans.3/60; for Rawlins, Ans.3/183.

6. See Ans.3/197–8.

7. Among the documents seized by Bernal from Gerard was a testimonial (?forged) from a Fr N.Lynch,O.P., of Santo Tomás in Seville, recommending him as a fit person to be received into a religious order.

Gerard's letter of complaint to the Congregation of Propaganda in Rome, dated May 1693, is in AP Serie II, vol. 65 (Collegi Vari).

Document 9. Richard Richardson's Will, 1730

This document is preserved among the Seville records at St Alban's, Valladolid,[1] because the writer, as will be seen, left half of his non-existent estate to St Gregory's and named one of the Irish priests there, Gerard Shaw, as his executor. The document throws interesting light on the Jacobite diaspora.

The testator, Richard Richardson, of Poulton, Lancs, after a life of exile and ill fortune spent in the Jacobite cause, ended up in the remote town of Guadalcanal, in the Sierra Morena, between Seville and Badajoz. There, on the 6th of June 1730, fearing the approach of death, he dictated his last will and testament to a local notary, using Gerard Shaw as interpreter. The fact that the old cavalry captain did not even have the ready money for his funeral did not prevent him making in imagination the bequests which, with better luck, he might have made in reality. The only tangible asset he had was an old fob watch which he hoped one of his creditors might accept in lieu of cash. His main hopes of a posthumous windfall rested with the ill-fated Mississippi Company which had crashed ten years earlier, and with the restoration of James III. In this unlikely event, half his estate was to go to St Gregory's and half to his next of kin in Lancashire, whose names, after a lifetime of exile, he could not remember.

Richardson was at Guadalcanal as overseer of the mines of San Antonio, but the success of this operation may be judged by the fact that he had to pay the workforce out of his own wages. The reference to these mines and to their concessionaires, Lady Mary Herbert and Joseph Gage, makes this document doubly interesting.

Lady Mary Herbert, born in 1685, was the daughter of the second Marquess of Powys, and her grandfather had been one of James II's most loyal followers, rewarded for his services with a dukedom. Joseph Gage was the second son of another Joseph, born a Gage of Firle, who in 1650, through his mother Mary Chamberlain, inherited the Chamberlain estate and castle at Shirburn, Oxfordshire. The baronetcy and estate were inherited by young Joseph's elder brother Thomas, who in due course was to conform to the Church of England, acquire a viscountcy and return to Firle after selling Shirburn. As a younger son, Joseph had to seek his fortune abroad. Both he and Lady Mary Herbert had been educated on the continent—Lady Mary at the Benedictine convent at Ghent, and Joseph Gage at the Jesuit college of La Flèche[2]—and their fortunes were to be made and lost there. They were together in Paris before 1718, when Gage was involved with the Irishman Richard Cantillon and the Scotsman John Law in floating the Louisiana, or Mississippi, Company.[3] Both Gage and Herbert made huge paper fortunes but failed to sell their shares before the bubble burst in 1720. According to Pope, who pilloried them in his *Epistle to Bathurst*, they tried to recoup their fortunes by mining for gold in Asturias, but Richard Richardson's will, corroborated by correspondence in the Caryll and Powys papers, shows that their mining operations were in Extremadura.[4] The project failed, but not before Lady Mary had ruined her family by sinking in the mines whatever resources remained from her speculations in Paris. She and Gage returned from Spain to Paris in the mid-1740's and were still in Paris in 1766 when they were visited by Horace Walpole. Despite a lifetime's companionship they never married.

Last Will and Testament of Richard Richardson, 1730 (Translation)

In the name of Our Lord God, Amen. Be it known to all who see this deed of will that I, Richard Richardson, residing in this town of Guadalcanal in the Province of Extremadura in the kingdoms of Spain, being a native of Poulton in the Province of Lancaster in the kingdom of England, legitimate son of Richard Richardson and of Juliana Parkinson his wife, deceased, one time captain of cavalry in the armies of His Majesty James the Second (whom God rest), King of England: being infirm of body and sound of mind, of such judgment, memory and understanding as it has pleased Our Lord to give me: Believing in the mysteries of the most holy Trinity, Father, Son and Holy Ghost, three distinct Persons and one true God; in the real Incarnation of the Divine Word, the institution of the Blessed Sacrament and all the other mysteries that our holy Mother Church teaches and confesses, in which faith by the mercy of God I have lived; being resolved to live and die as a Catholic and faithful Christian, and being afraid of death, I wish to compose my last will and testament, and for this I implore the Queen of Angels, Mary, the most holy Mother of God and Our Lady, that as the mother of sinners also she may obtain for me the pardon of my sins and the salvation of my soul. With this holy invocation I make the following dispositions:

First, I commend my soul to Our Lord God who made and created it in his image and likeness and redeemed it by his passion and death, and I commend my body to the earth of which it was formed.

And when His Majesty shall be pleased to remove me from this present life to the eternal, it is my wish that my body be buried in the parish church of Our Lady in this town. And in that which relates to my burial and masses, I make no dispositions, not having the immediate resources either in this town or in the kingdom of Spain with which to pay for them, and therefore I leave this to the Catholic goodwill and mercy of my executors. I declare that I have served for many years as captain of cavalry in the armies of His Britannic Majesty James the Second and others, for which I am owed at least forty thousand pounds sterling, and it is my will that if God sees fit to restore King James the Third, his son and successor, to the Crown of which he is deprived, the said sum should be recovered. The papers, deeds and other documents which record my services and certify what is owing to me are lodged with Patrick Blake, a native of the city of Galway in Ireland, now residing in the town of Lorient in the province of Brittany in France, together with my chests, clothes and other papers which I cannot recall in detail but which it is my will that the said Patrick Blake, or the person appointed by him, should hand over to my executors and heirs.

I declare that I am the owner of three shares, and a further tenth of a share, in the Missi Pipi [sic] Company in France, each share being worth fourteen thousand French livres. About eight years ago I entrusted the recovery of the dividend from the said shares to George Verdon, an Irishman residing in the same town of Lorient in the province of Britanny in France, part of which he has forwarded to me as recorded in my papers and books of account; it is my will that he should hand over any more dividends recovered and surrender any sums retained by him. So too any accrued interest owing to me which is in the possession of those persons who are in charge of the said Company should be recovered by my executors.

I declare that more than forty-two years ago I deposited four hundred pounds sterling with Mr Richard Sherburn, of Stonyhurst in the province of Lancaster in England, so that he should pay me an annuity on that sum according to the custom of the country; and the estate of the afore-mentioned person has now passed into the possession of His Excellency the Duke of Norfolk, Catholic Peer of Great Britain. The papers certifying my entitlement to the said annuity are in the possession of Mrs Effie Sanderson, if I remember rightly, widow of one N.Castels, who I think later married Mr John Wheatly in the City of London. And because I owed this lady one thousand two hundred pounds sterling she started to collect the said annuity. Ever since I handed over the said sum I myself have received nothing, and it is my will that if on the settlement of accounts still I owe anything to the said lady she should be paid, or else continue to exercise the aforesaid powers in order that the debt should be paid off.

I declare that I owe thirty silver pieces of eight to Mr Charles Cross, gentleman-in-waiting to the Duke of Sormont,[5] resident in Madrid, and it is my will that he should be paid this sum.

Also I owe a further two pesos to Mr John Dalton, His Excellency's tailor, and two more to one N.Taylor, both resident in Madrid, and it is my will that they too be paid.

To Mr Thomas Arundel, brother of Lord Arundel, resident in London, I owe twenty pounds sterling, and I owe another twenty to Mr Henry Robinson also resident in London at Lombard Street, who has in pawn some silver objects which are worth more than the sum owed him, and if he can be paid this debt I wish him to return the said silver, and although I have some other small debts I do not now remember what they are but it is my wish that they be paid on recovery of some of what is owed to me.

I declare that my suit of clothes and some small effects of little value are at the disposition of Father Gerard Shaw, whom I authorise to sell such belongings if necessary to pay for my burial and masses and to settle my debts.

I declare that at the behest of Mr Joseph Gage I have served for several months at the royal mines of San Antonio in this township, overseeing the works and workforce, and although I have been given various sums of money for this task it has all gone toward the costs of the said works and wages, as will be confirmed by the ledgers, for which reason I have nothing to declare.

To carry out the terms of this my will and its contents I name as my executors the aforesaid Mr Joseph Gage who is at present absent from this town but who is expected to return shortly, and the aforesaid Father Gerard Shaw, of the English College of the Society of Jesus in the city of Seville, chaplain to the said mines and those employed therein, whom I authorise to arrange for my burial and masses as they see fit and according to the wishes of the said Mr Gage, and should he be absent on the occasion of my death I rely on the Christian zeal of the said father to carry out my burial promptly and within the limits of what little funds I have.

I also give full authority to the most honourable Lady Mary Herbert, resident at the Court of His Most Catholic Majesty, daughter of His Lordship the Duke of Powys, Catholic Peer of Great Britain, in her own name and in that of the said Duke to request payment from each and every one of my creditors of the sums which I have mentioned as owing to me, so that when they are recovered and my debts are paid, the residue may be applied as stipulated below.

After completion of and payment for my will, my funeral and masses for my soul, and after settlement of my debts, as regards the remainder of whatever fortune and estate to which I may be rightfully entitled inside or outside Spain, being without immediate heirs, I wish half of it to go to my relatives, even though their names have not been known to me for many years, due to my separation from them and from my country; but it will be the responsibility of my executors to take steps to discover their identity in order to make my will known to them and to carry it out; the other half of my estate I bequeath to the aforesaid English College of St Gregory the Great in the city of Seville; and if Our Lord wills that these monies be recovered and realised, for his greater honour and glory and for the exaltation of his most holy name and the propagation of our holy religion it is my wish that the annual income produced may be used to increase the number of missionary students and that as a benefactor of the said College I may be granted annual suffrages as determined by the Rector, to whom I wish a copy of this my will to be sent together with such documents as he may need to take steps for the recovery of my estate, for which I grant him full powers.

I declare that Samuel Pearson, Englishman, on returning to the city of London, authorised me to recover a certain share of the wages owed to him for the work he did in the city of Toledo in laying pipes for the master engineer, and on learning that the said money was ready to be paid, I authorised some other English engineers who left these mines a few days ago in order to collect what was owed to them for the same reason, to collect the said wages, giving them a blank receipt so that they could receive the money and bring it to me here to be forwarded to the said Samuel Pearson. Because all this is well known to the said Father Shaw, it is my will that when they bring the said sum he should receive it and see that it is sent on to its rightful owner in the city of London.

I revoke and annul whatever wills, bequests, codicils or powers of attorney I may have made heretofore, whether in writing or by word of mouth or by any other means, which are now rendered invalid in and out of court, the only genuine will being that which I now make and which I wish to validate in the form which will be most acceptable in law.

And thus I make my will in this town of Guadalcanal on the sixth day of June, one thousand seven hundred and thirty.

The testator, known to me the notary, as I can testify, signed this in the presence of the witnesses Christobal González Triguero, Francisco Valverde and Pedro Pabón of this town.

The said Father Gerard Shaw also signed, being present and having served as interpreter of those statements of the testator which I could not understand.

The said Father, having read in his language all that is contained herein, stated that it corresponds to what the testator told him and what he wishes done, and he confirms this under oath.

The said Mr Richardson also declared that Mr John May, of the town of Chatham, near Rochester, England, owes him thirty or more pounds sterling, as will be confirmed by letters of his among the testator's papers, and he wishes this sum to be paid.

Likewise the said Mr Richardson declared that French and Rice, commercial partners in Seville, gave the said Mr Richardson fifteen, ten and six doubloons, and he gave them a bill of exchange to be paid on the account of the said George Verdon, and if the latter has not paid the said Messrs French and Rice the sum due to them, it is his wish that they be paid.

As for the debt to Mr Charles Cross, he adds that he wishes the latter to be given his fob watch, worth twenty-five pesos, and if he has cashed a promissory note which he gave him, then he wishes the six pesos over and above the debt should be returned to his executors in order to pay other debts, but if the said Mr Cross should not have cashed the note then he wishes him to be paid what is owed to him and to be given the watch also.

He also declared that he owes fifty-three French livres to Tempest junior in Covent Garden in the City of London, and he wishes this debt to be paid, and he added his signature witnessed by the aforesaid—Richardson—Gerard Shaw—in the presence of me, Miguel Geronimo Escutia.

[Hand changes] This corresponds with the original which is kept with the other documents of this year among my records, in certification of which at the request of the said executor Father Gerard Shaw I confirm it by my signature, Miguel Geronimo Escutia, public notary of His Majesty and of the Council of this town of Guadalcanal, at Guadalcanal, the thirteenth of July, one thousand seven hundred and thirty.

[Autograph] In witness (*locus signi*) of truth,
Miguel Geronimo Escutia

Notes

1. S lib.XV, C/158, 7 pp.folio.

2. Joseph Donne, *alias* Gage, and his brother Thomas were contemporaries of Henry Bedingfeld and of Lady Mary Herbert's brothers William and Edward Herbert, *alias* Grey, at La Flèche in 1702. See CRS 7/132.

3. Antoin Murphy, *Richard Cantillon, Entrepreneur and Economist*, Oxford 1986.

4. 'Epistle to Bathurst', lines 129–34, in *Alexander Pope: Epistles to Several Persons*, ed.F.W.Bateson, 1961, pp.103–4. The entry on Gage in the DNB is totally flawed by the fact that he is wrongly credited with the military career of Bonaventure Thierry du Mont, Conde de Gages, a Walloon general in the service of the King of Spain. For more information on Lady Mary's mines, see W.G.Nash, *The Rio Tinto Mine: its History and Romance*, 1904. Correspondence between Lady Mary in Spain and her father in England relating to the mines is in the Powys Castle papers, National Library of Wales. See Martin Murphy, 'Lady Mary's Mines; or, Pope's "Congenial Souls"', to be published in *Notes and Queries*, December 1992.

5. ? The Duke of Sermoneta.

Document 10. A petition to King Charles IV for the restitution of the College buildings, 1792.

At the suppression of the Society of Jesus, the English Colleges of Madrid and Seville were assumed to be the property of the Society, and their buildings and estate were therefore expropriated by the Crown. At St Gregory's an inventory was made of the College's effects, and its annuities (*juros*) were itemised in a list of the temporalities of the Andalusian province drawn up by the royal commissioners.[1] From this document we learn that by his will of 18 June 1649, Luis Téllez de Rivera left his entire estate to St Gregory's 'for the support of students' there preparing 'to go and suffer martyrdom in their native land'. In return the College undertook the obligation of one hundred masses a year and, on the feast of the Assumption, of providing a meal for the poor in the Royal Prison of Seville. Other annuities came from bequests by Iñes de Vera and Manuel del Río, and from a tax on goods sold in the territory of Calatrava ('alcavalas del partido de Calatrava de Andalucía')—a privilege originally bought by the first Rector with funds donated by Archbishop Rodrigo de Castro. The total income from these sources at the time of the suppression amounted to 175,517 maravedís.

In the early summer of 1767, the English bishops addressed a memorial to the Spanish ambassador in London, Prince Masserano, pressing their claim to the three Spanish Colleges.[2] The embassy chaplain, Gerard Shaw, was an alumnus of St Gregory's, which no doubt worked to their advantage. An enquiry was set on foot by the Madrid government, and on 14 September 1767 the Secretary of State, the Marqués de Grimaldi, communicated the decision of the King, Charles III, to Masserano. The three Colleges were to be 'reunited' in one establishment at Valladolid, and their revenues and property restored. As a result the buildings of St George's College, Madrid, were handed over to the Rector of St Alban's College, Valladolid, who subsequently sold them to the Duke of Alba. At Seville, however, the buildings of St Gregory's had already been ceded temporarily to the Royal Society of Medicine, which the King was reluctant to evict. He over-ruled the Council of Castile and his Fiscal by instructing that the Society of Medicine 'should have temporary use of the building until such time as he could decide on its ultimate destiny'. The Medical Society was to remain in indefinite possession of the buildings, in spite of further appeals by successive Rectors of St Alban's, Valladolid, claiming restitution or indemnification.[3]

Though St Alban's did not relinquish its claims, the Peninsular War and its aftermath led to a suspension of legal proceedings. An account of the college buildings written in 1844 noted the 'capacious' accommodation and the 'excellent gardens' with 'arches and stonework in the Moorish style, indicative of the antiquity of the house'. At that time the Church was occupied by the sisterhood of the Esclavas de Jesús y de María.[4] The case was eventually reopened in 1908, and in February 1913 the Dirección General de Propiedades del Estado upheld the English claim. This was over-ruled, however, by the Dirección General de lo Contencioso, and a subsequent appeal by the Rector of St Alban's was rejected by the Tribunal Gubernativo de la Hacienda. The case was again resumed in 1953 and finally ended in 1965, when the Valladolid College was indemnified for the expropriation of St Gregory's two centuries earlier.

Text[5]

Sire,

Joseph Shepherd, Rector of the Royal College of St Albans of the English in the city of Valladolid, with all due submission and respect begs to make the following representation to your Majesty.[6] Although the great majority of the English nation in the reign of Queen Elizabeth left the Catholic religion, there remained a few who were zealous for the Faith, for its preservation and propagation, and for the formation of priests to preach its doctrines to the remnants of the Catholics in the land. Owing to religious persecution, these men were obliged to flee from their country and establish in other lands colleges for the education of priests. In Germany, Italy and France, with the concurrence of the governments, colleges were founded. At that time Philip II was King of Spain. Under his protection the English Catholics and clergy received the help they so much needed, and were allowed to establish the College of St Alban in Valladolid, where English youths were educated for exercising the priesthood in their native land. Once this college was well established, various youths, in 1592 and 1593, set out from Valladolid and proceeded to found another college for the same purpose in Seville; which in effect was opened under the title of the English College of St Gregory in the houses belonging to the entailed estate of Don Fernando Ortiz and Doña Leonor Fernández de Fuentes. The English rented these houses till 1623, in which year they were able to buy them with their own funds and with the aid of subscription from various benefactors. We see from the title deeds drawn up on November 5th 1623 in favour of the College of St Gregory before the notary Nicholas Muñoz Naranjo, that the houses of the entail of Ortiz were bought for 71,500 reales. The College paid this amount with 36,300 reales—the proceeds of the sale of an annuity to Juan Infante, a citizen of Cadiz, which annuity had been destined for the maintenance of the students—and with 35,200 reales which were borrowed, 20,000 from Don Alonso de Armenta, and 15,200 from Don Fernando Antonio de Cenizo, both of whom were fully paid back by 1636. The College had previously bought other houses adjoining those of Ortiz. One was from the College of the Cardinal, in exchange for another house belonging to St Gregory's in the Collatio Omnium Sanctorum, as appears from the deed executed in favour of the English College before the notary Francisco Díaz de Vergara on December 27th 1596. Another house—where the College church now stands—was bought from the monastery of San Geronimo in Buena Vista, on the outskirts of Seville, as proved from a like deed of sale executed in favour of the College before the notary Pedro Almonacid on January 7th of the same year 1596. Another house was brought from the nuns of San Francisco de Paula in Seville, as evidenced by the duplicate deeds of sale drawn up by the same Almonacid on September 24th 1604 and by Geronimo de Lara on May 5th 1610. Another was bought from the nuns of Santa María de Gracia of the said city, the deed of which was executed before the notary Lara on May 28th 1608: by virtue of which the College of St Alban paid and still pays to this day 1000 reales of a perpetual annuity to the fabric of San Nicolás. And lastly another house was purchased from the canons of the Cathedral on September 14th 1600, as proved by a deed executed by the notary Gregorio de León the same day. All these buildings, united to the house of Ortiz, afforded a splendid opportunity for giving the form of a college to the dwellings of the students, whose great love and tender zeal for their religion were ever appealing in their favour to rescue them from the inconvenience and confinement of the buildings in which they were housed. It was decided, therefore, to rebuild at the College's own expense; and in fact this great work was finished by 1664. The expenditure on this undertaking from the College funds and from subscriptions amounted to 94,153 reales. To raise this money, the College sold a house it possessed for the sum of 6284 reales; it accepted a mortgage of 15,681 reales, which has recently been redeemed by the College of St Alban; it obtained loans from various individuals, who afterwards pardoned the debt—one of 40,218 and another of 29,903 reales; and from the College funds supplied the small balance necessary to pay off the expenses of the rebuilding of the establishment. Hence, all these costs, as well as those of the original purchase of the houses and sites, came from the funds and monies given by pious persons for the foundation and preservation of the College and the maintenance of its students, as proved by the facts narrated above and verified with exactness and clearness in the title deeds, which, if your Majesty wishes, the petitioner will be pleased to produce.

Wherefore, by logical and legal necessity, the material buildings of the College were owned and possessed by St Gregory's and the English mission in exactly the same manner as its other property; and this without anyone else, not even the expelled Jesuits, having any share whatever in this property. The Jesuits never had anything more than the direction and administration of the establishment; and even this only by special arrangement made with them in those early days when, owing to the dearth of priests in England, it was not easy to bring English secular priests to undertake the charge. All this was substantially admitted by King Charles III, your Majesty's father, when the Jesuits were expelled from Spain; and in the Royal Charter of Reunion of the Colleges given at the Pardo on February 11th 1779. For when representations were made to him through Prince Masserano, the Ambassador in London, by the Bishop of Debra, Dr Challoner, in his own name and in that of the English Catholic clergy, his Majesty, with the concurrence of his Council and the dictamen of his Fiscal, graciously hearkened to the petition and resolved that the College of St George in Madrid and that of St Gregory in Seville with all their funds and property should be united to the College of St Alban in Valladolid. Under this new system of government with an English Rector and English secular priests as professors the true object of all these establishments could best be achieved, and the foundations saved from the danger to which they had been exposed of being confounded with Jesuit establishments. It was the declared wish of His Majesty that no third person should be injured by the occupation of the temporalities of the Jesuits. In compliance with this Royal Charter, the Colleges of St George of Madrid and of St Gregory of Seville with all their funds and movable property were united with the English College of St Alban of Valladolid, *all except the actual buildings of St Gregory's, Seville*. Yet, as we have seen from the account of its acquisition, the material fabric of St Gregory's belonged strictly and wholly in full ownership to the College institution, forming a very substantial part of its assets and therefore included in the property ordered to be amalgamated with St Alban's. The building of St Gregory's, being thus isolated, was eagerly sought after, first by the College of Nobles, then by the Medical Society, and finally by the Beaterio de San Antonio, each body adducing various pretensions in the petitions which they formulated. The Royal Council, however, issued a decree on October 1st 1785 absolutely denying these pretensions, because the College of St Gregory 'belonged in full ownership to that of St Alban in Valladolid'. A certificate of this decree was ordered to be sent, and was sent, to the Camara [Privy Council] in order that the present petitioner might there continue his suit—as being on a point pertaining to the Royal Patronage—for the disposal of the building and the funding of its value for the maintenance of English students. The Camara, having in view the decision of the Courts of Justice and the dictamen of the Fiscal, had no doubt whatever as to the lawful owner of the edifice being the Rector of St Alban's, and on November 16th 1785 recommended to his Majesty the alienation of the edifices of the College and Church and the funding of the monies thereby realised in favour of the English College at Valladolid. His Majesty, however, in giving his decision on December 2nd of the same year, thought fit to order that his Royal resolution of the 30th October of the preceding year should be observed, which was a temporary concession of the buildings to the Beatas de San Antonio, reserving the right to take steps in due course to carry into effect the turning of St Gregory's into a Seminary for Andalusian Nobles as he had arranged before.[7]

Sire, the present petitioner respects this and all other Royal decisions of so kind and gracious a sovereign, and places at the disposition of his Majesty not only this building but all the other property which the zeal and piety of the benefactors bestowed on the Colleges; but urged on by the Bishops and Clergy of his country, he is obliged to work with them in under-taking this suit in the interests of the English colleges. Whilst alive to all the dictates of obedience and gratitude, he has studied this Royal Decree and what could have occasioned its dispositions, and he has come to the conclusion that the decision was based on one of two suppositions: either that the College buildings and church of St Gregory's were regarded as not being the property of the establishment, and therefore not to be included in the amalgamation of the College with that of St Alban's; or that this amalgamation was regarded as being a kind of gift to the College in Valladolid. Both these suppositions are false. The proof that the buildings of the College and Church did entirely belong to the English foundation, and that the amalgamation was not a gift or grant to the English community, is evident from the title deeds now presented to your Majesty, which were not included in the former petitions. By them it is shown beyond doubt that the College of St Gregory in Seville acquired with its own funds the sites and houses where at its own expense it erected the buildings in question without the assistance of the Royal Patrimony, or of the funds of the Jesuit Society, or of any other body. Likewise it is proved that the ownership was acquired by absolutely legitimate means, and this lawful possession was preserved till the expulsion of the Jesuits and the Reunion of the Colleges. Therefore it follows as a necessary consequence that the buildings were included in that Reunion as part of the establishment belonging to the English Mission. In confirmation of all this, St Alban's to this day bears the obligations created at the foundation and rebuilding of St Gregory's: it pays yearly the 1000 reales of perpetual annuity attached to one of the houses where the College in Seville is built; it has redeemed the 15,681 reales of the mortgage incurred in the rebuilding of St Gregory's; it fulfils the annual obligation of 52 low Masses and 4 sung Masses—which charge was undertaken to raise funds for the erection of the Church; it accepts the obligation for another 9 low Masses and 6 sung ones, the capital for which was invested in the purchase of the other houses. Wherefore it would be contrary to the gracious will of your Majesty that while the burdens attached to the College of St Gregory should be considered as being included in the reunion of the three Colleges, as part of the object amalgamated, the benefits from which those obligations arise should not be considered as equally included. The ownership, Sire, was vested in and always belonged to the establishment of the English College of Seville; or rather, to the English Mission. St Alban's acquired nothing from the Royal Charter at the Reunion of the three Colleges, since nothing was added to the Mission or its scope that it did not possess before. The mere translation of the establishments which the incorporation of the Colleges occasioned, for greater economy and better management, was not sufficient to cause any alteration in the ownership of the property, still less in the purposes to which, from the beginning, that property was dedicated, and which could be better realised in the state of union than in that of separation.

These considerations are founded on law, and establish an unquestionable right in favour of the College of St Alban, whose interests, like those of any third party, it is the wish of your Majesty to safeguard in dealing with the confiscated temporalities of the Jesuits. The petitioner, in profound gratitude for your resolute protection of a Seminary in which useful missioners are trained for labouring in England, humbly presents these arguments to you in hope that if you should find they refute the grounds on which the Royal decision of December 2nd 1785 was based, you may graciously accept them and grant the earnest request of the Bishops and Clergy of the Catholic Church in England. In view of all we have laid before your Majesty, we beg you to command that by virtue of the union of the College of St Gregory of Seville with that of St Alban of Valladolid, and as a necessary consequence of that union, the buildings of the College and Church of St Gregory be handed over to the Rector of St Alban's Valladolid, so that with the funds accruing therefrom a larger number of students may be maintained; or, if it be your Royal will to devote the buildings to some special purpose, we pray you to be pleased to allow to St Alban's an indemnity equivalent to the value of the property. Finally, the petitioner is always ready to prove before the Camara, where at present the suit is pending, all that he has herein manifested.

Notes

1. Simancas, Secretaría y Superintendencia de Hacienda, leg.331.

2. On the subsequent negotiations, see M. E. Williams, *St Alban's College, Valladolid* (1986), pp.72-3, 266-67; E. Henson in CRS 30/xlvi-xlvii.

3. Correspondence between the Medical Society and the Crown is cited in Antonio Hermosilla Molina, *Cien años de medicina sevillana* (Sevilla 1970).

4. F. González de León, *Noticia histórica y curiosa de todos los edificios . . . de esta . . . ciudad de Sevilla* (Sevilla 1844), 1, p.184.

5. From a copy of the translation in the Seville archive at ECV, Transcripts, leg.2.

6. For Shepherd, see M. E. Williams, op.cit., pp.74, 78-95, 100-16.

7. The College of Andalusian Nobles was planned by Pablo de Olavide (see p.28) but never realised. The 'beatas de San Antonio' were a community of religious women who at this time occupied part of the college buildings. On their disputes with the Medical Society, see A. Hermosilla Molina, op.cit.

APPENDIX: THE ESPINOSA LEGACY

In his account of St Gregory's reproduced earlier in this volume, Henry Piers wrote that its greatest benefactor was 'a widdowe in Civill, which gave unto Father Parsons for making up a Churche for the Colledge (wherein shee hirself should be buried and daily praied for) the sum of forteene thowsand crowns [ducats], and after the churche was builded which was finished at my being there, she bestowed three thowsande crowns for making of churche stuffe for the same. Right before the highe altar is her buriall place, under the which is a vaute which is covered with a verie fayre tombe stone, wherein is ingraven hir name and armes'.

The benefactress to whom Piers refers was Ana de Espinosa, widow of Alvaro Flores de Quiñones, Admiral of the Fleet of New Spain. Her wealth, however, was derived from her own remarkable family.[1] She was the daughter of Pedro de la Torre, treasurer of the Casa de la Moneda [Mint] of Seville, and his wife Juana Nuñez de Espinosa. She had three brothers, Pedro, Juan and Sebastian, all of whom were prominent financiers. All three, Pedro de la Torre Espinosa (1550–1596), Juan Castellanos de Espinosa (d.1601) and Sebastian Castellanos de Espinosa were imprisoned in 1589 on suspicion of peculation. Juan, the prime mover, was sentenced to death but used his influence in high places (he was a friend of Juan de Ibarra, Secretary of the Council of the Indies) to secure a reprieve. In May 1590 the brothers were given a lenient sentence and rehabilitated, their confiscated property being restored to them. Five years later, undeterred by this setback, Juan set up an exchange bank at Seville on a scale comparable to that of the Rialto at Venice, having bought the authorisation to do so for an inducement of 300,000 ducats. The nominal directors of the bank were his brother Pedro, his nephew Pedro de Mallea and the Genoese financier Agustín de Vivaldo, but Juan de Castellanos masterminded the ambitious undertaking, sponsored by influential patrons. After his brother Pedro's death in 1596, Juan returned from Madrid to Seville to head the reconstituted business.

The first signs of insolvency appeared in 1598. In May 1600, desperately short of funds, Juan persuaded the Council of Finances to appoint him Depositary of the *bienes de defuntos*—the capital belonging to emigrants who died in America without immediate heirs, which was repatriated to Spain in order to be distributed to claimants by the Crown. He bought this post—created especially for him—for an inducement of 133,000 ducats, a sum which he did not possess and which he was only able to pay after he had laid his hands on the American funds, the remainder of which he appropriated in order to fill the empty coffers of his bank. However even this windfall of more than 57 million maravedís (over 130,000 ducats) failed to stave off disaster. On 23 March 1601 he was officially declared bankrupt, his estate was seized, and he was confined in the prison of the Casa de la Contratación. The collapse sent shock waves throughout Seville. The majority of creditors lost 75% of their investment and claimants to the *bienes de defuntos* were left nothing. The consequences of the débâcle were felt at the very highest level, for the Asistente [King's representative] of

Seville, the Conde de Priego, had personally guaranteed the banker's credit-worthiness. The fate of Juan de Arguijo was notably spectacular. The Maecenas of his day, famed for his munificence and magnificence, he had been a guarantor of Castellanos as both banker and *depositario de los bienes de defuntos*. He now had to sell or mortgage his entire estate, including his palace (situated opposite the Jesuit College of San Hermenegildo, of which he was a patron), his art collection, effects, country estate and maternal inheritance. Only six years before he had staged a lavish reception at Seville for the Marquesa de Denia, the wife of Philip III's favourite the future Duke of Lerma—an occasion which had set new standards of extravagance in a city famed for profligacy.[2]

The chapel of St Gregory's had been built entirely on the proceeds of funds contributed by Ana de Espinosa and her two brothers, Juan Castellanos and Pedro de la Torre. Together they contributed 13,000 ducats, on condition that they and their descendants be granted the right of burial in the family vault before the high altar.[3] At the time of the benefaction, in 1595, the Espinosas were at the apogee of their fortunes, and Persons must have been well pleased with his coup in securing such rich and powerful patrons. The list of the college's other benefactors at this time includes other names closely associated with the Espinosa family, which suggests that they gave Persons the entrée to a wider network.[4] Besides Juan de Arguijo, already mentioned, there was Juan Vicentelo de Leca, who is recorded as having acted for Juan Castellanos de Espinosa in renting for him the palace of the Corso near the Puerta de Jerez in July 1595.

The chapel of St Gregory's was solemnly dedicated on the feast of St Andrew 1598, and no doubt the Espinosa family held pride of place among the distinguished congregation. Pedro de la Torre Espinosa had died two years earlier, but presumably the family exercised their rights in translating his remains to their new vault, splendidly surmounted by their coat of arms. Three years after the inauguration of their chapel, Pedro's brother Juan Castellanos de Espinosa died, bankrupt and disgraced, in the prison of the Casa de la Contratación, only a few months after his arrest. History does not relate the circumstances in which his body was interred at St Gregory's, but the continuing presence in front of the high altar of so controversial a patron must have been a considerable embarrassment for the college. After the *éclat* of Persons' initial success in Seville, when he enlisted the support of the wealthy and fashionable, the decline in the college's fortunes after the turn of the century may have been due in no small measure to the consequences of the Espinosa scandal. Doña Ana died in 1614, leaving a further sum to the chapel.[5] The family continued to exercise their burial rights, and later in the 17th century one Jeronimo de Mallea, a descendant of Doña Ana's nephew, instituted lengthy legal proceedings in pursuit of a claim to rights of patronage over the chapel.[6]

Notes

1. I am indebted for what follows to Guillermo Lohmann Villena, *Les Espinosa: une famille d'hommes d'affaires en Espagne et aux Indes à l'époque de la colonisation* (Paris 1968), pp.116–29.

2. See Jonathan Brown, *Images and Ideas in 17th century Spanish Painting* (Princeton 1978), pp.21–43.

3. Deed of gift in the Archivo de Protocolos de Sevilla (4 October 1595), Oficio 10, Marco Antonio de Alfaro 1595, libro 5, f.129. Henry Piers is incorrect in attributing the whole gift to Ana de Espinosa, who gave half the sum, the other half being contributed by her two brothers. A copy of her deed survives in the archives of St Gregory's at ECV (S V), witnessed by a number of students whose names were much distorted by the copyist.

4. For this list, see n.1, p.31. It is noticeable that when John Price, S.J., listed the names of these benefactors in March 1610 he did not mention any member of the Espinosa family.

5. Will of Ana de Espinosa, 28 June 1614, in Archivo de Protocolos de Sevilla, Oficio 9, Mateo de Almonacid 1614, libro 2, f.1219.

6. Dossier in ARSI, FG Tit.X/786.

INDEX OF PERSONS

Note: The names listed alphabetically on pp.48–104 and 107–14 are not included.

Acquaviva, Claudio, *S.J.* 7, 8, 163, 169
Ainsworth, John, *priest* 117, 124
Alan, Peter, *student* 168
Alcalá de los Gazules, *Duke of* 6, 20, 123–4
Alcázar, Juan Antonio del, *Seville councillor* 32 (n.16)
Alcázar, Luis del, *S.J., theologian* 15
Alemán, Mateo, *novelist* 2
Alexander VIII, *Pope* 128
Alfaro, Marco Antonio de, *notary* 201 (n.3)
Allen, William, *Cardinal* 6, 44
Almonacid, Mateo de, *notary* 201 (n.5)
Almonacid, Pedro de, *notary* 194–5
Andalusia Company 1
Anderton, Laurence, *S.J.* 115
Araoz, Antonio, *S.J., Rector of ECS* 44
Aray, Martin, *priest* 11
Arcos, *Duke of* 6
Arguijo, Juan de, *poet and patron* 20, 22, 32 (n.16), 35 (n.70), 200
Arkenstall, Giles, *merchant* 11, 162
Armenta, Alonso de 194
Armenta, Juan de, *S.J., Rector of ECS* 107
Arthur, Gregory, *S.J., laybrother* 162
Arton, William, *student* 162
Arundel, Thomas 189
Asoca, *Doctor* 32 (n.16)
Aston, William, *priest* 19, 168
Atkins, William, *S.J.* 33 (n.37), 105
Atkinson, Thomas, *Blessed* 117, 176, 179, 181 (n.18)
Avila, Hernando de, *S.J.* 15
Ayamonte, *Marquess of* 6

Bacon, Francis, *Baron Verulam* 11, 17
Bahamonde, *Doctor* 32 (n.16)
Baldwin, William, *S.J.* 175
Ball, William, *priest* 123
Ballinger, Henry, *student* 19
Bamber, Edward, *Blessed* 105
Barlow, Ambrose, *O.S.B., Saint* 121
Barnes, Andrew, *priest* 19, 168
Barret, Robert, *student* 19
Bassano, Jacopo, *painter* 121

Bazán, Juan, *chaplain* 45
Bedell, William, *Provost of Trinity College, Dublin* 70
Bedingfeld, Henry, *S.J.* 179
Bedingfeld, *Sir* Henry, *3rd Baronet* 192
Béjar, *Duke of* 6
Bell, Henry, *S.J.* 153, 159-60
Bellarmine, Robert, *S.J., Cardinal, Saint* 109
Benedictines 12, 20, 50, 51, 54, 57, 61, 70, 74, 75, 78, 79, 87, 88, 91, 96, 101, 104
Benstead, *alias* Hunt, Thomas, *Blessed* 9, 105, 115, 124
Bentivoglio, Guido, *nuncio* 180
Bernal, Juan, *S.J., Rector of ECS* 47, 182-3
Bertendona, Ximenes de, *S.J., Rector of ECS* 107
Bishop, William, *Bishop of Chalcedon* 85
Blackfan, John, *S.J.* 119
Blacklow. *See* White, Thomas
Blake, Patrick, *of Galway* 188
Blake, Valentine, *of Galway* 135-7
Blanco, Francisco, *Inquisitor* 32 (n.16)
Blanco y Crespo, José María 29
Blunt, Richard, *S.J.* 64, 101
Blunt, Thomas, *priest* 180
Bolen, Jaime, *Scotsman* 131-4
Bonner, Edmund, *Bishop of London* 162
Borghese, *Cardinal* 128
Boylan, Bartholomew, *student* 26
Briant, *brothers, students* 124
Bridgettines 77, 82, 93, 98-9
Browne, Anthony, *2nd Viscount Montague* 96
Browne, John, *Bristol merchant* 1
Browne, Thomas, *priest* 180
Burgo, Dominic de, *priest* 45
Bury, Anthony, *student* 125, 168

Cabot, Sebastian 1
Cabredo, Rodrigo de, *S.J.* 21, 23, 117
Cabrera, Juan de, *printer* 120
Calahorrano, Diego, *O.P.* 158
Cámeros, Francisco de los, *S.J., Rector of ECS* 107
Campion, Edmund, *S.J.* (*not the saint*) 25, 168
Campo, Gonzalo de, *Archdeacon of Niebla* 47
Cañas, Juan de, *S.J.* 157
Cantillon, Richard, *banker* 187
Caro, Rodrigo, *poet* 19
Carmelites 99
Carr, Robert, *Earl of Somerset* 181

Carvajal, Luisa de 15, 18, 21, 104, 116–18
Castañeda, Juan de, *S.J.* 4
Castellanos de Espinosa, Juan, *banker* 199–200
Castellanos de Espinosa, Sebastian, *banker* 199–200
Castels, N., *of London* 189
Castillo, Marcos del, *S.J., Provincial* 164
Castro, Ildefonso, *S.J.* 156
Castro, Melchior de, *S.J., theologian* 15
Castro, Rodrigo de, *Archbishop of Seville* 6, 9, 124, 193
Cecil, John, *priest* 5
Cecil, William, *Lord Burghley* 11, 20, 124
Cenizo, Fernando Antonio de 194
Cerda, Melchior de la, *S.J.* 15
Cervantes, Miguel de 2, 3, 9, 141
Cevallos, Manuel de, *priest* 28
Challoner, Richard, *Bishop of Debra* 25–27, 195
Chamberlain, George, *Bishop of Ypres* 7
Chamberlain, Mary, *wife of Richard Owen* 87, 187
Chapman, Stephen, *S.J.* 107
Charles III, *King of Spain* 27, 193, 195
Charles IV, *King of Spain* 193–8
Charles, *Prince of Wales, later Charles I, King of England* 13, 21, 118–20
Chatterton, Thomas, *priest* 168
Chauncy, Maurice, *Carthusian* 9
Cid, Miguel, *poet* 18
Clare, Elizabeth 79
Clavijo, Matías, *printer* 119
Clifton, Henry, *student* 124
Coloma, Alonso, *Bishop of Barcelona* 32 (n.16)
Comerford, Patrick, *O.F.M.* 118
Como, Fabricio, *S.J., laybrother* 172
Cooper, John, *priest* 124
Copley, Elizabeth, *wife of Reginald Knatchbull* 78
Copley, Margaret, *wife of John Gage* 109
Corby, *alias* Flower, Ralph, *S.J., Blessed* 105
Cordesses, Antonio, *S.J.* 159
Cordoba, Gaspar de, *O.P., Confessor to Philip II* 158
Corro, Antonio del, *Prebendary of St Paul's* 3
Cottington, *Sir* Francis 13, 33 (n.39), 121
Creswell, Joseph, *S.J.* 6–9, 12, 21–2, 31 (n.1), 116, 163–67
Cripps, *Captain, of Puerto de Santa María* 140
Cromwell, Oliver 121–2
Cross, Charles, *of Madrid* 189, 191
Croston, Peter, *pirate captain* 127
Cuenca, Juan, *Bishop of Cadiz* 167
Cuerva y Medina, Pedro de 45
Curtis, Richard, *S.J.* 19, 25, 168

Dalton, John, *tailor, of Madrid* 189
Derbyshire, Thomas, *S.J.* 157, 162
Davenport, Anne, *wife of Gregory Stanley* 97
Davis, William, *priest, musician* 16
Denia, *Marchioness of* 200
Devereux, Robert, *2nd Earl of Essex* 140–41
Díaz, Alonso, *S.J., Rector of ECS* 14, 107
Díaz de la Montoya, Fernando, *printer* 115
Díaz de Vergara, Francisco, *notary* 194
Digby, *Sir* Everard 64
Dodd, James, *priest* 26
Dominicans 25, 125, 186
Doria, Giovanni Andrea, *Prince of Melfi* 154

Eckelles, Constantine, *prisoner* 10
Egerton, Thomas, *student* 8, 123
Escalona, Catalina de Zuñiga y Sandoval, *Duchess of* 118
Escobar, Marina de, *Venerable* 110
Espinosa, Ana de, *benefactress of ECS* 8, 43, 138, 141, 199–201
Essex, *Earl of. See* Devereux
Evans, William 172
Everard, *alias* Talbot, William, *student* 168

Fairburn, George, *priest* 117
Farnese, Alessandro, *Cardinal* 128
Fearne, *Sir* John, *pirate* 127
Federíqui, Pablo de, *S.J., Rector of ECS* 107
Felton, Francis, *S.J.* 107
Ferdinand III, *Emperor* 98
Fernández de Fuentes, Leonor, *wife of Fernando Ortiz* 194
Fitzjames, Thomas, *priest* 182–3
Fixer, John, *priest* 5
Flack, William, *S.J.* 172
Flamenco, Diego de, *printer* 118
Flather, —, *Englishman at Jerez* 140
Fleming, Sebastian, *of Drogheda* 140
Fleming, Thomas, *O.F.M., Archbishop of Dublin* 70
Flood, Walter, *student of ICS* 182–3
Flores y Quiñones, Alvaro de, *Admiral of the Fleet of New Spain* 8, 141, 199
Flower, Charles, *See* Waldegrave
Floyd, Henry, *S.J.* 15
Forcer, Francis, *S.J.* 119, 162–67
Forcer, John, *S.J.* 67
Forth, James, *priest* 73, 89
Fowler, Francis, *S.J.* 163
Francis Borgia, *Saint* 3

Francis Xavier, *Saint* 19
Franciscans 56, 87, 97, 99
Fransam, William, *student* 34 (n.62)
French and Rice, *merchants of Seville* 191

Gage, Joseph, *of Shirburn* 187–92
Gage, *Sir* Thomas, *1st Viscount* 192
Gage, *family of Haling, Surrey* 109
Gages, Bonaventure Thierry du Mont, *Count of* 192
Garnett, Henry, *S.J.* 74
Gee, John, *spy* 103
Gerard, Henry, *student* 14, 182–6
Gerard, John, *S.J.* 100
Gil, *alias* Egido, Juan, *Canon of Seville* 3
Gifford, Mary, *wife of John Campion* 58
Gilbert, *Sir* John 135
Gilbert, Joseph, *of Norwich and Seville* 44
Godolphin, *Sir* William 93
Gómez, Bartolomé, *printer* 116
Gómez de Blas, Juan, *printer* 121
Gondomar, Diego Sarmiento de Acuña, *Count of* 180
Góngora, Luis de, *poet* 2, 15, 19
Gonzaga, Luis, *Saint* 109
González Triguero, Cristobal, *of Guadalcanal* 191
Granado, Diego, *S.J., theologian* 15
Green, *alias* Washington *or* Harris, Paul 16
Green, Richard. *See* Reynolds
Gregory XV, *Pope* 18, 119
Grimaldi, Jeronimo, *Marquess of* 193
Grinston, Dulcibel, *wife of Stephen Taylor* 98
Guise, Henri de Lorraine, *3rd Duke of* 156

Habington, Thomas, *of Hindlip, Worcs* 115
Hackshott, Thomas, *Venerable* 117
Halling, John, *student* 168
Halsall, Ann, *wife of Thomas Morris* 85
Harrington, *alias* Drury, Mark, *priest* 16, 168
Harrington, Nicholas, *priest* 19, 168
Haslewood, Catherine, *wife of Anthony Thorold* 98
Hatton, John, *student* 168
Hawkins, *Sir* Richard, *mariner* 137–41
Haydock, Richard, *Dean of Dublin* 135
Henry, *Cardinal Duke of York* 28
Henry, William 64
Herbert, *Lady* Mary 187–92
Herbert, William, *2nd Marquess of Powys* 187
Herrera, Fernando de, *poet* 9

Herrera, Francisco de, *painter* 29, 35 (n.71), 125
Hidalgo, Clemente, *printer* 21, 115-16
Higgins, Michael, *alias* Adam, *S.J.* 16, 107
Hinojosa, Juan Hurtado de Mendoza, *Marquess of* 120
Hippesley, Ferdinando, *of West Lavington* 75
Hojeda, Esteban de, *S.J., Superior of the Casa Profesa* 7
Hopton, Edward, *priest* 168
Hoskins, Anthony, *S.J.* 12, 159-60, 163
Houghton, John, *Saint* 9
Houghton, Peter, *of Leyland* 53
Howard, Philip, *O.P., Cardinal* 62, 182
Howard, Thomas, *8th Duke of Norfolk* 189
Hussey, Thomas, *Bishop of Waterford and Lismore* 28
Hutton, Anthony, *& Co., of Seville* 44

Ibarra, Juan Antonio de, *writer* 40
Ignatius Loyola, *Saint* 17, 19
Infante, Juan, *of Cadiz* 194
Inoiosa. *See* Hinojosa
Inquisition 10, 15, 124-5, 131-4, 155, 157, 180
Irish 25-8, 135-41, 152, 182-6

James, Thomas, *of Sanlucar, Consul* 6
Jáuregui y Aguilar, Juan de, *poet* 19, 21
Jáuregui, Miguel Martínez de, *Seville councillor* 22, 32 (n.16)
Johnson, George, *student* 123
Johnson, Thomas, *S.J., novice* 124
Johnson, William, *S.J.* (I) 155, 159-60, 162
Johnson, *vere* Purnell, William, *S.J.* (II) 21, 107
Jones, Frances, *wife of Peter Lewis* 80
Jones, Thomas, *Archbishop of Dublin* 135

Kemble, John, *Saint* 73
Kemp, Francis Boniface, *O.S.B.* 180
Kiernan, Terence, *student of ICS* 182
King, Adam, *spy* 33 (n.29)
King, John, *Bishop of London* 93
Knatchbull, *alias* Norton, John, *S.J.* 13, 172
Knatchbull, Thomas, *student* 79

Langley, John, *student* 128
Lara, Jeronimo de, *notary* 195
Laud, William, *Archbishop of Canterbury 102*
Law, John, *Scottish financier* 187
Lee, Abraham, *of Puerto de Santa María* 80
Lee, Edward. *See* Sheldon
León, Gregorio de, *notary* 195

León, Juan de, *printer* 115
León, Pedro de, *S.J., prison chaplain* 4, 131
Leopold I, *Emperor* 98
Lerma, Francisco Gómez de Sandoval y Rojas, *1st Duke of* 163-4, 168
Levison, Richard, *student* 124
Line, Anne, *Saint* 86
Lithgow, William, *Scottish traveller* 32 (n.27)
Longueville, *Sir* Henry 81
Lorençana, Bartolomé de, *printer* 117
Luca, Antonio, *S.J., Rector of ECR* 182
Lucero, Hernando, *S.J., Provincial of Toledo* 163
Lugo, Isabel de 45
Luna, Martin de, *S.J.* 21, 117
Luna y Mayorga, Antonio Vigil de Quiñones y Pimentel, *Count of* 66, 117, 170
Lynch, Nicholas, *O.P.* 186
Lynn, Thomas, *of Norwich* 81
Lyra, Francisco de, *printer* 21, 118-20

Mailer, Henry, *D.D.* 16, 172
Mal-Lara, Juan de, *humanist* 4
Malbrank, Francis, *of Cadiz* 182
Mallea, Jerónimo de 32 (n.20) 200
Mallea, Pedro de, *banker* 199
Mannock, John, *student* 168
Manrique, Alonso, *Archbishop of Seville* 2
Manwaring, Henry, *Captain, pirate* 127
Marin, Diego, *S.J., laybrother* 126
Martin, John, *student* 168
Martínez Montañés, Juan, *sculptor* 141
Maxey, Anthony, *Dean of Windsor* 181
Maxey, John, *S.J.* 175-7
May, John, *of Chatham* 191
Medinaceli, *Duke of* 124
Medina Sidonia, Alonso Pérez de Guzmán, *Duke of* 1, 5, 8, 123-4, 138, 153, 156, 164
Merchant Adventurers 1
Mississippi Company 187-9
Montague, *Viscount. See* Browne
Montano, Benito Arias, *humanist* 35 (n.70)
Montescarlos, Juan Manuel de Mendoza y Luna, *Marquess of* 153
More, Henry, *S.J.* 15
More, Thomas, *Saint* 9
Morris, William, *student* 19
Mota y Escobar, Alfonso de la, *Bishop of Tlaxcala* 23
Mottram, John, *student* 183
Mullins, John, *priest* 168

Muñoz Naranjo, Nicolás, *notary* 194
Murillo, Bartolomé Esteban, *painter* 14
Muscote, *alias* Fisher, George, *priest* 117

Newman, William, *priest* 125
Newport, Richard, *S.J., laybrother* 126
Norfolk, *Duke of. See* Howard, Thomas
Norris, John, *priest* 168
Nuñez de Espinosa, Juana 199

O'Casey, Roger, *student of ICS* 182-3
Olavide, Pablo, *Asistente of Seville* 28, 198
Oldcorne, George, *student* 168
Ortiz, Fernando 194
Ortiz y Sandoval, *Doña* María 43
Overbury, *Sir* Thomas 181
Oviedo, Juan de, *architect* 141
Owen, Hugh, *Welsh writer* 76
Owen, Lewis, *spy* 23

Pabón, Pedro, *of Guadalcanal* 191
Pache, Juan 45
Pacheco, Francisco, *Canon of Seville* 19-21, 32 (n.16)
Padilla, Martín de, *Adelantado of Seville* 6
Palacio, Toribio de, *S.J., laybrother* 161
Parkinson, Juliana, *of Poulton, Lancs* 188
Paul V, *Pope* 18
Paz, Alonso de, *benefactor of ECS* 160
Pearson, Samuel, *engineer* 190
Peralta, Francisco de, *S.J., Rector of ECS* 8, 12, 15, 21, 25, 107, 116-7, 142-62, 170, 180
Pérez, Bartolomé, *S.J., Provincial of Andalusia* 5, 154
Pérez, Diego, *printer* 118
Perry, Philip, *Rector of ECV* 29
Persons, Robert, *S.J.* 4-12, 20-22, 29, 31 (n.1), 112, 123, 138-9, 152-4, 157
Persons, Robert, *priest* (*not the above*) 168
Philip II, *King of Spain* 5, 6, 194
Philips, William, *student* 19
Pibush, John, *Blessed* 115
Pickford, John, *organist and consul* 16, 43
Piers, Henry, *of Tristernagh* 135-41, 199
Piers, James, *D.D., of Bordeaux* 135
Pigott, Thomas, *student* 19
Pimentel, Enrique, *Bishop of Cuenca* 119
Pineda, Juan de, *S.J., theologian* 15, 18, 117
pirates 12-13, 124, 127, 183

Plowden, Richard, *lawyer* 102
Pole, Gervase, *S.J.* 180
Pole, John, *S.J.* 124, 159
Pole, John, *student* 168
Pollard, Henry, *S.J.* 126, 168
Ponce de la Puente, Constantino, *Canon of Seville* 3
Pope, Alexander, *poet* 187
Porres, Francisco de, *S.J., Rector of Madrid* 167
Powys, *Marquess of. See* Herbert, William
Poyntz, Elizabeth 64
Price, John, *S.J.* 20, 31 (n.1), 162, 201 (n.4)
Priego, Pedro Carrillo de Mendoza, *Count of* 6, 123, 200
Puñonrostro, Francisco Arias de Bobadilla, *Count of* 124, 156

Ramírez, Luis, *S.J., Rector of ECS* 107
Ramos Bejarano, Gabriel, *printer* 118–19
Rawlins, Henry, *priest* 183
Raya, Antonio de la, *Bishop of Cuzco* 32 (n.16), 123
Redish, Alice, *wife of Sir Hamon Whichcott* 180
Reina, Cassidoro de la 3
René, Antonio, *printer* 117
Reynolds, *vere* Green, Richard, *Blessed* 105, 121
Ribera, Francisco, *Canon of Seville* 32 (n.16)
Richardson, Richardson, *cavalry captain* 187–92
Richardson, William, *Blessed* 105
Río, Manuel del, *benefactor* 193
Ríos, Romanus, *O.S.B.* 20
Roa, Martin de, *S.J., historian* 39
Robinson, Henry, *pawnbroker of Lombard Street* 189
Robles, Juan de, *writer* 19
Rodríguez, Bernardino, *Canon of Seville* 32 (n.16)
Rodríguez Gamarra, Alonso, *printer* 117, 170
Roelas, Juan de, *painter* 20, 29, 43, 125
Roffe, Edward, *priest* 168
Ruiz de Montoya, Diego, *S.J., theologian* 15

Saavedra, Juan de, *Constable of the Inquisition* 131
St George, William, *S.J., laybrother* 162
Salkeld, Henry, *student* 19
Salkeld, John, *S.J., later Rector of Churchstanton* 16, 34 (n.54)
Salucio, Agustín, *O.P.* 158
Sánchez, Francisco, *printer* 122
Sanderson, *Mrs* Effie, *of London* 189
Santander, *Doctor* 32 (n.16)
Santibañez, Juan, *S.J., historian* 41, 134
Sarmiento, Francisco de, *Bishop of Jaen* 154, 157–8
Savage, Paul, *student* 14, 129, 182–3

Saville, Mary, *wife of Thomas Whichcott* 170
Schondonck, Gilles, *S.J., Rector of St Omers* 172
Scots 119
Segura y Saenz, Pedro, *Cardinal Archbishop of Seville* 30
Sempill, Hugh, *Scottish exile* 119
Sepulveda, Francisco de, *Vicar of Baeza* 158
Sermoneta, *Duke of* 189, 192 (n.5)
Serrano de Vargas y Urrena, Juan, *printer* 118
Sessa, Antonio Folch y Cardona, *4th Duke of* 6
Sharp, *alias* Pollard, James, *S.J.* 178-9
Shaw, Gerard, *priest* 187-92, 193
Sheldon, *alias* Lee, Edward, *student* 168
Shepherd, Joseph, *Rector of ECV* 194, 198 (n.6)
Sherburne, Richard, *of Stonyhurst* 189
Sherburne, Thomas, *Vice-Rector of ECV* 29
Shirley, Robert, *Lord* 70
Shrewsbury, *Earl of.* See Talbot, George
Sidney, John, *student* 168
Simons, Joseph, *alias* Lobb, Emmanuel, *S.J.* 20
Simpson, William, *priest* 168
Skernett, Richard, *Galway merchant* 135
Smith, Edward, *O.S.B.* 125, 180
Smith, Richard, *Bishop of Chalcedon* 16
Smith, Robert, *student* 19
Somerset, *Earl of. See* Carr, Robert
Somerset, *Lady* Mary 90
Sotelo, Francisco, *S.J., Rector of ECS* 107
Southwell, Robert, *S.J., Saint* 83
Spanish Company 1, 5
Sparchford, John, *priest* 131-2
Spinola, Ambrosio, *1st Marquess of Los Balbases* 120
Spinola, *Master* 158
Sprott, Thomas, *Venerable* 115
Squyer, Edward, *alleged plotter* 11, 115
Stillington, Thomas, *Provost of St George's, Sanlúcar* 5, 153
Stone, Roger, *priest* 168
Stonor, John Talbot, *Bishop of Thespiae* 26
Suárez, Francisco de, *S.J., theologian* 17, 34 (n.54)
Sulyard, Elizabeth, *wife of William Wilford* 103
Sutton, Mary, *wife of Nathaniel Garnet* 68
Swinburn, John, *S.J.* 94, 182
Swinburn, Simon, *S.J.* 160

Talbot, Anne, *wife of John Hothersal* 74
Talbot, George, *9th Earl of Shrewsbury* 90
Talbot, William. *See* Everard
Tancard, Charles, *S.J.* 153, 160

Tarifa, *Marquess of* 6, 20, 123-4
Tassis y Acuña, Juan Baptista de, *Count of Villamediana* 9, 115-16
Taylor, Henry, *Dean of Antwerp* 98
Taylor, N., *of Madrid* 189
Taylor, Stephen, *of Bickerton, Yorks* 98
Téllez de Rivera, Luis, *benefactor of ECS* 44, 193
Tempest, —, *of Covent Garden* 191
Teresa of Avila, Saint 2, 8, 17
Thompson, John, *S.J.* 155
Thorne, Richard, *priest* 10, 123
Thorne, Robert, *Bristol merchant* 1
Thules, John, *Blessed* 117, 176, 179, 181 (n.19)
Tichborne, Henry, *S.J.* 124, 160
Tichborne, Nicholas, *Venerable* 117
Tilney, John, *student* 168
Tintoretto, Jacopo, *painter* 121
Tlaxcala, *Bishop of. See* Mota y Escobar.
Toledo, Pedro de, *Constable of Castile* 124, 153-4
Torre, Pedro de la, *Treasurer of the Casa de la Moneda* 199
Torre Espinosa, Pedro de la, *banker* 199-200
Travers, John, *S.J.* 127
Tregian, *Sir* Francis 120
Tyndall, William, *priest* 168

Urban VIII, *Pope* 128
Ussher, James, *Archbishop of Armagh* 70

Vaderfort, Jacobo, *S.J., Superior of the Casa Profesa* 163, 167
Valdelirios, *Marquess of, Commissioner in Paraguay* 47
Valdes, Juan de, *Inquisitor* 32 (n.16)
Valencia, Fernando de, *S.J., Rector of ECS* 107
Valverde, Francisco, *of Guadalcanal* 191
van Hardwick, Giles, *spy* 181 (n.18)
Vázquez, Miguel, *S.J., theologian* 34 (n.54)
Vega, Martin de, *S.J., Rector of ECS* 107
Vera, Iñes de, *benefactress of ECS* 193
Verdon, George, *of Lorient* 189, 191
Verstegan, Richard, *printer* 15, 33 (n.48)
Villar, Andrés de, *S.J., Procurator of St Hermenegild's* 14, 47
Vicentelo de Leca, Juan Antonio, *Seville councillor* 32 (n.16), 200
Vitelleschi, Muzio, *S.J., Father General* 110
Vivaldo, Agustín, *banker* 199

Wadsworth, James, *informer* 20, 33 (n.37)
Waldegrave, *alias* Flower, Charles, *S.J.* 168
Waller, Robert, *student* 8, 123
Walpole, Christopher, *S.J.* 160

Walpole, Henry, *S.J.* 8, 9, 21, 31 (n.1), 160
Walpole, Richard, *S.J.* 10, 11, 15, 123, 135, 137–8, 160
Ward, *Captain* John, *pirate* 127
Ware, Henry, *antiquary* 135
Ware, *Sir* James 135
Warford, William, *S.J.* 21, 116, 160
Weston, William, *S.J.* 4, 16, 107, 160–1, 163
Wharton, Thomas, *student* 34 (n.62)
Wheatley, John, *of London* 189
Whichcott, *Sir* Hamon 180
Whichcott, *alias* Saville, William, *S.J.* 170–81
White, Andrew, *S.J.* 163
White, Joseph Blanco. *See* Blanco y Crespo
White, *alias* Blacklow, Thomas, *theologian* 16, 168
Wilks, *alias* Tomson, —, *of Knaresborough* 98
Winwood, *Sir* Ralph 117
Wood, Anthony, *antiquary* 93
Worthington, John, *S.J.* 7
Worthington, Laurence, *S.J.* 162
Worthington, William, *S.J.* 159
Wrenno, Roger, *Blessed* 117, 176, 179

Yepes, Diego de, *Bishop of Tarazona* 31

Zapata, Juan, *Inquisitor* 32 (n.16)
Zaragoza, Jerónimo de, *S.J.* 15
Zurbarán, Francisco de, *painter* 9

INDEX OF PLACES

Agden, *Cheshire* 81
Aire, *Flanders* 87
Alarache, *Morocco* 13, 48, 124
Alcalá de Henares 93, 159
  Irish College 57
Andover 62
Antwerp 53
Anwick, *Lincs* 170
Ardee, *Co. Louth* 80
Ardfert, *diocese* 87
Armagh, *county* 80
Arras 72
Aycliffe, *Co. Durham* 96
Azores 108

Bableigh, *Devon* 93
Baeza 110
Babthorpe, *E.R. Yorks* 51
Ballymore Eustace, *Co. Dublin* 87
Barking 102
Barnborough, *W.R. Yorks* 85
Battle Abbey 85, 96
Beoley, *Worcs* 95
Berks 52, 76, 101, 107
Bermondsey 94
Bickerton, *Yorks* 98
Bierton, *Bucks* 74
Blainscough, *Lancs* 104
Boughton Blean, *Kent* 98
Bordeaux, *Irish College* 135
Brailes, *Warwicks* 85
Bridewell prison 83
Bridport 111
Brigg, *Lincs* 97
Bristol 1, 82, 112, 113
Bromley Hall, *Essex* 54
Brussels 171
  Benedictine convent 88
Bury St Edmunds 101

Calatrava, *Andalusia*
Cadiz 26, 67, 77, 108, 111, 113, 140, 153, 163, 182, 194
Caernarvonshire 65, 71, 76
Camborne, *Cornwall* 75
Cambrai 91

Cambridgeshire 50, 52, 67
Cambridge University 126–7
  Christ's College 48, 49
  Emmanuel College 86
  Magdalene College 127
  Peterhouse 113
Canterbury, *diocese* 58, 64, 68, 83, 97, 103, 113
Carlisle 93
Carmona 28
Carrickfergus 135
Cartagena 121
Castlejordan, *Co. Meath* 75
Chatham 191
Checkwell, *Dorset* 76
Chelles 50
Cheshire 54, 64, 81, 108
Chester, *diocese* 51, 73, 89, 90–1, 99, 103, 110
Chiswick 83
Chorley, *Lancs* 49
Churchstanton, *Somerset* 93
Cirencester 59
Civitavecchia 28
Clink, The, *London prison* 75, 103
Coimbra 93
Colchester 54
Comberford Hall, *Staffs* 61
Compostela. *See* Santiago
Conway, *Caernarvonshire* 76
Corby Castle, *Carlisle* 93
Cordoba 75, 81, 93, 104, 109, 112, 155, 162
Coria 139
Cornwall 16, 56, 75, 88, 89, 110
Cowdray, *Sussex* 52
Crosby Hall, *Lancs* 100
Croxteth, *Lancs* 54
Cumberland 74, 92

Daingean, *Co. Offaly* 92
Derbyshire 52, 53, 65, 70, 82, 85, 89, 94, 103, 108, 112
Devon 58, 69, 93, 97, 99, 100, 103, 104, 111, 127
Didlebury, *Salop* 96
Dieulouard 51, 52, 91, 96
Dillingen 109
Dinmore, *Herefords* 54
Dinton, *Wilts* 84
Docking, *Norfolk* 101, 113
Dorset 73, 76, 96, 100, 111, 112

Dos Hermanas, *Seville* 8, 37 (n.102), 45
Douai
 St Gregory's 57, 61, 88, 96, 101, 171
 St Bonaventure's 56
Drogheda 55, 140
Drumcar, *Co. Louth* 80
Dublin 26, 57, 61, 70, 80, 87, 135
Durham, *County* 61, 64, 65, 67, 69, 73, 75, 76, 96

Earswick, *N.R. Yorks* 67
Easington, *Co. Durham* 67
Easling, *Kent* 98
East Anglia 99
Ecija 67
Eden, *Co. Durham* 67
Essex 52, 54, 58, 59, 61, 76, 92, 101, 102
Eu 76, 104, 156
Exeter 69, 99
Extremadura 187–91

Farington Hall, *Lancs* 74
Farnworth, *Lancs* 104
Ferensby, *W.R. Yorks* 78
Ferrol, El 153
Firle, *Sussex* 187
Flintshire 90
Framlingham 74, 99

Galway 78, 135, 188
Garstang, *Lancs* 72
Ghent 59, 61, 64, 65, 75, 76, 78, 96, 103
 Benedictine convent 70, 78, 101
Gibraltar 77
Gloucestershire 59, 104
Godstow, *Oxon* 87
Golborne, *Lancs* 104
Granada 108, 112, 113
Grantham 98
Gravelines 171
Great Dunmow, *Essex* 76
Greenfield Abbey, *Flints* 90
Grosmont, *Yorks* 75
Guadalcanal 187–91
Guadix 110

Hadleigh, *Suffolk* 51
Haigh, The, *Wigan* 55

Hanley Castle, *Worcs* 101
Hants 53, 58, 62, 84, 89, 91, 92, 95, 101, 102, 103, 104, 107, 114
Harpswell, *Kent* 180
Hathersage, *Derbys* 52
Havant, *Hants* 101
Heaton, *Co. Durham* 80
Heighington, *Co. Durham* 69
Herefordshire 54, 81, 93, 109
Holborn 64
Holywell, *Flints* 90
Horwich, *Lancs* 100
Hough-on-the-Hill, *Lincs* 98
Huelva 26
Huntingdonshire 112
Hurley, *Berks* 107

Ingolstadt 109
Irthlingborough, *Northants* 90

Jerez 9, 28, 76, 110, 140

Kelsall, *Lincs* 108
Kempsford, *Glos* 104
Kent 65, 66, 72, 78, 98, 101, 114
Kentish Town 52
Kildare, *County* 63
Kilkenny 121
Killaloe, *diocese* 87
Kilmore, *diocese* 57
Kingston Lacy, *Dorset* 73
Kirkham, *Lancs* 29, 60
Knaresborough, *W.R. Yorks* 78, 98
Knockfergus 121

La Flèche 192
Lamspring 88
Lancashire 49, 51, 53-5, 60, 69, 72-4, 79, 80, 82, 84, 88, 95, 96, 100, 104,
    109, 111-112, 187-9
Lancaster 51
Leicestershire 55, 71
Lerwick, *Shetlands* 120
Leyland, *Lancs* 53, 74
Lichfield, *diocese* 71
Liège 53-5, 59, 61-2, 77, 88, 90, 99, 108-9, 111-2
Lierre 53
Lima 21, 141
Lincoln, *city or diocese* 53, 60

Lincolnshire 53, 86, 91, 96, 97, 103, 111, 114, 170
Lisbon 56, 67, 83, 86, 93, 95, 98–9, 102, 109, 120, 125
  Bridgettine convent 77, 82, 83, 93, 99
Little Crosby, *Lancs* 54
Llandaff, *diocese* 103
Llanfoist, *Mon.* 103
Llangattock, *Mon.* 85
Llanrothal, *Mon.* 76
London, Spanish chapel 26, 63, 75, 92, 94–5
Loreto 61, 76
Lorient 188
Louvain 71–2, 78, 90, 95, 99, 101–4, 109, 171
Lutterworth, *Leics* 71
Luttrellstown, *Co. Dublin* 70

Madrid, English College of St George 73, 79, 81, 90, 107, 109–11, 193, 196
Maelor Saeswyg, *Flints* 90
Maidstone 114
Malaga 26, 77, 109, 110, 111, 113
Mamorra, *Morocco* 127
Marchena 66, 109
Maryland 102
Maynooth 28, 75
Meath, *County* 26, 55, 63, 66, 75, 78, 135
Mechlin 56
Melilla 77
Mersham Hatch, *Kent* 78
Mexico 21, 23, 117
Middlesex 63
Midhurst, *Sussex* 50, 96
Monmouthshire 76, 85, 103
Montilla 25, 65, 93, 106, 107, 108
Moorfields, *London* 63
Morland, *Westmorland* 93
Morocco 13, 48, 124, 127
Morón de la Frontera 8, 158
Mortlake 79
Murcia 159

Naburn, *E.R. Yorks* 88
Naples 71, 113
Narraghmore, *Co. Kildare* 63
Ness Hall, *N.R. Yorks* 61
Newcastle-upon-Tyne 61, 80–1, 96
Newgate, *prison* 84
Norfolk 53, 68, 71, 81, 86, 101, 113

Northants 62, 90, 103
Northumberland 96
Norwich 81
Nottinghamshire 66, 108

Obarenes, Abbey of Santa María 50
Offaly, *County* 92
Oña, Abbey of San Salvador 54
Ospringe, *Kent* 98
Osuna 77
Oxburgh Hall, *Norfolk* 53
Oxford, *county and district* 49, 54, 58, 59, 70, 76, 81, 86, 87, 89, 101,
   112, 187
Oxford University 54
   Balliol College 55, 80
   Brasenose College 49
   Broadgates Hall (*now Pembroke College*) 162
   Christ Church 114
   Trinity College 96, 113

Padua 51
Paraguay 47, 104
Paris, St Edmund's 54
Peñon de Velez 77
Penzance 110
Peru 21, 23, 141
Petersfield 95
Philippines 57
Philipstown, *Co. Offaly* 92
Plymouth 110
Pont à Mousson 162
Poulton, *Lancs* 51, 87
Preston, *Lancs* 74
Proudston, *Co. Meath* 63
Puerto de S. María 6, 28, 77, 80, 140, 153, 182

Rheims 67, 75, 79, 84, 104, 108, 110
Richmond, *Yorks* 51
Río Tinto 192
Ripon 91
Rome
   English College 16, 135, 182–3

St Asaph, *diocese* 74, 87
St Germans, *Cornwall* 16, 89
St Kitts 125
St Malo 140

St Omers 12, 13, 16
Salamanca 108, 110
  Irish College 55, 78, 108, 110
Salisbury, *diocese* 113
Sanlúcar de Barrameda 1, 5-6, 16, 28, 50-1, 56, 62-3, 66, 70, 77-8, 86, 88, 98, 111, 114, 123, 126, 139, 153
Santiago de Compostela, Abbey of San Martín 75, 78
Scarisbrick Hall, *Lancs* 82
Scotney Castle, *Sussex* 55
Seaton, *Cumberland* 74
Seville
  Casa de la Contratación 24, 137, 199-200
  Casa de la Moneda 199
  Casa Profesa, *S.J.* 106
  Colegio de las Becas 28
  Colegio de Niños Nobles 196
  Colegio de San Hermenegildo, *S.J.* 4, 7, 14-15, 17-18, 47, 79, 90, 112, 113, 155, 200
  Colegio de la Purísima Concepción y de San Patricio (*Irish College*) 24, 25, 47, 182-86
  Colegio de Santo Tomás 28, 186
  Collación de Omnium Sanctorum 194
  Cruz del Campo 44
  Esclavas de Jesús y de María, *convent of the* 193
  Hospital de la Sangre, o de Cinco Llagas 137
  Reales Alcázares 13
  Regia Sociedad, *later* Real Academia, de Medicina 29, 193, 196, 198 (n.3)
  San Francisco de Asís, *monastery of Friars Minor* 136
  San Francisco de Paula, *monastery of Minims* 194
  San Isidoro del Campo, *Hieronymite monastery* 3
  San Jerónimo de Buenavista, *Hieronymite monastery* 194
  San Luís, *Jesuit novitiate house* 106
  San Nicolás, *church* 195
  San Pablo, *Dominican monastery* 25
  Santa María de Gracia, *Dominican convent* 195
  Santa María de la Victoria, *monastery of Minims* 43
  Santa María del Carmen, *Carmelite monastery* 11
  Virgen de la Antigua, *chapel of the* 136
  Virgen del Valle, *statue of the* 136
Shirburn, *Oxon* 59, 187
Shoreditch 52
Shropshire 63, 96
Sichem 173, 181
Sittingbourne, *Kent* 66
Somerset 87, 93, 112
South Kyme, *Lincs* 170

Spinkhill, *Derbys* 89
Staffordshire 50, 61, 80, 82, 86
Stamullen, *Co. Meath* 55, 66
Stonyhurst 88, 189
Suffolk 51, 59, 65, 67, 75, 76, 101, 103, 111
Surrey 79, 109
Sussex 50, 52, 55, 71, 76, 78, 79, 95, 96, 101, 102

Tarifa 77
Taunton 112
Thorverton, *Devon* 99
Tisbury, *Wilts* 94
Toledo 190
Tournai 112
Tredunnock, *Mon.* 85
Trigueros 85, 107, 110, 155, 162
Tristernagh, *Co. Meath* 135
Tunis 127

Uffculme, *Devon* 93
Ufton Nervet, *Berks* 76
Upholland 99
Ushaw 29
Utrera 137

Valladolid 12
Vejer 77
Vienna 98
Villagarcía 25, 58, 62, 108, 110
Vilna 96

Wales, *W.R. Yorks* 91
Wales, *Principality* 50, 59, 65, 71, 74, 76, 89, 92, 102, 103, 104
Warwicks 48, 85, 101
Waterford 26, 75, 135
Watten 50, 54, 56, 59, 61, 64, 77, 84, 88–90, 92, 96, 99, 107, 111
Wellington, *Somerset* 93
Welton, *Lincs* 96
Wereham, *Norfolk* 86
West Bretton, *W.R. Yorks* 56
West Grinstead, *Sussex* 76
West Mapledurham, *Hants* 95
West Lavington, *Wilts* 75
Westmorland 59, 80, 93
Whalley 96, 99, 109
Widnes 80
Wigan 55, 79

Wilts 75, 84, 94, 102
Wimborne, *Dorset* 100
Winchester 52, 93, 100
Windward Isles 22
Wisbech 50, 99, 161
Wolverhampton 80
Wolverton, *Bucks* 81
Worcestershire 82, 90, 94, 95, 101, 111
Wyke Without, *Winchester* 93

York 73, 75
Yorkshire 50, 51, 56, 60, 61, 67, 72, 75, 78, 83, 84, 85, 86, 88, 91, 92, 98, 99, 102, 108, 109, 112, 113
Ypres 59